THE NINE LIVES
OF PAKISTAN

Mourners outside the Bhutto family mausoleum during the funeral of Benazir Bhutto in December 2007

THE NINE LIVES OF PAKISTAN

Dispatches from a Precarious State

Declan Walsh

W. W. NORTON & COMPANY
Independent Publishers Since 1923

For information about permission to reproduce selections from this book, write to
Permissions, W. W. Norton & Company, Inc., 500 Fifth Avenue, New York, NY 10110

For information about special discounts for bulk purchases, please contact
W. W. Norton Special Sales at specialsales@wwnorton.com or 800-233-4830

Manufacturing by Lakeside Book Company

Library of Congress Cataloging-in-Publication Data

Names: Walsh, Declan, author.
Title: The nine lives of Pakistan : dispatches from a precarious state /
Declan Walsh.
Description: First edition. | New York, NY : W. W. Norton & Company, 2020. |
Includes bibliographical references and index.
Identifiers: LCCN 2020008294 | ISBN 9780393249910 (hardcover) |
ISBN 9780393249927 (epub)
Subjects: LCSH: Walsh, Declan—Travel—Pakistan. | Pakistan—
Description and travel. | Pakistan—History.
Classification: LCC DS377 .W35 2020 | DDC 954.91—dc23
LC record available at https://lccn.loc.gov/2020008294

ISBN 978-1-324-02025-7 pbk.

W. W. Norton & Company, Inc., 500 Fifth Avenue, New York, N.Y. 10110
www.wwnorton.com

W. W. Norton & Company Ltd., 15 Carlisle Street, London W1D 3BS

1 2 3 4 5 6 7 8 9 0

To Eamonn and Samuel

Who is without sin in the city of my beloved
— *Go Forth in the Streets Today in Your Fetters*
by Faiz Ahmed Faiz

CONTENTS

CONTENTS

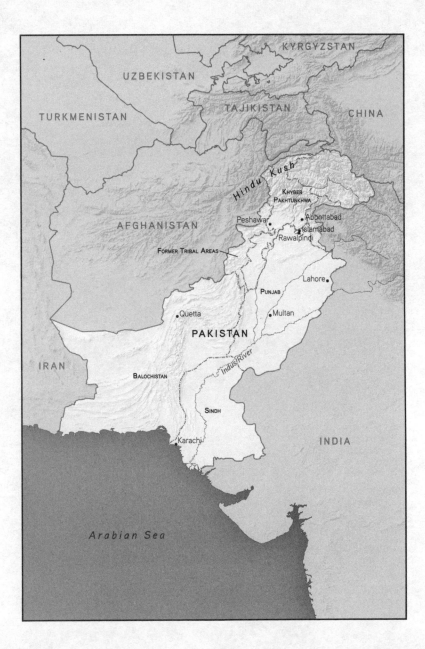

PROLOGUE

May 2013

On my last night in Pakistan, the angels come to spirit me away.

It is a balmy summer evening in Lahore, the ancient city of Mughal splendour, down by the border with India. Lying on my bed in the Avari, Lahore's grandest hotel, I stare at the ceiling and listen. Sounds of jubilation drift in: honks, hoots and cries; the urgent stampede of hundreds of feet. An historic election is under way, the kind that promises to reshape the destiny of a nation, and this is the street music of democracy, Pakistani style. Tens of millions of people have voted, forming impatient lines or elbowing their way into polling stations across this vast country, from the twinkling, snow-dusted Himalayas to muggy villages on the Arabian Sea. Here in Lahore, as the sun dips low, the most fervent citizens are parading down the Mall, the city's elegant tree-lined boulevard. They pass under my window – men tottering on cheap motorbikes, three to a seat, or scampering past on foot, waving placards emblazoned with images of cricket bats, tigers and arrows – symbols that help illiterate voters identify their chosen party.

On my phone, I scroll through scattered reports of election-day trouble: a gunfight outside a polling station in rural Punjab; a Taliban bombing in the port city of Karachi that killed eleven; and a clash between rival political factions in the restive province of Balochistan. Compared with the chaos of recent years, however, this is small-scale violence, and on the whole this election is shaping up to be a startling success. Pakistanis have voted in record numbers; the main parties have promised to accept the result; a winner is emerging. On my television, the prime-time anchors, gabby men in shiny suits, stride excitedly before giant screens, making feverish predictions.

But the triumph of the day transcends any one party. For the first time in Pakistan's history, an elected, civilian-led government has completed its term of office, and is about to hand power to another one. It might seem a small achievement, but in Pakistan it is stupendously good news. For sixty years, Pakistani leaders have departed power in handcuffs or coffins, expelled by military coups, rigged votes or lurid assassinations. A relatively clean vote: this is novel. Across town at the home of a well-known lawyer, my Pakistani friends are glued to the TV, exhilarated witnesses of history in motion, trading gossip and sipping bootleg Scotch. I wish I could join them. But I can't.

For one thing, a towering man with a sullen face stands outside my room, preventing me from leaving. His colleague is stationed at the end of the corridor, next to the lift. Two more are positioned in the lobby. They work for Inter-Services Intelligence, the military's powerful spy agency, known as the ISI. Plainclothes ISI operatives can be found in towns and cities across Pakistan, low-key but ubiquitous, like pigeons on a power line. With experience, it is easy to spot them, with their tinted-window jeeps, hand-held radio sets and air of unspoken menace. In Urdu, Pakistanis call them *farishtay*, or angels – a double-edged euphemism that refers both to the traditional white longshirts typically worn by ISI men, and to the vast uncircumscribed powers at their disposal.

The angels, as everyone knows, can knock on any door, flout any law, question or harass or even abduct any citizen. Tonight,

I am the object of their attentions. After nine years in Pakistan, I have been ordered to leave. Their job is to ensure that I go.

❧

The trouble started three days earlier in the capital, Islamabad. I was at a pre-election party hosted by an American friend, where foreign diplomats and well-heeled Pakistanis nibbled on seekh kebabs, when my phone rang with an anonymous number. The caller announced himself as a police officer and ordered me home immediately. He offered no explanation. I arrived home after midnight to find two vans filled with police officers parked at my gate. An older bearded man, in civilian clothes, stepped forward and handed me an envelope marked 'By Special Messenger'. He urged me to open it. 'It is informed that your visa is hereby cancelled in view of your undesirable activities,' read a letter on government stationery. 'You are therefore advised to leave the country within 72 hours.'

The Special Messenger flashed me an awkward smile and then, in the finest tradition of subcontinental bureaucracy, politely asked me to sign for my own expulsion order.

Bewildered, I went inside. I had been working as a correspondent in Pakistan for almost a decade, first with the *Guardian* and then the *New York Times*. It was a long time, certainly; foreign reporters usually cycled out after three or four years. But I didn't see this coming.

Certainly, there had been difficulties. The Pakistani security services tapped my phone and intercepted my email. I received threats of legal action, often for outlandish sums of money – in one case, by a retired military dictator demanding $5 million. Months earlier, I'd received a death threat from someone who claimed to be with the Taliban. ('Next time we will take action,' he said.) Pakistani journalists who helped me had been abducted and beaten by the security forces; one had been forced into exile. But I had grown to love Pakistan, too – a country of hidden delights, endearing absurdities and some of the closest friendships I had ever experienced. My work took me to corners of heart-stopping beauty and plunged me into strange, inspiring or heart-rending situations. I had made my peace with Pakistan, and I thought Pakistan had made its peace with me. 'Undesirable activities': what did that mean?

The next morning, I raced across town to the information ministry, seeking to undo the expulsion order. It was rare for the Pakistanis to kick out an accredited foreign reporter and the acting minister, Arif Nizami – himself a journalist – claimed to know nothing of the expulsion order. He shuffled some papers, offered tea, and posed an odd question. 'Have you been to Quetta recently?' I kept going. In the manicured garden of the Serena Hotel (the lobby was presumed to be bugged), I met an American diplomat who informed me the ISI was the source of my difficulty. 'We're going nuclear on this,' she said. I never saw her again. Late that night came a message from the agency itself: a senior ISI official, a suave and charming man I'd met for breakfast on the veranda of the Serena, sent a private message via a mutual acquaintance. 'The order has come from the top,' he said. 'It is not reversible. You should start packing.'

What an infuriating moment to be told to go. Pakistan's most unpredictable and consequential election in years was taking place the next day. Nawaz Sharif, a two-time former prime minister, was vying for power with Imran Khan, the country's most famous cricketer. Both men were from Lahore, 160 miles to the south, where the battle would be decided. Unusually, given Pakistan's history of rigged votes, nobody was sure who would win.

It had been forty-eight hours since I received the expulsion order. Pakistan had a day to vote. I had a day to leave. I threw a hastily packed suitcase into a car and set off for Lahore.

Sharif's previous term of office ended abruptly, in 1999, with the coup that brought the army chief, Pervez Musharraf, to power. In exile, Sharif spruced up his image with a tuft of hair implants to disguise his balding pate. He campaigned in the company of a caged tiger, his party's mascot, an unfortunate animal that was paraded across the country. Opponents made fun of Sharif's prodigious appetite, but the middle classes of Punjab loved him as one of their own, and at boisterous rallies, exultant supporters hailed him as the 'Teflon Tiger'. The actual tiger was less fortunate: it died of heat exhaustion before the campaign was over.

Khan generated no shortage of electricity; the question was whether he could convert it into votes. After captaining the national cricket team to a World Cup victory in 1992, he became Pakistan's premier playboy, a friend of Mick Jagger with a string of high-society girlfriends. As his cricket career waned, the sports hero turned to Islam and politics, and his marriage to an English heiress twenty-two years his junior, Jemima Goldsmith, ended in divorce. Now, after years in the political wilderness, his popularity was soaring again. Tall and craggily handsome at sixty, Khan retained his star quality, and adoring young Pakistanis flocked to rallies that had the buzz of a pop concert. He railed against American drone strikes and promised to eradicate corruption within six months. Progressives scorned him as an idiot savant – one paper dubbed him 'Im the dim' – and worried that he was a Trojan horse for the political ambitions of Pakistan's generals, to whom he was notably deferential.

Clearly, each candidate had drawbacks. Yet the election was a blast of sweet relief to weary Pakistanis. The country of 180 million people had been through a hellish period, the worst since its blood-soaked independence in 1947. A relentless wave of Taliban attacks had killed thousands of Pakistanis, as many as 150 in a single bombing. The former prime minister, Benazir Bhutto, had been assassinated. The teenage education activist Malala Yousafzai had been shot in the head. CIA drones fired missiles into the tribal belt; frequent power blackouts plunged entire cities into darkness. Two years earlier, a team of American Navy SEALs raided a three-storey house in Abbottabad, next to Pakistan's top military academy, and shot Osama bin Laden in the head. Somehow, democracy had survived.

Arriving in Lahore, I found a city gripped by election mania. Voters jammed into polling stations, determined to cast their ballots. Even the city's pampered elite, more frequently seen in glossy magazines or at fashion shows, shrugged off their apathy. At one polling station, wealthy women in sunglasses yelled at polling staff; outside, giddy young people waved thumbs splashed with the purple dye that proved they had voted. A family of Imran Khan supporters cruised past in an open-top sports car. 'Look who's coming – the tiger hunter!' they shouted.

I shared their sense of relief. For years, my reporting from Pakistan had been filled with notes of chaos. Too often, I deleted the phone numbers of contacts who had died. Friends took comfort in conspiracy theories or sank into despondency. Now, that most delicate and precious thing – faith in the power of a vote – appeared to be taking root. 'The nation is fighting for its right,' Fouzia Qayyum, a beaming bank clerk in her twenties, told me at a polling station.

Best of all, the military, which had rigged so many earlier elections, was keeping out of it this time. Or so it seemed.

As I drove away from the polling station, a khaki jeep raced alongside and pushed my car off the road. A soldier jumped out and ushered me back to a checkpoint, where an officer delivered a lecture. I was supposed to be leaving the country, he chided, not covering the election. Eventually I made it to a friend's house, but ISI goons turned up at the gate and declared me an 'enemy of the state'. I was packed off to the Avari Hotel until the next flight out of the city. Stranded in my room, I filed an election story and chatted with friends who managed to talk their way past the guard. Again and again, they asked: what have you done to be thrown out?

I still had no idea. For almost a decade, I had puzzled over the workings of this perplexing, fascinating country, teasing out its nuances and arguing with those who chose to view its problems in stark black-and-white. But that night, as I sat in the Avari, it seemed to boil down to one hard truth: the military always wins. When the ISI men come to the door, the illusion of a democratic state melts away. Nobody can stop them – no judge, no lawyer, no ambassador, not even a minister. The angels rule.

And so, at four in the morning, I left, traipsing down the hallway with my suitcases, trailed by three ISI men who refused to help but, in a comical flourish, insisted on cramming into the lift with me. A friend was waiting in the lobby: Cyril Almeida, a senior journalist with *Dawn*, Pakistan's newspaper of record, who, furious at the news of my expulsion, insisted on driving me to the airport. We took off, gliding through the deserted streets in a convoy of four-wheel-drives and motorcycles with flashing lights. The election revellers had collapsed into their beds, their passions spent; Nawaz Sharif had emerged victorious and would be the next prime minister. In the distance, a pink light glowed on the horizon.

Then I was in the departure lounge, alone. I thought of the friends I was leaving behind, my life in Pakistan, and I wrote on

Twitter: 'Here I go. Hard to believe this is happening.' A voice over the loudspeaker called my flight.

In a land of riddles, here was yet another one. It wasn't until years later that I would learn, through a call from a mysterious stranger, why the angels had expelled me. But that explanation made sense only as the culmination of a much longer journey through the glorious chaos of Pakistan. During my time in the country I had made trips to the wildest, most far-flung and downright odd places. But the journey also took me deep into the psyche of the country where, as it turned out, I had poked an unexpectedly tender spot.

It all started, almost a decade earlier, with a glass of beer.

THE NINE LIVES OF PAKISTAN

Pilgrims in the Indus, Sehwan Sharif

1

Insha' Allah Nation

Land of Broken Maps

In the summer of 2004, I drove from my new home in Islamabad to the dowdy garrison city of Rawalpindi, about fifteen miles away. The road led down a chaotic, fume-choked highway where tiny yellow taxis weaved around hulking rainbow-coloured trucks, their flanks painted with delicate floral motifs. After passing the army's General Headquarters, I turned onto a quieter road and pulled up outside a quaint-looking, Victorian-era building. A pungent odour of brewing hops wafted through the air. The owner waited inside.

Minoo Bhandara perched behind an antique desk in a dimly lit office, resplendent in a three-piece suit despite the hundred-degree weather outside. He was in his sixties, a portly man with tinted glasses and a vaguely impish smile. A fan whirred overhead. 'I'll be with you in a minute,' he said, signing some papers. The walls were lined with framed antique cartoons that depicted pearl-skinned British soldiers in battle, firing at wild-eyed tribesmen or spearing them with bayonets – century-old company calendars. The Murree Brewery had been founded in 1861 to slake the thirst of the soldiers of the Raj, as British rule in colonial India was known. Now it was listed on Pakistan's stock exchange. 'We're one of the country's biggest taxpayers,' Bhandara boasted.

His success was puzzling. Prohibition had been in effect in Pakistan for a quarter-century, and any Muslim caught slugging one of Bhandara's lagers could be sentenced to eighty lashes from an oil-soaked whip. Yet Murree Brewery was doing a roaring trade, largely on the back of sales to God-fearing Muslims, Bhandara cheerfully admitted. Trade was so strong, in fact, that the company was expanding into foreign markets. A new line of single-malt whisky was being casked in the cellar; 'Have a Murree with Your Curry' was the marketing slogan in Britain.

Bhandara pressed a bell to summon an attendant. 'A beer?' he enquired with a raised eyebrow. It was nine thirty in the morning. I gratefully accepted.

I'd been in Pakistan a month or so by then, and the breakfast beer would prove the first of numerous riddles in the country. At that point, though, I was struggling to warm to my new assignment. Islamabad seemed dull and bloodless, a shimmering monotone of broad avenues and gaudy mansions. It was a chessboard capital, a low suburban sprawl that was divided into square neighbourhoods named after grid references or primary colours. My guesthouse was in F-7/3; the sleepy main shopping drag was the 'Blue Area'. Houses were built in a bewildering range of styles – imperial Rome, Spanish hacienda, seventies chic. Public monuments included a replica of the mountain where Pakistan exploded its first nuclear device in 1998, and replica missiles that appeared to be pointed in the direction of the Indian border. At night, rich kids drag-raced their fathers' saloon cars under the Margalla Hills, swerving to avoid the wild hogs that ambled from the bushes. Getting a drink involved ridiculous subterfuge. 'Special tea, sir?' the waiters at the Marriott hotel would ask archly, proffering a teapot filled with bootleg Chianti.

Pakistanis from more spirited cities sneered at Islamabad's antiseptic calm. 'Don't tell me that you live in that Hicksville,' a peroxide-haired fashionista told me in Karachi. Westerners took a perverse pleasure in the capital's isolation from the chaotic country it ruled. 'Islamabad: only half an hour from Pakistan,' diplomats would quip at stuffy parties where gloved attendants served gin-and-tonics on the terrace.

The torpor of Islamabad mirrored the wider mood of the country, then in the grip of its fourth bout of military rule. The generals had ruled directly for half of Pakistan's history since independence in 1947, always seizing power with an air of feigned reluctance. The civilians had screwed things up again, they would mutter – time for a stiff dose of military discipline to set things right. The latest khaki messiah was Pervez Musharraf, the army chief who had ousted Nawaz Sharif five years earlier. A photo of Musharraf, broadcast on state TV in the early hours of the coup, was unpromising: a macho-looking officer in fatigues and brandishing a pistol, with a cigarette dangling from his lips. But Pakistanis quickly warmed to him. In contrast with Sharif, who had become erratic and autocratic in power, Musharraf turned out to have an endearing manner and a caddish charm. He played golf and tennis, smoked cigars, and sat in the front row of fashion shows where he flashed a cheeky smile at the models. He gave himself the title of 'chief executive' and made extravagant promises of eradicating corruption. At an early press conference, Musharraf posed for the cameras with his wife, his mother and his Pekinese dogs, Dot and Buddy – an image that enraged conservative clerics, who were unsure whether they hated dogs or women more, and delighted just about everyone else. Meanwhile, Sharif was taken to a remote fortress over the River Indus, stripped of property worth $8 million and later dispatched into exile at a palace in Saudi Arabia.

By the time I reached Pakistan, in 2004, the Musharraf magic was fading. The military leader had organised a referendum on his popularity that was supposedly approved by 98 per cent of voters, followed by an election that the ISI tilted in his favour. People grumbled, but it was too late. Parliament had been reduced to a toothless talking shop, stuffed with cronies and sycophants, and Musharraf's political rivals languished in exile – a state of affairs that suited the Americans just fine.

The United States and Pakistan had been feuding and falling in love for decades. People often compared their tempestuous, co-dependent relationship to a bad marriage, but it was more accurately the worst kind of forced marriage – a product of shared interests rather than values, devoid of genuine affection and scarred by a history of dispute and betrayal. It started during the Cold War, in the 1950s, when the Americans ran a secret base in Peshawar from which Gary Powers, the pilot of a U-2 spy plane, took off before being shot down over the Soviet Union in 1960. The two countries forged a momentous partnership in the 1980s to expel the Soviets from Afghanistan, declaring victory in 1989. But barely a year later Washington slapped painful sanctions on Pakistan over its covert nuclear weapons programme. Stung, the Pakistanis made crude jokes about being treated like a used condom, and then eight years later exploded a nuclear bomb anyway. The September 2001 attacks on America threw them together again. President George W. Bush needed Pakistan's help with the war in Afghanistan – American supply lines ran through Karachi – and with the hunt for the fugitive Osama bin Laden, who, as far as anyone could tell, had slipped into Pakistan's tribal areas. Bush hailed Musharraf as his 'buddy' and lavished him with F-16 warplanes and billions of dollars in aid. The Pakistani leader reciprocated with terrorist scalps: Pakistan's intelligence services rounded up hundreds of al Qaeda suspects and shipped them to Guantánamo Bay and CIA 'black sites' – secret prisons in Poland, Thailand and Afghanistan – where many were tortured. Grateful American officials heaped praise on Musharraf's 'controlled democracy'.

'You have to realise,' one State Department official told me over beers in his Islamabad garden, 'that this is the best we can hope for.' He didn't even have the decency to blush.

Pakistan's relations with India, meanwhile, bobbed along at a low ebb. A few years earlier, the two countries had flirted with mutual annihilation when an attack by Pakistan-backed militants against India's Parliament building caused the mobilisation of one million soldiers in both countries, raising the possibility of a nuclear war. Now they were back to more mundane tit-for-tat. An Indian diplomat invited me for Sunday brunch at her home. I arrived to find her standing at the door, sheened with sweat and proffering apologies. The electricity had been cut off, most likely by the Pakistani spooks who harassed the other guests as they arrived, and there was no air-conditioning. The diplomat shrugged. 'Don't worry,' she said nonchalantly. 'We do the same to their people in New Delhi.'

Pakistan was once a hopeful prospect of the post-colonial world. In the 1960s, when its economy was on a par with Singapore's, cheering throngs greeted the American president, Dwight Eisenhower, as he toured Karachi in an open-top limousine. Jackie Kennedy visited in 1963, jaunting around the garden of the military ruler, Field Marshal Ayub Khan, on the back of a camel. Indians, whose leaders were closer to the Soviet Union, laboured under a suffocating bureaucracy and a socialist economy; Pakistanis had Coca-Cola, imported Toyotas, and a modern new capital. But disaster struck in 1965 in the form of a misbegotten war with India, triggered by Pakistani attempts to instigate a revolt in the disputed territory of Kashmir. Pakistan lost, and the mishaps kept piling up: assassinations, insurgencies, more military coups, and, through the 1980s, an influx of guns, narcotics and refugees from war-torn Afghanistan.

The greatest calamity by far occurred in 1971, with the secession of East Pakistan. The country was an oddly shaped entity from its birth, composed of two 'wings' – East Pakistan, on the Bay of Bengal, and West Pakistan, centred on Karachi and Lahore – that were separated by a thousand miles of hostile Indian territory. The awkward arrangement was exacerbated by discrimination and racism. The East Pakistanis were poorer and more dark-skinned than their Western cousins, who disregarded the Bengalis' language and treated them with condescension. The inevitable uprising, following an election in 1970, met with a brutal response. Pakistan's army, aided by Islamist militias, massacred Bengali villagers, executed intellectuals and raped an untold number of women. American diplomats warned privately of 'selective genocide', but the Nixon administration, mindful of its alliance with Pakistan, turned a blind eye to the atrocities. India sided with the Bengali rebels, decisively tipping the military balance, and in December 1971, Pakistan's generals submitted to a humiliating surrender. WAR TILL VICTORY read the headline in *Dawn*. East Pakistan became Bangladesh.

It was a devastating blow – not only because the Bengalis accounted for half of Pakistan's population and held one-third of its territory, but because their departure had shattered a foundational myth: that Pakistan was the sole homeland for the Muslims of South Asia.

After 2001, when the attacks on America thrust Pakistan to global prominence, the country occupied an uncomfortable place in the Western imagination, as a crucial yet perfidious ally. Daniel Pearl of the *Wall Street Journal* was kidnapped from Karachi in 2002 and beheaded nine days later. News stories were invariably accompanied by photographs of rabid-looking clerics torching American flags. Successive opinion polls ranked it among the least popular countries on Earth. If Pakistan was a person, Christopher Hitchens wrote, he would be 'humourless, paranoid, insecure, eager to take offence and suffering from self-righteousness, self-pity and self-hatred'; Thomas Friedman of the *New York Times*, visiting Peshawar, complained of 'cold stares and steely eyes'.

'Those eyes did not say, "American Express accepted here",' Friedman wrote. 'They said, "Get lost."'

Once I had settled in, though, a more complex and interesting country came into view, softer around the edges than its dour image suggested, where people loved to let their hair down.

An early revelation was Basant, Lahore's spectacular spring fiesta. Kites filled the skies over the Old City, where giddy boys coursed through the narrow streets, in the shadow of the ancient Lahore Fort, tugging on strings as they did battle in the sky. On the rooftops, I mingled with city grandees who chewed kebabs at lavish parties in traditional *haveli* mansions. The forbidden pleasures were at street level. One night I attended a rave party at an abandoned bakery, where young Pakistanis high on the drug Ecstasy bopped to a throbbing techno beat. Another time, I ended up at a party hosted by an underground gay collective. HOT BOYZ read the sign on the door. Outside, several hundred men danced to the top Bollywood hits, some in dresses and lipstick, others with heavy moustaches. I lingered awkwardly on the edge of the crowd, until a man in a sequinned dress – a *hijra*, as Pakistan's third sex are known, who make money dancing at weddings or begging in traffic – beckoned me onto the floor.

Pak is the Urdu word for 'clean', so Pakistan translates literally as 'Land of the Pure'. But the pockets of permissiveness, at odds with the country's reputation, weren't limited to the party scene. I visited art exhibitions that explored Islamist violence or the intimacies of the heart. In the countryside, I visited religious shrines where Hindus and Muslims worshipped side by side in a tradition that stretched back centuries. Climbing to a remote valley in the Hindu Kush, I met the Kalash, a tiny tribe of animist believers supposedly descended from Alexander the Great, who carefully guarded their traditions.

My story on the Murree Brewery was a cliché of foreign correspondence – nearly every newly arrived reporter had covered it – but the company's unlikely success spoke to a broader truth about Pakistan. Despite its harsh Islamic laws, every neighbourhood had a semi-official bootlegger, which made it as easy to order a bottle of whisky as a pizza. (The whisky usually arrived more quickly.) Newspapers carried advertisements for clinics that treated alcoholism. Nobody had been lashed with an oil-soaked whip for decades. At Murree Brewery, Minoo Bhandara led me to a first-floor window where he pointed to a grand, white-columned house across the street: the residence of President Musharraf who, it was widely known, was partial to a dose of Johnnie Walker premium blend Blue Label in the evening.

※

I rented a house on the Islamabad chessboard, a four-bedroom villa with a capacious garden, bought a 1967 Volkswagen Beetle (of a marque known to Pakistanis as a 'Foxy') for scooting around the city, and acquired three dogs, all strays. Spike and Luna came via friends; Pookie straggled through the front gate as a puppy. When I told a visiting American diplomat, who was versed in the ways of the intelligence world, that Pookie was a 'walk-in', he shot back: 'Well, I hope she brought some useful information.'

I hired a housekeeper named Mazloom Raja, a gentle man in his fifties with speckled hair that he frequently dyed black, in the style of Musharraf. Mazloom meant 'The Suffering One', which was apt. He seemed weighed down by the tribulations of a working-class life: squabbling relatives, scheming young men seeking to bed his daughter and regular attendance at funerals for unfortunate relatives struck down by disease or accidents.

When I was out, I realised, he sneaked into the TV room to catch up on Bollywood movies. He could be excessively deferential. When Mazloom started to call me 'sir', I asked him to use my name. He shuffled awkwardly.

'Yes, sir,' he replied.

Autumn arrived, and with it Ramzan, as Pakistanis and Indians call the Muslim holy month of fasting and prayer. Pakistanis advertised their piety with long faces during the day, when restaurants were closed, and donned their finest duds at night, when they gorged on rich food and socialised until it was time for *suhoor*, the predawn breakfast. As my car idled at a traffic light, a young man on a bicycle – a student at a *madrassa* religious seminary, judging from his wiry beard and hitched trousers – rapped on the window of my Beetle and proceeded to admonish me for chewing gum. I told him I was a Christian. No matter, he shot back testily. 'Pakistan is a Muslim country.' A rule was a rule.

Or was it? The country's most notorious *madrassa* was the Darul Uloom Haqqania, a vast complex near Peshawar whose 4,000 students were taught a harsh, fundamentalist brand of Islam. In the 1980s, when the *madrassa* churned out radicalised students who later crossed the border to fight in Afghanistan, it was informally known as the 'University of Jihad'. Its head was a stern, henna-bearded cleric who liked to claim that his students included the Afghan Taliban's top leaders. But he also had his mortal weaknesses. I heard accounts that, some years earlier, the Pakistani intelligence services had caught the cleric on camera at an Islamabad brothel with two other people, at least one of whom was a prostitute. Subsequently, the cleric, Maulana Sami ul Haq, was informally known in political and media circles as 'Sami the sandwich'.

In Pakistan, it seemed, prose could be as rich as poetry. Novelists such as Mohammed Hanif, Mohsin Hamid and Kamila Shamsie were gaining global acclaim for their artful depictions of the country. But daily life offered the best material. 'We have no need for magic realism,' a lawyer friend told me. 'We just have realism.'

❦

In a country of contradictions, it made sense to visit the opposition. I flew to Dubai, where I found Benazir Bhutto at her suburban villa. She sat in a gilded armchair, tapping on her BlackBerry and picking from a box of chocolates. A Mercedes was parked outside. 'Do help yourself, Mr Walsh,' she purred, at once imperious and intimate.

Foreigners were never quite sure what to make of Benazir. As a young woman, she was the object of global admiration, the whip-smart, eloquent daughter of a Pakistani prime minister. She went to Radcliffe and then Oxford, where she drove a sports car, was known as 'Pinky', and entranced posh young Englishmen with her regal airs. In the 1980s, she led a gutsy campaign against a brutal military dictator, General Zia ul Haq, who had overseen the execution of her father. Returning from exile, in 1986, the streets filled with fervent supporters clamouring for a glimpse of the steely thirty-three-year-old beauty – 'that wisp of a girl that the generals were scared of', as the revolutionary poet Habib Jalib put it. Two years later she was prime minister, the first woman to hold that position in a Muslim-majority country, glamorous and commanding. The fairytale soured. Her two terms of office, from 1988 to 1990 and 1993 to 1996, were marred by disappointments. She sparred endlessly with the army, failed to reform Pakistan's misogynistic laws, and, along with her husband, developed a reputation for mouth-watering corruption. Benazir denied the accusations, but after she fled into exile, in 1997, lurid details spilled out: Swiss bank accounts, a lavish English country estate and jewellery splurges at the Bulgari and Cartier showrooms in Beverly Hills. She claimed it was inherited wealth. 'I mean, what is poor and what is rich?' she said to a *New York Times* journalist.

The Bhuttos were one of South Asia's great political dynasties – part Greek tragedy and part *The Godfather*, a sweeping story of hope, hubris and tragedy, written against the backdrop of four decades of tumultuous politics, frequently in blood. It started with Benazir's father, Zulfikar Ali Bhutto, a swashbuckling lawyer-turned-politician who came to power in 1971. Bhutto mesmerised Pakistanis with his heady oratory and buccaneering style, vowing to renew their pride after the debacle of the secession of East Pakistan. Riding the socialist wave of the era, he pledged land reform and wealth redistribution, and secretly launched Pakistan's effort to build a nuclear bomb. He gave no quarter to anyone. On a visit to the White House in 1963, the story went, President John F. Kennedy was so impressed with Bhutto, then Pakistan's foreign minister, that he said: 'If you were an American, you would be in my cabinet.' To which Bhutto is said to have replied: 'If I were an American, you'd be in mine.'

An enthusiastic drinker, he brushed aside conservatives who tried to use it against him. 'At least I don't drink the blood of the people!' he proclaimed at a rally. 'Long may our Bhutto drink!' roared his supporters. Ultimately, though, many were bitterly disappointed. Bhutto ruled with a ruthless, arrogant touch. He jailed critics, including former allies, failed to deliver key reforms, and implemented a clumsy nationalisation programme that wreaked havoc on the economy. Discontent fed street protests that Bhutto tried to head off with a sop to conservatives: a ban on his beloved booze. It was too late. In July 1977, the army chief, General Zia, a pious man with an obsequious manner and a gleaming smile, ousted Bhutto in a military coup. Zia had been Bhutto's hand-picked choice only a year earlier, on account of his apparent lack of ambition. In 1979, following a trial on trumped-up murder charges, Bhutto was hanged in the courtyard of Rawalpindi jail.

But in killing Bhutto, Zia had resurrected his legacy. The traumatic execution created a powerful cult of martyrdom around Bhutto, made a villain of Zia, and anointed Benazir as the presumptive saviour of Pakistan's battered dreams of democracy. Tragedy struck again. In 1985, Benazir's younger brother Shahnawaz was found dead in a holiday apartment in the South of France, mysteriously poisoned. In 1996, her other brother, Murtaza, was gunned down by the police outside the family's Karachi mansion, at a time when Benazir was prime minister. The Bhutto mausoleum, an imposing structure that towers over the family's feudal lands in the countryside of Sindh, filled up fast.

Now Benazir, the survivor, was marooned in Dubai, held at arm's length by her latest military foe. As we talked, she complained that General Musharraf was rounding up her supporters: 'Five thousand of our workers have been arrested in Lahore. There's teargassing taking place on the border between Punjab and Sindh as we're speaking, right now.' She sighed. 'We want elections. They're not listening.'

Her husband bounded into the room, flashing his trademark Cheshire-cat smile. Asif Ali Zardari had been released from jail in Pakistan weeks earlier, after twelve years in detention. Benazir pined for her husband during their long years of separation, she told me. But to many Pakistanis, Zardari was 'Mr Ten Per Cent', for his supposed cut from crooked government deals.

Their marriage, in 1987, was South Asia's most notorious arranged match – Benazir, the haughty feudal princess, and Zardari, the hard-partying Karachi playboy whose father owned a cinema in the city. As prime minister, Benazir had been embarrassed by his garish indulgences, such as the polo stables, large enough to house forty ponies in air-conditioned comfort, built at taxpayer expense on the grounds of the prime minister's official residence. Benazir claimed to be ignorant of her husband's moneymaking schemes. But later, when the details came out – about the foreign bank accounts with tens of millions of dollars – it was harder to play innocent.

Like any good dynasty, the Bhuttos had their share of feuds. Amid the rice fields of Sindh I met Benazir's uncle, seventy-three-year-old Mumtaz, who sat on the veranda of his century-old house receiving a line of peasants who touched his feet before speaking. Over the course of a sumptuous lunch, Mumtaz talked about his 15,000-acre property, waxed lyrical about his recent holiday on Italy's Amalfi coast – 'We stayed at the Hotel Splendido; absolutely heavenly' – and attacked his estranged niece. 'She destroyed her father's household,' he said, 'and she'll make a deal with anyone to get into power, by any means.'

In Karachi I shared a meal with Benazir's twenty-six-year-old niece, Fatima. Her nose curled at the mention of her aunt. 'Oh, you mean Mrs Zardari,' she said. Fatima accused Benazir and Zardari of orchestrating the police shooting that killed her father, Murtaza, and was writing a book that would describe them as a villainous pair. By all accounts, the shooting was a complicated business, but Fatima was driven by unyielding certainty. 'She's a nasty piece of work,' she said of her aunt.

Benazir, who had wailed in anguish after the death of Murtaza, sidestepped my enquiry about her niece's rage. 'She's a sweet girl, very nice,' she said. 'I hope that one day her eyes will open.' Her major concern was to find a way back to Pakistan. Delicate talks with General Musharraf were already under way. But the struggle was no longer just about democracy versus dictatorship, she said. There were worrisome signs that the forces of Islamist extremism were gathering strength inside Pakistan – soon Pakistanis would have to decide what kind of country they wanted. 'Will our future be obscurantist or enlightened?' she asked.

※

As fascinating as Bhutto was, political leaders told only part of Pakistan's story. It dawned on me that I was learning most from what you might call the offstage encounters of my job. Pakistan was full of people who wanted to talk. Their motivations differed, but I realised that their stories were the threads that might help me make sense of this hurly-burly country. The most revealing encounters, when I felt I was really getting to grips with how Pakistan worked, were not with the larger-than-life politicians but with these secondary characters – people in the smaller headlines, or no headline at all – who were willing to speak with frequently astonishing candour.

One evening I was invited to have a drink with a businessman. He lived in an elegant bungalow on a leafy street, where I found him sunk into an armchair, a dog snoozing at his feet, in a room that was adorned with expensive art, mostly Islamic calligraphy in dramatic swirls of blue and gold. A servant walked in bearing a silver tray, an ice bucket and a bottle of Johnnie Walker Black Label. My host, who was occupied chopping a small pile of white powder with his credit card, motioned to the bottle. 'Help yourself,' he said.

I had come to learn about graft, a subject on which my host considered himself an unrecognised authority. By his own admission, he had passed cash-filled envelopes to ministers, bureaucrats and generals in exchange for favours and government contracts. 'You guys in the West call it corruption,' he said. 'We call it a reasonable cost of business.' This was an important part of the Pakistan story. To justify the military's decades-old domination, the generals routinely described graft as an incurable condition of the country's political class. Many Western experts agreed. The businessman saw it differently. In Pakistan, everyone was on the take, he insisted; only their methods differed. He explained the rules of the game. Bribes were paid on a sliding scale: 10 per cent for small contracts, 5 per cent for anything worth $10 million or more; 3 per cent for everything else. Now and then, international bodies such as the World Bank forced the authorities to adopt anti-corruption measures, such as tendering and shortlists. He sighed. 'Paperwork,' he said.

'Look,' he said, 'there are fifty ways to fix a game, and 90 per cent of the time here in Pakistan the game is fixed. I may not agree with the system, but it's the only way to survive.' He sympathised with the politicians' plight. It could cost tens of thousands of dollars to get elected in Pakistan, he said. Plates of steaming *biryani* had to be bought for tents filled with impoverished constituents; buses had to be hired to transport them to polling stations; cash handouts had to be provided to ensure their votes. Once in office, 'they have to find a way to make the money back.'

Of course, they appreciated the good life, too. The servant walked back in, holding the businessman's phone, and whispered in his ear. A car had pulled up outside the front gate. My host stopped chopping the white powder, decanted it into a small plastic bag that he sealed inside an envelope, then handed it to the servant, who carried it to the driver of the car at his gate. 'Cocaine,' the businessman said, saving me the embarrassment of asking. 'For a politician. He happens to be a friend of mine. I'm sure he's got some girl coming over, so he rang to ask if I had any.' Times had changed, he noted. Before, powerful Pakistanis demanded cases of expensive Scotch to sweeten a deal; now they wanted a more powerful buzz. 'I always keep a little lying around, just in case,' he said.

The key to meeting the right people was *sifarish*, an intercession from a well-connected friend. *Sifarish* was a kind of magic carpet in Pakistan. With the right push, it could take you just about anywhere – to distant tribal forts, to army bases in Waziristan and to hidden corners of the cities. Truths could also be gleaned from the small things, like the way people drove. Pakistanis swerved into traffic without looking, veered between lanes, and rarely signalled when they were turning, which made it hard to predict where anyone was going. Drivers honked horns and flashed lights but observed a strict social hierarchy: hulking four-wheel-drives barged heedlessly through packs of diminutive, locally made Suzukis. On the roadside, police officers took bribes.

The crime pages of the newspapers were written in a charming, old-fashioned diction that was a holdover from colonial times. Police detectives were 'sleuths', suspects who refused to speak had 'kept mum', and anyone who spoke to a reporter had 'told this scribe', which brought to mind a medieval monk hunched over parchment in his cell. My favourite term was *miscreant*, used to describe lawbreakers of any kind, from petty thief to terrorist mastermind. Pakistan had a lot of miscreants.

People like to get involved in the reporting. I once wrote a story about child marriage while on a domestic flight to Islamabad from Multan. As we prepared to land, the passenger behind me tapped my shoulder. 'I've been reading your story,' he said. 'Nice job. Could I offer a few suggestions on how to improve it?'

Under the surface, there lurked a mischievous sense of humour. In Karachi I went to see Mahmood Shaam, the editor of *Jang*, Pakistan's biggest-selling Urdu-language paper, who was just back from a tour of the United States. The State Department had funded his travel, as part of a cultural-exchange programme intended to foster grassroots ties between the two countries and overcome their history of mistrust. The experience prompted Shaam to write a book about his experience. He handed me a copy. A dramatic cover depicted the Statue of Liberty being swarmed by F-16 warplanes and surrounded by explosions.

I asked Shaam to translate the title, which was in Urdu. A wry smile flashed across his face.

'Visit America Before America Visits You,' he said.

My notebooks filled with scenes and characters: a Dirty Harry cop who enforced the law by breaking it; a poetry-quoting tribal chieftain, readying for war at his desert fort; a coquettish movie star who shocked Pakistanis by posing topless for an Indian men's magazine. I started to receive, as well as make, requests for *sifarish*. I was out on a Saturday evening when I received a strange phone call from a political contact. The man was standing with a police officer, he said, at a venue named the Cathouse. 'Don't you remember telling me about the Cathouse?' he asked, sounding stressed. 'Could you explain that to the officer?' I had no idea what he was talking about. The line was cut.

I heard nothing further until days later when I read a newspaper report about a police raid on an Islamabad brothel, run by Chinese and Ukrainian women, called the Cathouse. 'Many bigwigs among regular visitors of "Cathouse"' read the headline. A video of the raid appeared on YouTube that showed, at one moment, my contact standing in a hallway, a police officer by his side, yelling into his phone. 'Don't you remember telling me about the Cathouse?' he asks.

As time went on, and Pakistan came to be seen in the foreign press as a threat to global security, on a par with countries like North Korea and Iran, friends began to resent how their country was portrayed. Mostly Western-educated, their lives were punctuated by dinner parties, swanky weddings and foreign vacations. They resented being lumped in with the 'fundos', as fundamentalists were pejoratively known, and, as Islamophobia swelled in the West, felt their identity as Muslims was coming under siege. Why didn't I report on 'the real Pakistan', they asked, showing photos of verdant valleys from their weekends in the northern mountains, or taking me to glitzy fashion shows in five-star hotels, where organisers made breathless claims that models in tank tops were somehow standing up to the Taliban.

Yet nostalgia and denial could not mask the cruel, ugly and downright terrifying side of Pakistan. Hateful currents swirled close to the surface of daily life. Extremists attacked Christians, Shias and other minorities – gunning them down in the streets, torching their homes and blowing up their places of worship. Discrimination was enshrined in the law. Members of the Ahmadi faith, considered heretics by orthodox Muslims, had to renounce a central tenet of their faith to get a passport. Justice was a function of income: the rich and well connected could steal, kill and avoid their taxes with wide impunity. Women were subjected to heinous violence – shot, stabbed or strangled, often by their own families – in the name of 'honour'. Others were burned with acid, their faces melting in agonising pain, all for the rage of a jealous or insecure man. Such crimes were so banal as to barely merit a few inches in the papers, alongside the other tales of heartbreaking desperation: a maid found hanging from a fan in her employer's living room; a rickshaw driver, driven crazy by poverty, who killed his children, his wife and then himself. As much as anything, those small stories presented a searing indictment.

※

One day I purchased, for about a dollar, a map of Pakistan. Printed by Haqqi Brothers of 22 Urdu Bazaar, Karachi, it depicted Pakistan in bright, bold colours. But a note in the corner sounded a note of hesitation. 'Boundaries and other information on this map may not be authentic,' it read. The caveat spoke volumes about the psychology of insecurity in Pakistan, one of a handful of countries – the other notable example is Israel – whose borders were drawn by faith.

At independence in 1947, Pakistan had been carved from the flanks of British India by Muhammad Ali Jinnah, a nattily dressed lawyer who, fearing Hindu domination, sought to create a Muslim homeland. Yet decades later, as my map illustrated, only one-sixth of Pakistan's borders had been formally agreed. To the north, a dispute with Afghanistan had festered for decades. The Afghans claimed that a chunk of northwestern Pakistan, as far as the Indus river, was rightfully theirs, fuelling endless conflict. To the east, in the high Himalayas, an old border argument with China had been resolved, but not formally settled. South of that, the map traced the deepest scars: Kashmir, a stunning mountainous territory of snow-capped peaks and emerald valleys.

But if maps evoked Pakistan's external insecurities, its most sensitive borders lay inside the country, which was riven by ethnic, tribal and sectarian fault lines, a place of head-spinning contradictions. One day, a street would fill with rioters protesting against an obscure insult to the name of the Prophet Muhammad. The following day, rich folk would gather to party in a mansion along the same street, clinking their glasses in a Gatsby-like bubble. Depending on who you asked, Islam or the army were supposed to be the glue holding the place together. Yet both, in their own way, seemed to be tearing it apart. People stumbled from crisis to crisis, hoping to find answers. But they remained elusive. More concept than country, Pakistan strained under the centrifugal forces of history, identity and faith. Could it hold?

Pakistanis themselves seemed unsure. Some took refuge in conspiracy theories, hoping to make sense of the paradoxes through lurid accounts of Indian, American or Israeli meddling. Others indulged in weary self-flagellation. 'The whole trajectory of this place is wrong,' wrote Cyril Almeida in *Dawn*, the newspaper established by Jinnah. 'What does it matter where you're coming from if down is where you're headed?' It was a country of sighs and regrets, the only I had been where some of its own citizens quietly regretted it had ever come into being. Early in my stay, I visited the Parliament building in Islamabad. Inside the cavernous chamber, querulous deputies hurled abuse at each other as Jinnah watched wearily from a giant portrait. Fakir Syed Aijazuddin, a writer from Lahore, noted that Pakistan recalls Julian Barnes's definition of a net as 'a collection of holes tied together with string . . . less a country than a mesh of voids, bound by coils of self-interest'.

To me, Pakistan resembled one of those old Japanese puzzle boxes, comprised of secret compartments and hidden traps, which can only be opened in a unique, step-by-step sequence. One afternoon, as I sat in my garden with a friend, considering the latest convulsion, he suddenly threw up his hands in exasperation. 'That's the difference between us,' he said. 'You are always looking for answers. I have trouble with the questions.'

In my darker moments, it seemed the only thing holding it all together was blind faith. '*Insha'Allah* it will happen,' people said, all the time.

Insha'Allah translates as 'If God wills it', and I heard it everywhere. On my first trip to Pakistan, as the plane descended to Islamabad, the pilot addressed the cabin: '*Insha'Allah* we will be landing shortly,' he announced, somewhat disconcertingly. The phrase was hardwired into the national psyche – a code, a philosophy, a comfort blanket to get through tough times. Sure, things were hard, people admitted. But Pakistan would stumble through, as it had always done – *Insha'Allah*.

Were they right? About three years into my stay, things really began to fall apart.

Abdul Rashid Ghazi

2

Red Zone

The Reluctant Fundamentalist

The Holiday Inn in downtown Islamabad wasn't much to look at: a nondescript slab of seventies architecture, tucked behind a popular food market, with a greasy buffet and an antiseptic whiff in the corridors. But on a steamy night in the summer of 2007, it afforded the best available vantage point on an extraordinary showdown.

The walls of room 203, where I was staying, quivered gently as an orange flash flickered in the sky. A helicopter, its engine buzzing like a chainsaw, swooped overhead. Then came an unmistakable sound: the soft suck of a bullet whistling past my window.

The gunfire was coming from the Red Mosque, an egg-shaped, ruby-domed building about 400 yards down the street. For days, the police and military had been pummelling it with gunfire and rockets in an effort to flush out its occupants: a motley coalition of teenage students and hardened jihadis that was led by a pair of radical clerics, who were brothers. In the early days of the siege, it had been possible to catch glimpses of the fighters on the mosque roof, hunched behind sandbags, squeezing off bursts of automatic gunfire. There were hundreds of girls inside, too – students at the sprawling girls' *madrassa* next door, clad in all-covering, jet-black cloaks. Some escaped during lulls in fighting, blurry shadows that stumbled from bullet-pocked walls, sprinting into the waiting arms of their distraught parents.

A Waco-style siege in the heart of sleepy Islamabad — it was a bizarre turn of events, as jarring and disconcerting as a pitched battle in downtown Brussels or Washington, DC. The Red Mosque was located within a mile of the institutions of Pakistan's see-saw democracy: the Parliament, the Supreme Court and the modernist, American-designed Presidential Palace, now occupied by the army chief Pervez Musharraf. The mosque was built in the 1960s, when a Greek architect carved Islamabad from the rock-strewn plains of northern Punjab, but was overshadowed in the 1980s by the completion of the Faisal Mosque – a soaring, blindingly white edifice, funded by the king of Saudi Arabia, that nestled at the foot of the Margalla Hills. Still, the Red Mosque retained a certain cachet. The traders, teachers and bureaucrats who kept Islamabad humming thronged its hall for Friday prayers, in such great numbers that they frequently spilled onto the street. Among them were officers from the military's ISI spy agency, whose low-key headquarters was a five-minute drive away.

The neighbourhood around the Red Mosque had been officially designated a 'Red Zone', ringed with barbed wire and sealed off from the rest of Islamabad. A curfew was imposed, the electricity was cut off and residents were forced to stay inside their homes, listening anxiously as the battle raged outside. A few nights earlier, commandos from the elite Special Services Group, which Musharraf once commanded, stole up to the perimeter of the mosque and tried to blast their way through, triggering a fusillade of fire from within that killed two soldiers, including the lead commando. Now the press was being kept well back and so, in an effort to get closer to the action, I checked into the deserted Holiday Inn a few streets away.

I flipped on the television. The mosque's spokesman and deputy leader, Abdul Rashid Ghazi, was on air, speaking by mobile phone from a bunker inside the besieged compound, engaged in stormy negotiations with Musharraf's snowy-haired interior minister, Aftab Ahmad Sherpao. It wasn't going well. The minister implored Ghazi to lay down his arms. Ghazi responded with spitting defiance, raging against Musharraf, his voice chipped and strained after days of pulsating violence and sleepless nights. The phone signal faded and Ghazi's voice trailed off, obscured by hiss and static, as if he was calling from a storm-hit town, or a distant planet. There was a beeping noise, then silence. 'Hello? 'said Ghazi, his voice betraying a hint of desperation. 'Hello?' Sherpao had hung up.

After midnight, a fresh barrage of gunfire jolted me from my bed. I pulled on my trousers and clambered up the emergency staircase, guided by the glow of my phone, heart pounding. Once on the rooftop, I felt my way through a deserted barbecue restaurant to the roof edge, to peer over the parapet. The Red Mosque was still out of sight, obscured behind a line of trees, but the battle unfolded in stereophonic sound: thunderous booms, undulating waves of gunfire, more flashes in the sky, then silence. Down below, soldiers perched on an armoured vehicle in the hotel car park, and sewage pooled in empty streets strewn with piles of uncollected rubbish.

The pampered residents of Islamabad grappled with this surreal turn of events. Stray gunfire tumbled from the sky, killing a construction worker at a five-star hotel and shattering a window in the home of the British defence attaché. The silky golf lawns at the Islamabad Club, a favoured haunt of bumptious military officers and senior bureaucrats, were deserted. At night, diners sat on the balcony of a French restaurant, watching the skyline light up with the red glow of exploding ordnance. Nobody made jokes about sleepy Islamabad any more.

I finally fell asleep. The following morning, Ghazi was back on television, newly defiant. 'We may be martyred,' he declared. 'But we will not surrender.'

It felt like a bluff. I knew Ghazi. He had always struck me as a politician, not a martyr. He would find a way out.

Not for the first time in Pakistan, I was entirely wrong.

❀

'Have you seen *Best of Baghdad*?' Ghazi inquired, proffering a cup of milky tea.

It was a Friday morning, four months earlier, and we were seated cross-legged on the floor of a cramped room behind the Red Mosque. A slender young man with a wispy beard sat hunched over a computer, making DVD copies of movies. *Best of Baghdad*, it turned out, was one of them: a fifteen-minute slice of jihadist propaganda that focused on the exploits of an insurgent sniper fighting the American occupation in Iraq. The video had several sequences, all roughly the same: the camera tracks a group of American soldiers patrolling in the distance. A sniper's shot rings out. One of the Americans crumples to the ground, clutching his wound. His panicked comrades swarm around.

'Wonderful,' said Ghazi, smiling as he turned to face me. 'Of course, Islam does not allow us to kill the innocent. But the Americans are invaders.'

Jihadi puffery aside, I rather liked Ghazi. He was in his early forties, with round glasses, an unkempt beard and the curious, earnest manner of an obliging university professor. He spoke fluent English in soft, mellifluous tones and had a warm, engaging manner, always with a smile dancing on his lips. His cheery manner contrasted with the mosque's sour-faced leader, his older brother Abdul Aziz, who on Fridays would climb the pulpit to inveigh against the United States or to praise Osama bin Laden, an old family friend. Ghazi painted himself in the softer tones of a principled, picaresque rebel. His political heroes included Che Guevara and Fidel Castro, and he relished debate with Western visitors, when he demonstrated a knack for the apposite sound bite, framing his arguments for Islamic rule in universal notions like social justice and civic responsibility. 'Do you remember Giuliani's *zero tolerance*?' he said to me, referring to New York Mayor Rudy Giuliani's anti-crime initiative during the 1990s. 'We're just doing like him.'

He was referring, in fact, to the vigilante campaign being waged by the female teenage students at Jamia Hafsa, the *madrassa* next door to the Red Mosque, who had burst into the spotlight with an unusual protest. The girls hailed mostly from poor, conservative families in the rural hinterland of Islamabad and further afield in northwestern Pakistan, often from communities where women of all ages were usually hidden from view. Now they had burst into the spotlight. Clad in long black cloaks and wielding wooden staves, the girls had seized control of a nearby children's library to protest about a government initiative that angered Ghazi – a push to shut down the many illegally built, ideologically radical mosques which had mushroomed around Islamabad and Rawalpindi in previous years. It could be seen as an unorthodox kind of empowerment.

At first, Islamabad's middle-class residents viewed their antics as a kind of absurdist street theatre. 'Chicks with sticks' read one newspaper headline. But as the protests dragged on, the sniggering died out. Photographs showed a phalanx of these black-clad students posing at the gates of the *madrassa*, their sticks held aloft, like the guardians of a medieval citadel. Some told journalists they would become suicide bombers – until then, a rarity in Pakistan – unless their demands were met.

'Young people,' said Ghazi. 'So enthusiastic.'

Outside the door of the room where we were sitting stood a young man wielding a Kalashnikov rifle. I had noticed other guards scattered across the compound. 'All our weapons are licensed,' Ghazi assured me. 'Purely for self-defence.'

The occupation of the children's library was a first step towards a greater goal, Ghazi declared: the imposition of Islamic rule across Pakistan. Like Saudi Arabia? I asked. No, he said. The Kingdom had been corrupted by oil-rich, America-loving monarchs; Ghazi envisioned a system that mirrored the rule of the Prophet Muhammad in seventh-century Arabia. Already, male students at the mosque wore their baggy *shalwar* pants hitched above the ankle, and grew their beards to the length of a fist, in imitation of Muhammad's reputed style. 'Pakistan was established on the basis of Islam, and that system should be implemented,' Ghazi said firmly.

Few Pakistanis share that view, I noted: the religious parties won just 11 per cent of votes in the previous election. Ah, yes, Ghazi countered, but who was talking about democracy? 'Islam is about selection, not elections,' he said.

'So many people are uneducated and behave like sick sheep,' he continued. 'They need a guiding hand. For example, a drug addict doesn't know what is good for himself or his family, never mind the interests of his country. But he has the same vote as a person who is intellectually strong, who understands what is good. That is the problem with democracy.'

The *azaan*, or call to prayer, rang out. Ghazi swallowed the last of his tea and excused himself, handing me a copy of *Best of Baghdad*. As I left, worshippers filtered into the mosque under the wary gaze of police officers assembled outside. Young men with scarves around their faces perched on the mosque roof, bamboo staves gripped tightly in their hands. Above them fluttered the Red Mosque flag – a pair of crossed swords against a black background – which bore a striking resemblance to the Taliban standard.

❈

Men with clamorous dreams of Islamic revolution are nothing new in South Asia. The first notable *jihad*, or war of resistance, occurred in 1831 in Balakot, a town in the lush Himalayan foothills. In military terms, it was a disastrous flop. A revivalist Muslim preacher named Sayyid Ahmad, who sought to create an Islamic state among the Pashtun tribes, led hundreds of followers into battle against a contingent of Sikh invaders. But a band of tribesmen who had promised to stand with the cleric betrayed him, so when Sayyid Ahmad charged from a mosque, crying '*Allahu Akbar!*', he was promptly slain. Yet, defeat became victory. Among his followers, he was revered as the quintessential Islamic warrior, braving impossible odds in the name of God, ready to embrace martyrdom. Still today, his grave is a shrine for pilgrims who come to pay their respects. The lush hills around Balakot, meanwhile, are dotted with secretive training camps where modern-day Pakistani jihadis train for battle against Indian forces in Kashmir.

In the second half of the nineteenth century, *jihad* became the frame for resistance to British colonial rule in northern India. A succession of charismatic clerical rebels became the scourge of the Raj, leading bands of guerrillas who harried and fought the imperial army. The British, for their part, portrayed the clerics as sinister fanatics, and caricatured them with nicknames such as the 'Mad Mullah of Malakand'. In the early 1900s, Lord Kitchener, the commander-in-chief of the British forces, derided one irksome opponent, a rebel cleric named Mullah Powindah, as a 'pestilential priest'. In the 1940s, nearly forty thousand troops hunted an elusive mystic known in London as 'The Scarlet Pimpernel of Waziristan'.

Paradoxically, the creation of Pakistan, in 1947, diminished the clerics' importance. Although the new nation was a homeland for Muslims, religious leaders rejected the notion that the nation-state, then a new-fangled concept, could contain the grandeur of the Muslim *ummah*, or community of believers. They sought a caliphate. Their rejectionism was a grave strategic mistake. In the early decades of Pakistan's existence, army generals and powerful bureaucrats ruled the roost, leaving the clerics in the cold. The power of mullahs slipped. By the early 1970s, they had come to occupy a modest place on the social ladder in towns and villages, somewhere between the tailor and the teacher. Clerics instructed children in the Qur'an; officiated at births, weddings, and funerals; and were the object of gentle mockery for their fondness for *halwa*, a syrupy dessert.

Their fortunes were transformed, in 1977, by the arrival in power of General Zia. Born into a modest, socially conservative family in southern Punjab, Zia rejected the whisky-swilling ways of the aristocratic, pseudo-British officers who had led the army since 1947. 'I said prayers instead,' he said. After ousting Zulfikar Ali Bhutto in July 1977, the military dictator embarked on an ambitious drive to reshape Pakistani society.

Zia introduced a slew of harsh Islamic laws that sought to turn Pakistan away from its roots in the rich cultural soil of South Asia in favour of a harsh, unyielding brand of Islam imported from the sands of Saudi Arabia. Criminals were flogged in public, female television presenters had to cover their heads, and the crime of blasphemy – any perceived insult to the Prophet Muhammad – became a capital offence. In the courts, women became second-class citizens whose testimony was devalued to half the worth of a man's, which made it impossible to prosecute for rape. Muslim preachers turned up on military bases, giving sermons to officers and rank-and-file alike, and Zia turned for political support to religious parties like the Jamaat-e-Islami – Pakistan's version of Egypt's Muslim Brotherhood – which usually won only a small fraction of the vote.

Following the execution of Bhutto in April 1979, Zia would have become an international pariah – 'We Also Hang Our Prime Ministers' sneered the headline in *The Economist* over a photo of a smug-looking Zia – were it not for a fortuitous calamity in neighbouring Afghanistan. Soviet tanks rolled into Kabul in December 1979, signalling the start of a momentous confrontation whose effects would reverberate across Pakistan – and the world – for decades. Afghan resistance fighters, known as the *mujahideen*, took up arms to fight the Red Army occupiers, in a war that become known the *jihad*. The CIA and Saudi intelligence funded the fight, to the tune of billions of dollars, but Zia was in charge. His ISI ran a network of guerrilla training camps in northern Pakistan and managed a vast covert war machine that funnelled Kalashnikovs, Stinger missiles and bundles of hard cash to the *mujahideen*, especially the most radical Islamists among them. Soon, Zia was being feted in Western capitals as an indispensable Cold War ally.

The *jihad* wrought tremendous change inside Pakistan. A countrywide network of radical mosques and *madrassas*, funded by Saudi Arabia, sprang up across the country. The mosques served as way stations for the thousands of foreign volunteers who were arriving in Pakistan from across the Muslim world, in the hope of joining the righteous fight against the godless communists. Many viewed the *jihad* as a moral cause, much like the European volunteers who went into Spain to fight Franco in the 1930s. They included Osama bin Laden, the callow, twenty-three-year-old son of a Saudi billionaire, who landed in Pakistan at the start of the war, straight from college.

Zia perished in 1988, when his C-130 aircraft mysteriously nose-dived into a field, its propellers spinning at full speed. One popular theory had it that a nerve-gas canister hidden in a crate of mangoes had incapacitated its crew. The culprit was never identified: by then, Zia had so many enemies that investigators hardly knew where to start looking. All that remained of the dictator was his jawbone, which was buried inside a tomb at Islamabad's Faisal Mosque. But Zia had bequeathed a poisonous legacy to his country.

The Afghan war forged a new generation of Pakistani jihadis – fired-up young fighters, driven by a hardline Islamist ideology and burning with a new sense of purpose. And it left behind a network of radical mosques and madrassas, led by emboldened clerics, where new generations of jihadis could be shaped. An Ivy League of hard-line institutions sprang up in the big cities. In Karachi, there was Binori Town, memorably described by the French writer Bernard-Henri Lévy as 'the house of the devil'. Not far from Peshawar stood the Darul Uloom Haqqania, the gigantic seminary run by the 'Father of the Taliban', Maulana Sami ul Haq. Islamabad had the Red Mosque.

Its founder and chief cleric was Muhammad Abdullah Ghazi, a fire-and-brimstone preacher who became a confidant of General Zia. Through the 1980s, the Red Mosque hosted a stream of foreign fighters bound for Afghanistan, including bin Laden, who became a family friend. Abdullah volunteered his own family into the fight too: his oldest son, the po-faced Abdul Aziz, joined the fighters heading north. His other son, though, proved a bitter disappointment.

As a teenager, Abdul Rashid Ghazi chafed against the dictates of his preacher father. He attended a regular high school and later enrolled at Quaid-i-Azam University – a verdant, modern campus on the edge of the capital where he studied international relations and history, read Nietzsche and Rousseau, and mixed easily with fellow students, including women. 'A normal, moderate student who was well adjusted to the co-educational system. Not a firebrand,' recalled Naeem Qureshi, a history professor who taught him between 1987 and 1989. Qureshi showed me a faded photo from that time, taken during a class picnic in the Margalla Hills, which showed a fresh-faced Ghazi standing curiously over a young woman as she stirs a pot of chicken curry. Also in the photo was Malik Ahmed Khan, the son of a Punjabi landowner, who befriended the cheery young student. 'He had such a sweet voice, and he would sing for all of his class fellows,' said Khan, who noted that Ghazi was otherwise fascinated by computer technology and had a reputation for elaborate practical jokes.

After graduation, Ghazi worked for the education ministry and the United Nations cultural organisation, UNESCO, where he arrived at work in a snappy suit with a red pocket handkerchief. (Ghazi jokingly called this his 'glamour boy period.') He travelled to France for work and groused to friends about his older brother, whom he found too rigid in this thinking. Ghazi's 'Western' ways infuriated his father, Abdullah, who admonished him for bringing shame upon the family and declared that, upon his death, control of the Red Mosque would pass to Abdul Aziz.

Even so, Ghazi also did a short stint fighting alongside the *mujahideen* – more excited, friends said, by the glamour and adventure of the war, than by any strictly religious aspect of it. 'He loved the vehicles and the danger and the gossip,' his friend, Malik Khan, told me. And despite their differences, the father and son made a trip together in 1998 to Tarnak Farms, a militant camp on the outskirts of Kandahar, in southern Afghanistan, where they met with bin Laden. Months later, al Qaeda bombed the United States embassies in Kenya and Tanzania, drawing a salvo of American cruise missiles that pulverised militant training camps in southern Afghanistan. In Islamabad, Abdullah declared war on the United States. 'As far as Islam is concerned, it is now permissible to kill Americans,' he said in one Friday sermon. As worshippers filed out of the Red Mosque, they chanted, 'Jihad till the last drop of blood.'

Two months later, Abdullah was assassinated. A gunman opened fire on the sixty-three year old cleric as he strolled across the courtyard of the Red Mosque, inflicting fatal injuries. Ghazi was devastated. Although Shia extremists took the blame for the shooting, Ghazi suspected that the Pakistani military was behind it. 'He said they used his father for *jihad*, then threw him away,' Malik Khan told me. With his confidence in the rule of law shattered, and haunted by feelings of guilt, Ghazi's life veered in a radical new direction. He moved back into the Red Mosque under his brother, Abdul Aziz. The snappy suits were replaced by a baggy *shalwar kameez* and Palestinian keffiyeh; he grew a thick beard and was fired from his job at the education ministry. He drifted into the orbit of Islamist groups he had once rejected. In early 2000, the mosque hosted Masood Azhar, a Pakistani cleric who had been freed from jail in India after fellow militants hijacked an Indian Airlines jetliner and forced it to land in Afghanistan. Standing beside an armed guard, Azhar urged worshippers to fight for Kashmir, drawing chants of 'Al-jihad! Al-jihad!'

The brothers' sense of purpose was galvanised by the 2001 attacks on America. The Red Mosque instantly became a platform for popular fury over the American invasion of Afghanistan. On Fridays, Abdul Aziz rose to the pulpit to denounce Musharraf, hail bin Laden and propagate anti-Semitic conspiracy theories like the claim that Jews had advance knowledge of the 9/11 attacks. For some Western correspondents, rowdy demonstrations that erupted outside the mosque embodied the widening gulf between Pakistan and the West. 'Their faces were drawn narrow with hate, and they were all looking at me,' wrote one Canadian journalist.

Some of this fury, with its flag burnings and declarations of holy war, had a performative aspect. But the sense of betrayal with Pakistan's military was deeply felt. Musharraf's alliance with President George Bush, which earned Pakistan over one billion dollars a year in assistance, infuriated conservatives. In 2004 Abdul Aziz caused uproar with a *fatwa* declaring that Pakistani soldiers who died fighting al Qaeda in the tribal areas should not receive a Muslim burial. Charged with sedition, the two brothers were forced to go on the run. Later, the police discovered explosives in the trunk of Ghazi's car; there were reports he was planning to bomb the United States Embassy.

Musharraf, walking a narrow line between his American allies and the jihadis his military had long supported, deployed his minister for religious affairs, Ijaz ul Haq, to smooth things over. As the eldest son of General Zia, the minister's credentials were impeccable, and he negotiated a deal with the brothers. Months later, they were back at the mosque. But the détente was short-lived. 'We will not stop teaching jihad just because America doesn't like it,' Ghazi said.

Ghazi's trajectory reminded me of the eponymous anti-hero of Mohsin Hamid's 2007 novel *The Reluctant Fundamentalist*, about a worldly Pakistani student who becomes a virulent critic of the United States after 2001. It wasn't just a question of events in Pakistan; in our conversations, he railed against the war in Iraq, the detention camp at Guantánamo Bay and the brutal abuses of Abu Ghraib. Yet he retained the courteous manner and open-minded curiosity of his student years. His *madrassas* offered instruction in English, science and computers, as well as in the Qur'an. He welcomed foreign visitors at his quarters, charming and cajoling them. 'Suavely convincing,' judged one. He joined a delegation of religious leaders that travelled to South Africa, at the UN's expense, to learn about HIV prevention. Others on the trip found him endearingly naive. During a demonstration on condom use by a South African health worker, Ghazi leaned over to a United Nations official, Bettina Schunter. 'What's a dildo?' he asked. Back in Pakistan, Ghazi invited Schunter, who is American, to supper with his wife and their eight-year-old daughter at their apartment behind the Red Mosque.

In June 2007, Farid Esack, a South African scholar who was teaching for a semester at the International Islamic University in Islamabad, paid a visit to Ghazi at the Red Mosque. Their approaches to Islam could hardly have been more different. A clean-shaven, liberal theologian, Esack loudly denounced anti-Semitism, argued for new interpretations of Islamic scripture to permit homosexuality, and had battled religious conservatives over the rights of women. He counted Nelson Mandela as a friend. Yet the two men instantly struck up a rapport. Ghazi peppered the South African with questions about Mandela's life in prison, and they chatted for hours about revolutionaries like Che Guevara and Fidel Castro. 'He didn't have serious knowledge of history or revolutionary events,' Esack, who as a teenager studied in a Karachi *madrassa*, told me. 'But he certainly saw himself in that mould, as the righteous moral rebel.' Esack, was fascinated to learn that Abdul Aziz's wife ran her own HIV programme for women inside the radical *madrassa*. He noted that Ghazi was very much under the spell of his older brother. 'Abdul Aziz had a serious hold over him,' said Esack.

But in the streets outside, the mosque's stick-wielding students were taking their vigilante campaign to a new level. A self-declared 'vice and virtue' squad stormed through a local market, confiscating DVDs from stores that sold Indian and Hollywood movies. The movies were piled outside the Red Mosque and set ablaze for the benefit of TV cameras. They raided a local brothel and dragged its madam back to the Red Mosque, where she was forced to make a humiliating public confession. In sermons, Abdul Aziz accused diplomats' wives of 'spreading nudity' in Islamabad and issued a *fatwa* against Musharraf's tourism minister, Nilofar Bakhtiar, over a photograph that showed her hugging a French skydiving instructor after a jump for charity. 'A sinful hug,' he declared. Weeks later, Bakhtiar resigned, citing security fears.

The mosque's FM radio station declared that Quaid-i-Azam University, Ghazi's alma mater, had become a 'brothel' and suggested that uncovered female students risked having acid thrown in their faces. SHARIA OR MARTYRDOM, read a banner on the mosque walls. At Friday prayers, children wearing toy suicide vests walked among the worshippers.

❀

Malik Ahmed Khan, the old college friend who had remained in touch with Ghazi down the years, tried to persuade the cleric to change course. In long debates, he warned that Ghazi had gone too far. But his friend was becoming withdrawn, less open to challenge. 'He had these new beliefs about fighting and killing,' Khan told me. 'He had become brainwashed.'

❀

The official history of Pakistan records that Islam arrived on the Indian subcontinent at the tip of a sword. In AD 712 less than a century after the death of the Prophet Muhammad, a teenage Arab commander named Muhammad bin Qasim landed on the coast of Sindh, near Karachi. His mission was twofold: to punish Sindh's Brahmin rulers, whose pirate ships had been raiding passing Arab fleets, and to spread the new faith. Mounted on camels and armed with a giant catapult, bin Qasim's force battled up the Indus River, sacking every town they crossed.

What some histories omit to mention, though, is that bin Qasim departed India soon after his conquest, and that Islam only truly took root on the subcontinent many centuries later, with the arrival of ambulatory mystics of a more peaceable disposition. The Sufis, as the mystics were known, focused on the spiritual aspect of their Muslim faith, emphasising closeness to God over outward displays of piety, and preached coexistence with other religions. Hindus and Sikhs worshipped at their glittering shrines, where a relatively tolerant version of Islam took deep roots that endure today.

In the summer of the Red Mosque, I escaped Islamabad and travelled hundreds of miles south to one such shrine, at an ancient settlement on the banks of the Indus, where the biggest party in Pakistan was taking place.

Sehwan Sharif perched on a hill overlooking the river, a labyrinth of ramshackle houses and winding alleys that huddled around a twinkling crown of Sufi shrines. I arrived at two in the morning with Isambard Wilkinson, a friend from the *Daily Telegraph*, after a day-long journey up a battered highway. Even at that hour, people were flooding in: snake charmers and drummers, circus dancers and cigarette sellers, con artists and mendicants and miracle-men. Mostly, though, they were pilgrims, bedraggled families from ragged villages and crowded slums across Sindh and Punjab, disgorged by a stream of overloaded buses that wheezed to a halt on the main street. The town had a carnival air. Stalls offered dripping wedges of Ferrari-red watermelon; a fairground lured customers with dancing monkeys and a rickety Wall of Death; burly, half-clothed men, lathered in suds, stood in an open-air shower. A choir of angel-faced boys perched on the steps of their bus, singing a cappella.

A conga line surged forward, led by a fierce-looking man with kohl-lined eyes: a *fakir*, or Sufi initiate. Behind him, people jiggled and held each other by the waist. I stepped forward and was swept away, borne through the serpentine streets on this exuberant tide, headed for a luminous dome that glittered in the distance.

About a million Pakistanis converge on Sehwan every year during *Sha'ban*, the eighth month of the Muslim calendar, to pay tribute to Usman Marwandi, a thirteenth-century Sufi mystic popularly known as Lal Shahbaz Qalandar. Born in present-day Afghanistan, Qalandar was an ambulatory poet and philosopher, who wandered through the region before settling on the banks of the Indus. This was his 755th *urs*, or death anniversary, and his image adorned billboards and amulets and the stores selling pilgrim tat: a bearded figure with a beatific gaze and a roguish glint in his eye. Lal means 'ruby', after the colour of his cloaks, and his life story had become embroidered with fanciful legends: that he lived in the trunk of a giant tree, or had mystical powers that allowed him to transform into a falcon. His philosophy of interfaith tolerance resonated widely in a land with multiple religious personalities. Hindus and Buddhists flocked to his shrine, and over the centuries he boosted Sufism's reputation as the folk faith of the poor, infused with irreverence and a bawdy sense of humour. 'I have no concern but carouse and rapture,' wrote Jalaluddin Rumi, Sufism's most celebrated philosopher-poet. 'I have no tale to tell but tipsiness and rapture.'

The conga line deposited me before a pair of golden gates where the *dhamaal*, a kind of religious rave, was under way. Hundreds of people were crammed into a small courtyard, dancing frantically to a hypnotic drumbeat that filled the moist air. Barefoot women in red jived and spun like dervishes, their sweat-drenched hair whipping against the men behind them, who pogo-jumped in unison and thrust their hands in the air. Others pressed up against the shrine's gates, whispering silent invocations. The sweet odour of hashish drifted from a group of rheumy-eyed elderly men sucking from a waterpipe, who beckoned me to join them. A lanky *hijra* with smeared lipstick caught my eye and winked extravagantly.

The drumbeat rose and fell; fireworks exploded and fizzled in the sky; a roar went up. I scribbled frantically, globs of sweat drenching my notebook, entranced.

A rickety stairwell led to a rooftop, where snoozing families lay under the stars, oblivious of the din. Stepping over them, I reached a ledge that overlooked the shrine. It had a Las Vegas aesthetic, its elegant onion-shaped domes garlanded in flashing lights and a tacky neon windmill. Yet it seemed to glow in the steamy night, pulsing with a mystical energy, unspeakably lovely. I got chatting with my neighbour, a middle-aged woman in a headscarf. She had come from Peshawar, in the northwest, in defiance of conservative relatives who considered Sufism a form of heresy. 'We have a lot to learn from these people,' she said, pointing to the dancers. 'We believe from the head, but they believe from the heart.'

Sufism is not all song and dance. It has many schools of thought and practice, some quite conservative. Adherents to Sufism have also carried out extremist violence. Yet in general, Sufis practice their faith through a mystical connection with God and have little time for dreams of a new global caliphate, a central objective of the Islamic State and al Qaeda extremists. Prominent Sufi mystics favoured tolerance over obedience and were suspicious of those who preached frown-faced piety. In his poem 'The Saintly Sinner', Sheikh Mohammed Ibrahim Zauq, a poet laureate of the nineteenth-century Mughal court, wrote of the mullahs:

He preaches morals and pines for paradise, but this too
is true:
He will give his life for houris,* he also loves to screw.

* In Islam, *houris* are the beautiful young virgins who await the faithful in paradise.

On my second night in Sehwan, I found myself at the feet of Syed Baryal Shah, one of several *pirs*, or holy men, who plied their trade at the shrine. A burly, half-shaven man in a lustrous red necklace, Shah cut a lordly figure, perched on a leopard-skin rug laid across a raised platform. Throughout the evening, *murids*, or devotees, streamed into his air-conditioned chamber to kiss his turquoise rings, offer tribute and seek help for their earthly woes. Shah offered his blessing in return for a consideration. One family arrived with a mentally impaired boy. 'He suffers from shadows on the brain,' a relative explained. Shah was nonchalantly chewing betel nut, spitting its oily brown juice into a silver dish held aloft by an assistant. He puffed up his chest and splashed a mix of oil and spices on the boy's head. '*Mast Qalandar!*' he exclaimed, invoking the powers of the saint. The boy seemed unmoved but his parents looked pleased. Moments later, the family shuffled out, after palming a wad of rupees to Shah's assistant, a portly man with a teddy-bear face and a toothy grin.

The assistant invited us backstage, so to speak, into the *pir*'s private room. A pair of dainty women's slippers were positioned outside. Three glasses were produced and filled with local moonshine. 'Holy water,' said the assistant, clinking my glass and Isambard's.

We left the next morning, rumbling down the bumpy highway back to Karachi. Despite its size, the festival had gone largely unnoticed. A small item in *Dawn* noted that forty-two pilgrims had died from drowning and heatstroke during the festivities. We stopped at a greasy roadside café, where we joined a group of exhausted *hijras*, also coming from Sehwan, who slumped on rope beds, smoking cigarettes and sipping tea, savouring the pause in a long road trip.

If Sehwan offered a powerful repudiation of the steel-edged versions of Islam that had been imported into Pakistan under General Zia, the tide was turning against it. Extremist seminaries such as the Red Mosque had proliferated since the 1980s, funded by donations from oil-rich Gulf countries. The seminaries were a magnet for the poor, offering children as young as five free food, clothing and a rudimentary education. Students woke at dawn and learned the Qur'an by heart, rocking back and forth for hours on end, parroting an Arabic that few could understand. Sexual abuse, a horrifically common crime, was swept under the carpet.

Textbooks taught that *A is for Allah* and *J is for Jihad*; after 2001, one illustrated the word for *collision* with a jetliner slamming into the World Trade Center. Teachers downplayed democracy in favour of a chimeric new caliphate that would span the Islamic world – from the lost kingdom of Al-Andalus in Spain to the islands of western Asia. I once sat in a dingy *madrassa* in Quetta facing Maulana Noor Muhammad, a pro-Taliban scholar. Behind him, on the wall, was a giant map of this imaginary realm. Yet for the poor, these *madrassas* were better than the alternative. Pakistan's public schools consistently ranked among the worst in South Asia, and the countryside was littered with 'ghost schools', where teachers collected a wage but never showed up. The *madrassas* tapped into a powerful vein of discontent, offering their impoverished students an intoxicating promise: that the shimmering pleasures enjoyed by Pakistan's dissolute elite also could be theirs – although not until the next life.

'All the major institutions of our country have failed to solve its problems,' Abdul Aziz told a journalist at the Red Mosque. 'Military rulers failed. Democratically elected leaders failed. And the judicial system has failed too. Everyone failed, and because of that, there is a vacuum. Somebody's got to fill it.'

❋

In late June 2007, the Red Mosque 'vice and virtue' squad raided a Chinese massage parlour in F-8, close to my home. The vigilantes – ten burka-clad women and young men carrying sticks – abducted six Chinese women whom they accused of being sex workers, and hauled them back to Jamia Hafsa, a *madrassa* run by the Red Mosque that was located in a salubrious Islamabad neighbourhood. The following morning, Abdul Rashid Ghazi summoned the press. 'Islam says that when you see some kind of wrongdoing, you must stop it with your own hand,' he said. 'The students stopped it.' Hours later the Chinese women, draped in all-covering burkas, were released, after the city authorities promised Ghazi they would crack down on other massage parlours. Musharraf's hand had been forced.

China and Pakistan had been steadfast allies for decades. China sold missiles and warplanes to Pakistan; helped develop its secretive nuclear weapons programme; and asked no difficult questions – unlike the irksome Americans. Pakistan repaid the favour following the Tiananmen Square massacre in 1989 when it was among the few foreign leaders to openly support Beijing's brutality. The bond between the two countries was 'higher than the mountains, deeper than the seas, and stronger than steel', as Pakistani and Chinese officials loved to say. The massage parlour incident strained that bond. It was certainly true, as Ghazi charged, that some of Islamabad's Chinese-run establishments offered much more than massages. (Several senior Pakistani politicians were said to be among their clients.) But Beijing was also investing hundreds of millions of dollars in Musharraf's pet projects, such as the new deep-water port he was building at Gwadar, on the Arabian Sea. China expected its citizens in Pakistan to be protected.

The massage parlour raid in Islamabad became a concern at the highest level in Beijing, where President Hu Jintao received regular briefings as the drama unfolded. Days later his subordinates delivered a sharp dressing-down to Pakistan's interior minister, Aftab Ahmad Sherpao, who happened to be visiting China. Over the phone, Musharraf told Hu he was 'ashamed' of what had happened. The army's top commando and paramilitary units were ordered to take up position around the Red Mosque. Tensions soared, although few foresaw the bloody events that were coming.

On 3 July, I was having lunch at the Marriott Hotel with the prime minister's press secretary, Mahreen Aziz Khan, when I received a text message: 'Shots fired at the Red Mosque'. My guest was as surprised as I was. By the time I reached the mosque, twenty minutes later, volleys of bullets were whipping through the trees in the suburban streets surrounding it. I ducked into an alley, taking cover beside a line of crouching soldiers. Within a few hours, a government building opposite the mosque was on fire and a Pakistani cameraman, caught in the crossfire, lay dead.

Farid Esack, the South African scholar, happened to be inside the mosque when the shooting started, and he stayed until nightfall. As the clashes intensified, he was struck by the unnerving sense of calm and purpose among the students. 'They weren't panicking,' he recalled. 'This was the jihad they had spoken about. And it was the jihad they were ready to die for.'

Days later, Abdul Aziz was arrested trying to escape from the mosque disguised under a burka – an old trick of rebel clerics in the subcontinent. But instead of a glorious escape, Aziz was betrayed, it seemed, and the gleeful Pakistani authorities took full advantage. That night, security officials produced Abdul Aziz on a national television station, still in female dress, and forced him to lift back the veil to reveal his bearded, scowling face. If this humiliation was intended to discredit the clerics in the eyes of ordinary Pakistanis, though, it risked backfiring. Many Pakistanis were already deeply ambivalent about the confrontation between rebel clerics and a state they distrusted, and their greatest sympathies lay with the parents whose children were trapped inside the mosque. The TV stunt with Abdul Aziz only deepened their distrust.

As the siege deepened, I walked through a nearby working-class neighbourhood with Griff Witte, a correspondent with the *Washington Post*. We happened upon a government clerk at the modest house he shared with two brothers. Traumatised after days of gunfire, they visibly struggled to make sense of events. 'This is the cause of the Jews in your country,' Rabbani said, stabbing a finger at Griff. 'Everything is in the control of the Jews.' It struck me that he wasn't necessarily a fanatic – just a poor, disillusioned man with limited prospects, prone to prejudice and conspiracy theories, who, confronted with the great inequalities around them, saw in Islam an expression of rebellion. I thought of the socialist undercurrent in many of Ghazi's arguments and realised that was part of their genius.

Life in the capital acquired a surreal quality. Residents trapped in the Red Zone endured sweaty nights punctuated by the rattle of gunfire and could buy food only from government supply trucks that weaved through the empty, rubbish-strewn streets. After I checked into the Holiday Inn, I grappled with a dilemma: was it reasonable to ask Mazloom to bring over my bulletproof Kevlar jacket, previously used on military embeds in Afghanistan, given the possible danger to him? We met halfway, but even so it felt incredibly strange to drive through placid Islamabad in a bulky armoured vest.

Ijaz ul Haq and other mediators tried to find a way out of the crisis. Ghazi pleaded for safe passage for his elderly mother, trapped inside the compound, who, he said, was dying. There was speculation that he had become a prisoner of the jihadis doing the fighting, and that surrender was impossible. Farid Esack felt that, following the televised humiliation of his brother, Ghazi had little choice but to stay. 'He had to be martyred to avenge the honour of his brother,' he said. A solution to the crisis slipped away.

On the seventh day of the siege, Special Services Group commandos penetrated the mosque compound, and after thirty-six hours of room-to-room combat, reached the basement bunker where Ghazi was holed up. There is no reliable account of what happened next. By some accounts, Ghazi refused to surrender. By others, he had no option. Either way, Abdul Rashid Ghazi was dead. The body of his mother, who apparently had died several hours earlier, was found nearby.

When I visited the shattered complex a day later flies swarmed over the bloodstained floor and the prayer hall had been reduced to rubble. Walls painted with Quranic verses were riddled with bullets. In the basement where Ghazi made his last stand, the walls were blackened and studded with explosive marks. The army presented the remnants of Ghazi's arsenal: stacks of ammunition, grenade launchers and gas masks. There were also stacks of jihadi DVDs, such as *Best of Baghdad*.

Pakistanis breathed a sigh of relief, glad to put this traumatic episode behind them. In fact, their troubles were just beginning.

The Red Mosque siege would prove to be a watershed in the history of modern Pakistan, the first flame of a jihadi firestorm that within a few short years would threaten to consume the country. One month later, a suicide bomber struck the dining hall at a military base outside Islamabad, killing twenty soldiers from Zarrar Company, the commando unit involved in the siege. Violence exploded in the tribal belt, along the border with Afghanistan, and soon reached deep into Pakistan's big cities. In September 2008, an explosives-laden truck rammed into the

Marriott Hotel, where politicians whispered in the lobby and the waiters served wine in teapots. When I reached the hotel, moments after the blast, I found a sixty-foot-wide crater where the front gate had once been. In the lobby, bodies were strewn around the X-ray machine at the entrance, and rescuers carried the body of a woman whose head was partly missing. Three hundred people had been killed or injured. Baghdad, it seemed, had come to Islamabad.

Ghazi was buried in his ancestral village amid the swaying cotton fields of southern Punjab, 400 miles from Islamabad. Thousands of mourners attended his funeral, crushing against his coffin as men in black turbans shouldered it to a grave. News footage showed Ghazi's open coffin, his head resting on a blood-stained pillow. Police officers watched from a distance. Osama bin Laden, who had just moved his family to a new safe house in Abbottabad, in northern Pakistan, issued an audio message of support. Ghazi was a 'hero of Islam', he declared.

Abdul Aziz, on temporary release from prison, led the prayers. 'Our struggle will continue. There are many Ghazis living to be martyred,' he declared over his brother's grave. '*Insha'Allah*, Pakistan will soon have its Islamic revolution.'

Islamabad Expressway

3

The Prodigal Father

Jinnah's Pakistan

Every summer, in a far corner of the Hindu Kush, horsemen converge on the Shandur Pass – a majestic grassy arena ringed by snow-dusted peaks – to join in battle. This is not war but sport: polo, or rather its spirited local variant. Over three days, rival teams clash in pullulating contests where the action is fast, freewheeling and largely unencumbered by rules. Riders thunder down the pitch on sweat-soaked horses – men with ruddy faces and chipped teeth, swinging mallets in wide intoxicated arcs, striking man as often as ball. Few wear helmets; there is no referee in sight. Each game lasts fifty minutes, an eternity compared with the more genteel edition played in Westchester or Buenos Aires. Spectators roar their passions and gasp for breath. At 12,000 feet, oxygen is precious here, but the altitude is cruellest on the animals. Now and then, a horse crumples to the ground, legs twitching, in the throes of a heart attack. Attendants rush over and the unfortunate beast is carted off. Play resumes. Riders tumble, noses are bloodied, the ball cannons back and forth, and, when a goal is scored, the crowd leaps to its feet – squinting old men in wool caps and teenage hotshots in cheap sunglasses, fisting the air in triumph or groaning with anguish. When the final whistle blows, ballyhooing boys storm the pitch, slobbering kisses on their favourite players and shouldering them to the trophy stand, where the Chitral Scouts, proud para-militaries in dress uniform, stand guard over the silverware. THE SPORT OF KINGS, AND THE KING OF SPORTS, reads the battered, hand-painted sign at the entrance to the pass.

The Shandur Polo Festival was one of Pakistan's hidden gems: a magical mountain party with the air of a medieval pageant. I went as often as I could. The teams came from Chitral and Gilgit, rival kingdoms that once settled their differences with weapons, now keeping score with sport. Reed bands offered a squealing soundtrack, undercover bookies mingled in the crowds (gambling is illegal in Pakistan), and a motley assortment of local grandees filled the stands. At night they gathered around a blazing bonfire to sing, jig and discreetly swig from bottles of mountain liquor, under a giant sky framed by saw-toothed peaks and flaming stars.

One year, in between matches, I paused at a stall to buy some *jalebi*, swirls of sticky orange confectionery. It came wrapped in recycled pages from a child's copybook. Licking my fingers, I began to read.

The pages contained a short essay about the life of Muhammad Ali Jinnah, the dapper lawyer who founded Pakistan in 1947. Pakistanis often refer to Jinnah as Quaid-e-Azam, or The Great Leader, and he remains a ubiquitous presence, staring out from faded portraits that hang over cramped courtrooms and smoke-filled government offices. Schoolchildren learn to recite his life story – or a version of it much like the one on the crumpled pages in my hands. Written in wobbly script, it portrayed Jinnah as a pious leader of unerring judgement who had pursued the creation of Pakistan with unshakeable resolve. Growing up in Karachi, it recounted, he spurned playground games and lectured fellow pupils on the virtues of cleanliness. Later he chose to study law at Lincoln's Inn in London, because 'there, on the main entrance, the name of the prophet

Muhammad (Peace Be Upon Him) was included in the list of great lawyers of the world.' As a politician, he peppered his speeches with religious references. 'A great Muslim thinker and writer,' the essay read. 'The Quaid's speeches are full of the message of Islam.'

Much of this starchy portrait was fanciful, distorted or plain wrong. Jinnah wore Savile Row suits, drank Scotch and was said to enjoy a ham sandwich. He could barely say his prayers, and his marriage to a Parsi woman twenty-four years his junior, in defiance of social and religious conventions, scandalised Indian society. Lincoln's Inn does not, in fact, list the Prophet Muhammad among 'the great lawyers of the world', although his image does feature in a giant fresco in the dining hall that would shock orthodox Muslims, who consider pictorial depictions of the Prophet to be blasphemous. And Jinnah's faith in Pakistan wavered wildly: even as independence loomed in the mid-1940s, he seemed unsure about what kind of country he wanted – or whether he wanted a country at all.

Yet my anonymous essayist might be forgiven for getting it wrong. For much of his life, Jinnah was purposefully vague about his beliefs; even today, he remains an enigma – aloof and distant, a half-sketch awaiting completion. He stares down from official portraits, inscrutable and rake-thin, sinking into an armchair with his legs neatly folded, giving away nothing. Pakistan's warring ideological tribes have appropriated every aspect of Jinnah's life – his words, his deeds, even his clothes – in service of their arguments. In the 1980s, regime Islamists on state television stripped Jinnah of his wool suits and gleaming spats to present him in a traditional *sherwani* longcoat. Official histories airbrushed inconvenient facts – that he was born a Shia in a Sunni-majority country, or that his wife was a Parsi and his daughter married a Christian. His speeches, like his shirts, can be tailored to any occasion: conservatives cite Jinnah's desire to create an 'Islamic state'; liberals cling to his soaring appeals for tolerance.

I sought out Jinnah's biographer. At eighty-one, Zawwar Zaidi had giant white eyebrows and a fragile stoop, but his eyes lit up as he recalled how he drove Jinnah around northern India in the 1930s and 40s, in a horse and carriage, to campaign for the creation of Pakistan. 'It was such a thrill,' he said, recalling their *nara*, or chant: '*Pakistan ka matlab kya? La ilaha il-Allah.*' ('What is the meaning of Pakistan? There is no God but Allah.') Zaidi stirred his tea and issued a weary sigh. It turned out to be such a terrible disappointment. 'When you look at a poor man, with his clothes tattered, what is the feeling? It is so disturbing to look at people with no future for their children.' It wasn't just Pakistan, he continued. Across the Indian subcontinent, inequality was rampant. His voice quivered. 'In this part of the world the feeling . . .' A tear trickled down his cheek. 'The feeling is almost dead.' We finished our tea and he walked me to the door. Three weeks later, he died.

Such introspection was rare; Jinnah mostly inspired heated polemics. In Indian popular culture, he was portrayed as a vainglorious and spiteful figure, hell-bent on obtaining Pakistan at any price. In Pakistan he was a spectral presence, remembered yet unknown, the prodigal father of the nation.

Every time I returned from a trip, I would pass Jinnah, perched on a hilltop near the Islamabad airport, his gaunt features frozen in a giant iron monument that depicted him in profile. On the slope below, Pakistan's national slogan was written in giant letters that mimicked the famous Hollywood sign: FAITH, UNITY, DISCIPLINE. One time I noticed that several letters had fallen over, lending the monument a dishevelled air. Jinnah still stared imperiously into the distance, grave and impenetrable as ever, watching the departing airliners vanish into the clouds.

The manipulation of history in the service of a nationalist myth is not unique to Pakistan; many countries, including the United States, spin their founding fathers in mystical gossamer. But Jinnah's blurry image was symptomatic of a broader malaise: decades after his death, Pakistanis were still bitterly at odds over the most basic questions about their country.

'Lord in heaven,' groaned the commentator Ayaz Amir on Independence Day in 2007, weeks after the Red Mosque siege. 'After sixty years of existence, still stuck at the beginning.'

❦

I wrote this book with a photograph of Jinnah on the wall over my computer – not the dour, black-and-white image that adorns government offices but a portrait in dazzling Technicolor, glowing with modernity. Jinnah poses rakishly before a pair of French windows, resplendent in white linen suit and gold cufflinks, a cigar balanced between his teeth. At seventy, his silken hair is carefully slicked back and a glossy lawn stretches in the background. In another context, he might pass for a plantation owner, or a card shark in a casino. But the eyes tell another story. Jinnah regards the camera with studied intensity, eyes glinting with restlessness, even anxiety. It suggests the gaze of a man who has gambled at the table of history, won big – and now wonders whether he won more than he bargained for.

The photograph was taken in September 1947, at what should have been a moment of intoxicating triumph. A month earlier, on 7 August, Jinnah had flown into Karachi aboard the British viceroy's Silver Dakota plane, to a delirious reception. Exultant supporters crashed through the airfield fence when he stepped from the plane in sunglasses, flashing a movie-star smile. People ran alongside as his limousine raced into Karachi, then a sleepy colonial port in the throes of a jolting transformation. Day and night, trains wheezed into its railway stations bearing a groaning tide of migrants – Muslim pioneers who had abandoned their homes in northern India, drawn by Jinnah's magnetic promises of this Muslim Zion. Karachi's population had doubled in a matter of months, and its streets buzzed with an electric air of anticipation. *'Pakistan Zindabad!'* people cried. 'Long Live Pakistan!'

On the evening of 13 August, Jinnah hosted a banquet for the departing British viceroy, Lord Louis Mountbatten, who came decked out in his finest military splendour. The following morning, the two men toured Karachi in an open-top Rolls-Royce, waving at the cheering throng. Speeches were made, handshakes exchanged, and a green-and-white standard – a star in the lap of a crescent – was run up a flagpole and left to flutter in the warm breeze of the Arabian Sea. Pakistan was born.

It was an odd creation, certainly, consisting of two giant territories known as 'wings' that lay 1,000 miles apart: West Pakistan, centred on Karachi and Lahore, and East Pakistan, sliced from the Indian province of Bengal. Pakistan was a lumpy stew of tribes, tongues and cultures; most of its borders were contested; only a minority of its people could speak the official language, Urdu. Western cynics abounded. 'A slick political trick,' judged *Time* magazine.

Jinnah was undaunted. In his inaugural address to the Constituent Assembly – an august gathering of the *pirs*, *rajas* and *nawabs* of the territory that now comprised Pakistan – the *Quaid* hailed his new-born as the resurrection of the lost glories of Muslim rule. He harked back to the Mughal era, centuries earlier, when Muslim emperors reigned over the subcontinent through the richest kingdom on the planet – a vast realm that stretched from Kabul to the river Kaveri, bursting with gold, jewels and spices and counting one hundred million souls, fully one-quarter of the world's population. The Mughals were aesthetes, too, patronising exquisite art forms, not to mention the Taj Mahal, the world's greatest monument to love. But the arrival of British colonists in the seventeenth century heralded the slow decline of an empire that formally collapsed in 1857. The last Mughal emperor, Bahadur Shah II, a doddering old man with a fondness for poetry, became a figurehead for Indian rebels in the Great Rebellion. After his ousting by the British, he was exiled to Burma.

Now, Jinnah told the Constituent Assembly, Muslims had a second shot at a self-ruling dominion, albeit in the guise of a modern nation-state. 'The whole world is wondering at this unprecedented cyclone revolution,' he declared. It was also a stunning personal triumph. As Jinnah's admiring biographer Stanley Wolpert put it: 'Few individuals significantly alter the course of history. Fewer still modify the map of the world. Hardly anyone can be credited with creating a nation-state. Muhammad Ali Jinnah did all three.'

So why, then, as he stood under the photographer's arc light, could Jinnah not muster a smile? Partition, the act of severing British India in two, had become a botched job of epic proportions. Months of simmering tensions among Muslims, Hindus and Sikhs had exploded into a frenzy of communal violence. Gangs armed with crude weapons roamed the streets and fields, hacking, stabbing and shooting enemy religionists. Riots surged through the cities; villages went up in flames. Columns of terrified refugees, up to fifty miles long, snaked across the bleeding land. Ghost trains pulled into stations carrying nothing but corpses. The promised land had become a charnel house.

Jinnah was distraught. As he pulled on his linen blazer for the photographer on that bright September morning, he was painfully aware of the dark forces his historic victory had unleashed. Over breakfast, he discussed the latest harrowing reports with his loyal spinster sister, Fatima, furtively dabbing his moist eyes with a handkerchief. Physically drained and plagued by a hacking cough, Jinnah secluded himself in Governor-General's House, smoking and pacing the halls, issuing desperate appeals for an end to the bloodletting. Nobody, it seemed, was listening.

Partition was a messy business everywhere. As the British Empire crumbled in the first half of the twentieth century, new nations were hurriedly carved from blood-soaked maps. I was born in one of them. Ireland won independence from Britain in 1921 but the civil war that followed split the island, north from south, two years later — an uneasy arrangement that festered until the 1970s, when an explosion of sectarian unrest consumed Northern Ireland. 'The Troubles', as the conflict was known, were largely confined to the North but occasionally spilled into the Republic, where I grew up.

One warm summer's evening in 1979, when I was six, one of the most notorious killings of the era took place an hour's drive from our home. A thirty-foot boat chugged from the harbour in Mullaghmore, a village in County Sligo, carrying Lord Louis Mountbatten, the seventy-nine-year-old peer and confidant to the royal family, and several of his family members. As the trawler faced into the Atlantic swell, a member of the Irish Republican Army, watching from shore, remotely detonated a bomb on board. The explosion lifted the boat from the water, instantly killing Mountbatten but also three others — Mountbatten's fourteen-year-old grandson, an octogenarian female relative and a teenage deckhand. The IRA justified the brutal attack by referencing the establishment credentials of their target, a second cousin once removed to Queen Elizabeth II who sat in the House of Lords and counted Queen Victoria as his godmother. Yet Mountbatten's Irish links were limited.

Apart from his annual summer holiday at Classiebawn Castle, the handsome manor overlooking Mullaghmore, the elderly aristocrat had no direct role in Ireland's rancorous split. And if Mountbatten was truly to answer for the iniquities of British rule, then surely it related to his role in another colonial decoupling, many decades earlier, during his brief yet catastrophic stint as the last viceroy of British India.

Mountbatten flew into New Delhi in March 1947 at a moment of grinding change. World War II had beggared Britain and shattered the mystique of empire. Saddled with enormous debts, London scrambled to quit its colonies, first among them British India – a sprawling mini-continent once prized as 'The Jewel in the Crown', now a burdensome and querulous possession of some 400 million people. Battle-hardened Indian soldiers, back from the trenches of Europe and North Africa, demanded greater rights. Britain owed India $6 billion for wartime provisions and wages. A short-lived mutiny aboard a Royal Indian Navy ship docked off Mumbai (then Bombay) in 1946 sent a powerful signal: Britain's grip was slipping. Prime Minister Clement Attlee dispatched Mountbatten to New Delhi with a ship-breaker's charter: to dismember the property and dispose of it within fifteen months. He did it in five.

Mountbatten was accompanied by his chic wife, Edwina, a freewheeling heiress and socialite, and trailed by a contentious wartime record. As an admiral in the navy, Mountbatten commanded the disastrous raid on Dieppe in 1942 and later scuttled a ship off the coast of Crete, which earned him the sniggering nickname 'master of disaster'. Tall, assured and strikingly handsome, Dickie, as his family knew him, had an easy elegance and counted famous figures like Charlie Chaplin among his friends. He was also vain, obsessed with royal genealogy, and relished any chance to don his decoration-studded dress uniform. 'A glamour boy,' grumbled General Joseph Stilwell, an

American officer who served under him in Singapore. 'Enormous staff, endless walla-walla, but damned little fighting.'

'I am,' Mountbatten admitted, 'the most conceited man I have ever known.'

In New Delhi, Mountbatten had ample opportunities to indulge his love of pageantry. The viceroy's palatial residence boasted 340 rooms, 12 indoor courtyards and 500 servants; he arrived at ceremonial events wearing a giant velvet cloak with gold chains; his wife swept by in a shimmering gown. Yet the political task at hand was the most delicate thing of all. India, it was agreed, should gain her freedom. But could the British exit without leaving chaos in their wake?

The most sensitive task – that of tracing the new border between Pakistan and India – fell to Cyril Radcliffe, a London barrister of distinction who had never previously set foot in India. When Radcliffe arrived in June of that year, Mountbatten lodged him in a cottage in the grounds of Viceroy's House and gave him forty days to complete the job – an impossible deadline. India was a vast country, one of the most ethnically diverse on earth; its new frontier with Pakistan stretched thousands of miles across a thickly-populated patchwork of farms, villages and soaring mountains. Every flick of Radcliffe's pencil had the potential to uproot or enrage entire communities. Matters were most sensitive in Punjab and Bengal – behemoth provinces with millions of Hindus, Muslims and Sikhs, now to be sliced in two. Radcliffe was aided in his work by a government commission. But much of the time he was secluded in his cottage, poring endlessly over giant maps and bundles of documents, drenched in sweat from stress and the stifling heat.

The British anticipated trouble. An eruption of citywide violence between Hindus and Muslims in Calcutta a year earlier left 4,000 people dead and presented an ominous portent. 'Grave communal disorder,' wrote Norman Smith, the director of the

Intelligence Bureau, in January 1947, 'is a natural, if ghastly process tending in its own way to the solution of the Indian problem.' The partition plan of 3 June allowed just seventy-two days for the transition to independence, during which time three provinces had to be divided, civil and armed services bifurcated, assets shared out. Intelligence reports warned that entire communities were arming themselves. Whatever happened, the British were determined to stay out of it. Thousands of British troops stationed in India were packed onto steamships headed for Europe; those left behind were ordered to avoid any trouble unless British lives were at risk.

Haste, incompetence and cynicism collided with catastrophic results on 14 August, when Pakistan was granted independence. (India was born a day later.) As Dickie and Edwina Mountbatten flew back to New Delhi from Karachi, they could see columns of refugees trailing across the plains of Punjab, where smoke rose from torched villages. Gangs of Muslim, Hindu and Sikh men prowled the land. Women were raped, mutilated and cast into wells. Unborn children were wrenched from the wombs of their slain mothers. Astonishingly, the new border between Pakistan and India had not been finalised, with Radcliffe still holed up in his cottage at Viceroy's House, mulling the last painful decisions. The Punjab Boundary Force, a hastily assembled, ad hoc unit intended to keep the peace, collapsed and was quickly disbanded. Back in New Delhi, the Mountbattens took the evening off to watch the latest Bob Hope movie, the romantic comedy *My Favorite Brunette*.

By October, at least half a million people were dead and the greatest refugee exodus in human history had been unleashed – a vast tide of Hindus, Sikhs and Muslims washing back and forth across Radcliffe's cursed line. (Historians argue over the final death toll, with some estimates as high as two million.) The British military suffered seven fatalities. Pakistan and India were plunging into war over Kashmir, the Muslim-majority but Hindu-ruled princely state in the Himalayas. Back in London, Radcliffe burned his papers and refused his £3,000 fee, vowing never to return to India. 'There will be roughly eighty million people with a grievance who will begin looking for me,' he wrote. 'I do not want them to find me.' A year later, he was awarded a knighthood.

In retrospect, it is striking that Britain's shameful role in partition has not received harsher scrutiny. Certainly, it was the end point of an empire rooted in violence and sectarianism. British officials had long exploited India's religious fissures to divide and rule, pitting Muslim against Hindu. Their rule was underwritten by pitiless counter-insurgency campaigns and periodic massacres, such as the shooting of unarmed protesters at Amritsar in 1919 and Peshawar in 1930. But the sheer ineptitude and cynical abandonment of partition – more hit-and-run than divide-and-rule – meant that whatever exalted idea the British had of their empire, or themselves, drained into the blood-soaked fields of Punjab.

Yet while imperial haste explains the calamitous course of partition, blame for the split itself lies elsewhere. India's elite was dominated by distinguished men of privilege (and they were all men) who spent years locked in argument over what shape India, a continent as much as a country, should take after independence. Those leaders had undertaken the most vital challenge of their era. Tragically, they failed to surmount it.

❧

As *swaraj*, or independence, drew closer in the mid-1940s, the burden of negotiating India's post-independence dispensation fell on two of its most capable leaders: Jawaharlal Nehru of the Indian National Congress and Muhammad Ali Jinnah of the All-India Muslim League. Lawyers by training and Anglophiles by inclination, Nehru and Jinnah were a refined blend of English education and subcontinental pedigree, perfect gentlemen of empire who, on the face of it, had everything in common.

In his youth, Jinnah yearned to tread the boards. Born into a family of Gujarati merchants based in Karachi, he left for London in the 1890s to work at a shipping agency before turning to the law. He graduated from Lincoln's Inn at the age of twenty, exhilarated by the politics and fashions of England. Jinnah wore a monocle, hustled at billiards, and toyed with the idea of becoming an actor. A stern letter from his father convinced him to return to India, where he satisfied his yen for performance before the stuffy colonial judges of the high court in Bombay (today's Mumbai), where his brilliant litigating style made him a rising star. He bought a smart house in a ritzy neighbourhood and embraced the cause of Indian nationalism, which was suddenly gathering steam. Jinnah's manner could be cool, even prickly – a friend once quipped that she needed a winter coat to sit in his presence – and he rejected the exaggerated deference shown by many educated Indians towards their imperial masters. During one court hearing, a British judge cried 'Rubbish!' as Jinnah argued his case. 'Your honour,' Jinnah shot back, 'nothing but rubbish has passed your mouth all morning.'

Jinnah stirred scandal in 1918 with his marriage to 'the Flower of Bombay', Ruttie Dinshaw, the witty and charming daughter of a wealthy merchant. They met on holiday in Darjeeling and, despite a twenty-four-year age gap, had shared interests in horse riding and literature. But Ruttie's Parsi father, aghast at her marriage to a Muslim, disowned his daughter. Following their small wedding ceremony, Ruttie arrived at Jinnah's home carrying little more than her pets.

Jawaharlal Nehru hailed from the upper reaches of the Hindu community, the scion of an aristocratic, wealthy family. His father was a prominent barrister and politician from a Kashmiri Pandit family, and Nehru was raised on a palatial estate where a French tutor shaped his early views. He went to school at Harrow and Cambridge in England, graduating in 1910, having polished his vowels and honed his formidable rhetorical skills. Like Jinnah, he had cosmopolitan tastes, but his politics were further to the left, with a magnetic charm and wit that were offset by quick flashes of temper. He flung himself into the struggle for Indian independence, and fell under the wing of Mahatma Gandhi, the mystical sage whose tactics of peaceful resistance infuriated the British and brought global fame to their cause. Gandhi teased Nehru as 'our Englishman'.

Yet for all that Nehru and Jinnah held in common, they loathed one another with a passion. Where Nehru was ebullient and charismatic, Jinnah was imperious and distant. Nehru disparaged Jinnah as a 'mediocre lawyer' and 'the reactionary Muslim Baron of Malabar Hill', a reference to the upscale Bombay neighbourhood where Jinnah had a mansion; Jinnah fumed at Nehru's grandstanding and railed against his 'atheistic socialism'. But they were brought together by the drive for freedom, under Gandhi's guiding hand. The independence movement swelled through the 1920s as Gandhi led mass meetings and, in 1930, the Salt March, an act of mass civilian disobedience to protest against British taxes on salt production. The Salt March brought global fame to India's independence movement and attracted millions of fervent followers at home. Gandhi crossed the continent-size country by train, surviving on a diet of toast, grapes and goat's milk. Nehru flung himself into the campaign and repeatedly landed in jail. Jinnah preferred to agitate from within the wood-panelled halls of the colonial legislature. Those differences of political tactics presaged a wider split inside the independence movement.

The prospect of independence posed a thorny dilemma for India's Muslims. They had suffered crippling discrimination for almost a century, sidelined in India's civil service and under-represented in its colonial assemblies since Muslim officers led the failed anti-colonial uprising of 1857 (still known to some as 'the mutiny'). In an independent India, Muslims should advance on merit. But there was equally a danger that democracy could deepen the discrimination, or even make it permanent. Hindu voters outnumbered Muslims by two to one in India. With religion emerging as the organising force of politics, Muslims worried about being permanently marginalised. The British Raj, the fear went, would become the Hindu Raj.

The nominally secular Congress Party often employed the symbols of Hindu spirituality in the cause of nationalist politics. The freedom struggle's unofficial anthem, *Vande Mataram*, was an appeal to a Hindu goddess; in his speeches, Gandhi urged his followers to worship cows, in line with Hindu teachings. Jinnah publicly admonished Gandhi. It was madness to mix religion and politics in a country like India, he felt. But it was Gandhi, bold and inspiring, who electrified the Indian public, leaving in his shade the grey-suited Jinnah, beloved of neither mainstream nationalists nor India's colonial rulers. Then he suffered a devastating loss. In 1929 his wife, Ruttie, from whom he had separated a year earlier, died in Paris at the age of twenty-nine, after gulping a fistful of sleeping pills. 'Try and remember me beloved as the flower you plucked and not the flower you tread upon,' she wrote in one of her last letters to Jinnah. 'I have loved you my darling as it is given to few men to be loved.'

Jinnah was heartbroken. A year later, his political career on the ropes, he abjured politics and retreated to London to practise law.

In London, Jinnah established himself as a figure of professional success and considerable means. He shared a grand mansion in Hampstead with his sister, Fatima, and young daughter, Dina, bought properties in Mayfair and toured the city in a gleaming Bentley driven by an English chauffeur. As one of England's most sought-after barristers, Jinnah earned the equivalent of one million pounds a year; he attended the theatre, played billiards and acquired so many tailored suits and silk ties that his daughter teased him as 'a dandy'. For the most part, he avoided Indian politics, but there was one prophetic encounter.

At a black-tie dinner at London's Waldorf Hotel in 1933, a young man from Lahore named Choudhry Rahmat Ali marched up to Jinnah and pushed a pamphlet into his hand. NOW OR NEVER: ARE WE TO LIVE OR PERISH FOREVER? it read. Ali, a student at Cambridge, proposed a radical idea: that the Muslims of South Asia, unable to prosper in India, should break away and establish their own homeland. This new country, Ali explained, would be named after its five constituent parts: Punjab, Afghania (an alternate name for present-day Khyber Pakhtunkhwa Province), Kashmir, Sind and Balochistan (the source of the 'stan'). Ergo, Pakistan.

Jinnah was unimpressed. 'My dear boys, don't be in a hurry,' he told Ali and his three co-signatories when they sought his support. 'Let the waters flow and they will find their own level.'

But the students had called it right. A clamour for Muslim representation was surging across India, and it was about to sweep Jinnah away. After his return to Bombay in the mid-1930s, Jinnah became leader of the Muslim League and established himself as the self-styled 'sole spokesman' of India's Muslims. He came under the spell of Allama Muhammad Iqbal, a poet and philosopher who floated the idea of a Muslim homeland in 1930, and began to sprinkle his speeches with Islamic references. In 1940, Jinnah presided over a meeting in Lahore that formally called for an independent Muslim state.

What that meant, though, changed over time.

Jinnah initially advocated a post-independence dispensation in which India's Muslim-majority provinces would enjoy a high degree of autonomy. That plan was trenchantly opposed by the Congress Party, led by Nehru, which advocated a strong centre anchored in Delhi along British colonial lines. The British government, recognising the inevitability of its exit from India, sent successive delegations to New Delhi in an effort to break the deadlock.

But Muslims were also divided among themselves. Some clerics welcomed a Muslim homeland as a chance to restore the Muslim caliphate that collapsed with the Ottoman Empire in 1924; others spurned the notion that the Muslim *ummah* could be contained in this new-fangled thing called a nation-state. Then there were those who viewed Islam as a cultural, rather than a political identity, and yearned for a secular democracy.

Still others wanted no change at all.

Saadat Hasan Manto, a scriptwriter for Radio India, was one of India's burgeoning talents. A hard-drinking man with thick glasses and a scabrous sensibility, Manto lived in Bombay, where he churned out scripts at a prodigious rate, sometimes starting at breakfast and finishing by dinner. Quality was variable, but his true metier, to which he turned in his spare time, was the short story. Here Manto excelled, producing work of acuity and humour that still shines today. Manto had a keen eye for the exotic, the earthy and the lewd, creating characters grounded in the raw realities of the Indian street: prostitutes and alcoholics, layabouts and obsessives. Like many intellectuals, he grew suspicious of the nationalist fervour sweeping India in the 1930s and came to distrust both Nehru's Congress Party and Jinnah's Muslim League.

Many other Indians shared his worry. Muslims, Hindus and Sikhs had lived cheek-by-jowl for centuries, mostly in peace. They attended one another's weddings and funerals, and sometimes even worshipped at the same shrines. In Amritsar, Manto's hometown in northern Punjab and the site of Sikhism's holiest shrine, the writer drank heartily with Hindus and sang with Muslims. All of them were Indian. They liked India the way it was. Why change it?

Confusingly, Jinnah spoke to both sides of the argument. In addresses to Muslim community leaders, the *Quaid* spoke of an 'Islamic state' and embraced the 'Two-Nation Theory' – the idea that Islam and Hinduism were distinct social and cultural orders that could never coexist. '*La ilaha il-Allah!*' chanted his supporters. 'There is no God but Allah!' But in newspaper interviews, Jinnah was far vaguer about the role of religion in any future state, and he appeared to shield his true intentions and personal beliefs behind lawyerly formulations.

Jinnah's ideological tango on Islam foreshadowed an ambiguity that would become the refuge of Pakistani leaders for decades to come, mostly to disastrous effect. And Jinnah may not even have wanted a country at all. The historian Ayesha Jalal has unearthed evidence that, for many years, the demand for Pakistan was little more than a bargaining ploy, a threat to wring concessions from the reluctant Congress Party. It was a risky strategy. The talks with Nehru spluttered, stalled, and then were rapidly overtaken by events on the ground.

The Calcutta riots, in August 1946, sounded the alarm for India's slow-boil political tensions. Four thousand people died in frenzied clashes between Muslims and Hindus; foreign reporters arriving in Calcutta compared the heaped corpses with the horrors they had recently witnessed at Auschwitz. The unrest spread, and soon the poison of communal hatred was pumping through the veins of British India. Hindus campaigned for *swaraj* (independence); Muslims had a different cry: *Pakistan!*

❧

As partition hove into view in early 1947, the talks between Jinnah and Nehru focused on the terms of the divorce. The arrival of Lord Mountbatten and his wife exacerbated their choleric relationship. Mountbatten instantly struck up a friendship with Nehru, whom he found warm and engaging, but he was turned off by 'frigid, haughty' Jinnah. 'He might be a psychopathic case,' Dickie confided to his diary. The three men argued fiercely over Punjab, the behemoth province with millions of Hindus, Muslims and Sikhs. Jinnah wanted the province in its entirety for Pakistan, arguing that it was the backbone of his new state. But Mountbatten sided with Nehru, who wanted to divide the province in two. Enraged, Jinnah protested that he was being handed a 'maimed, mutilated and moth-eaten' country.

The triangle was further complicated by Mountbatten's wife, Edwina. It was an unguarded secret that the couple had an open marriage. Edwina slept with both genders, counting an American golf star and allegedly a West Indian cabaret performer among her lovers, while Dickie embraced their reputation for unconventional behaviour. 'Edwina and I spent all our married lives getting into other people's beds,' he later remarked. But it was Edwina's close friendship with Nehru that elicited the most sensational speculation. 'She and Jawaharlal are so sweet together,' Mountbatten wrote to his daughter Pamela. 'They really dote on each other.' Were they lovers? Many Muslims saw it as a fresh slight – not only were the British siding with the Hindus, they were also sleeping with them.

Still today, exactly what transpired in those tortured negotiations is a matter of heated debate. Indians portray Jinnah as the great spoiler, a stubborn megalomaniac who, faced with a losing wager, insisted on doubling down. Pakistani scholars point to the intransigence of Nehru and the Congress Party, which stubbornly refused to make concessions to Muslim concerns. As the storm gathered around them, Jinnah and Nehru failed to anticipate how bad it would get. Jinnah refused to sell his beautiful mansion at Malabar Hill in Bombay, believing that after partition he would be able to return to India regularly, perhaps even spend his winters there. But by the time Jinnah landed at Karachi in August, there was no turning back.

In New Delhi, Nehru delivered one of the most famous speeches of the twentieth century. 'Long years ago,' he began, 'we made a tryst with destiny. And now the time comes when we shall redeem our pledge; not wholly or in full measure, but very substantially. At the stroke of the midnight hour, while the world sleeps, India will awake to life and freedom.' Later that night, he went to see Mountbatten, who offered a glass of port. 'To India!' they toasted. But outside the gilded gates, a holocaust was underway.

Riots rippled across the Punjab, where women were gang-raped in great numbers, their bodies flung into wells. Riots surged through Lahore and New Delhi, where refugees cowered in graveyards and disease-ridden camps. A British journalist visiting the hospital in Sheikhupura, in late August, found patients with savage injuries: hands hacked off, bloodied stumps that swarmed with flies. In nearby fields, flames rose from burning homes and vultures wheeled in the skies.

'Such rivers of blood have flowed,' wrote Saadat Hasan Manto, 'that even the heavens are bewildered.'

An exodus of biblical proportions accompanied the carnage. Fifteen million people fled their homes – Hindus and Sikhs into India, Muslims into Pakistan – in one of the largest migrations in human history. Among them was Pervezuddin Musharraf, a Muslim official at the Indian foreign office, who abandoned his home in New Delhi to make the perilous train journey to Karachi. Musharraf was accompanied by his wife and a four-year-old son, Pervez. Stowed under the seat was a tin box containing 400,000 rupees destined for the coffers of Pakistan's new foreign ministry. As the train crossed Punjab, refugees clinging to its roof, the four-year-old stared out in horror. Sixty years later, now president of Pakistan, Pervez Musharraf claimed to recall the scene: bodies littering the tracks and trains that pulled into stations 'carrying nothing but the deafening silence of death'.

Saadat Hasan Manto refused to move at first, reluctant to leave his home for the unfamiliar land of Pakistan. But then the bloodthirsty air reached Bombay. News reports brought graphic accounts of rape, abduction and pillage, and even close friendships became strained. One evening in 1947, Manto was drinking with a Hindu actor named Shyam when the conversation turned to a massacre in Rawalpindi. 'When I was hearing about the atrocities committed by Muslims,' Shyam told him, 'I could have killed you.' His friend's candour rocked Manto, who realised that India had irreversibly changed. Soon afterwards, he gathered his family and boarded a ship to Karachi.

Pakistan was no promised land. Lahore's small film industry had collapsed in partition, so there was little money in script-writing. Manto drank heavily, pining for the lost pleasures of Bombay. But then he channelled his pathos into his writing. A series of short stories and essays, mostly in Urdu, captured the moment. In deadpan prose, Manto probed the psychology of partition with an unsparing eye, revealing its tragedies and absurdities, becoming its foremost chronicler. 'When I think of the recovered women, I think only of their bloated bellies – what will happen to those bellies?' he asked. Would the children so conceived 'belong to Pakistan or Hindustan?'

Manto's most celebrated short story 'Toba Tek Singh' is a dark parable set in a lunatic asylum at the height of partition. The inmates are to be separated along religious lines – Muslims to Pakistan, Hindus and Sikhs to India. But first they must solve a conundrum: which country do they live in? 'If they were in India, where on earth was Pakistan?' Manto wrote. 'And if they were in Pakistan, then how come that until only the other day it was India?' The main character trapped in this dilemma is Toba Tek Singh, an elderly Sikh who is named after his hometown in Punjab. In the final scene, he suffers a breakdown on the newly drawn border between the two countries, paralysed in no-man's-land and unable to move. 'There, behind barbed wire, on one side, lay India. And behind more barbed wire, on the other side, lay Pakistan,' Manto wrote. 'In between, on a bit of earth that had no name, lay Toba Tek Singh.'

※

In the months after partition, the leaders of Pakistan and India were confronted with the bitter fruits of their failures. Riots gripped New Delhi where Nehru, independent India's first prime minister, roamed the streets like a man obsessed, raging and emotional, pleading with citizens to halt the carnage. Nehru ordered the army to shoot rioters on sight, converted his vast garden into a campsite for Muslim refugees, and clashed with cabinet hard-liners who wanted to leave the Muslims to fend for themselves. Nehru could barely hide his contempt for those who advocated turning India into a 'Hindu Pakistan', as he put it. 'The whole idea of a theocratic state is not only medieval,' he fumed, 'but also stupid.'

But the hard-liners were emboldened. On a cold January evening in 1948, Gandhi was shuffling across a lawn in New Delhi, leaning on the shoulders of two young women, when a Hindu supremacist named Nathuram Vinayak Godse stepped from the crowd. Godse greeted Gandhi, touched his feet in a mark of respect, then produced a Beretta pistol and shot the frail seventy-eight-year-old three times in the chest, killing him. Godse, who belonged to a neo-fascist Hindu group called the R.S.S., was furious at Gandhi for his conciliatory attitude towards Muslims, and for his insistence that Pakistan should receive its fair share of the assets of the former colonial state.

Mountbatten stayed on for six months, his time partially spent on a fastidious division of the contents of the Viceroy's House between India and Pakistan, down to the library books, kitchen spoons, and musical instruments of the Raj brass band. Edwina threw herself into the relief effort, working to help the camps of the sick and displaced. It was the start of a charity career that ended in 1960 with her death in British North Borneo at the age of fifty-eight, with a pile of Nehru's letters by her bed.

In Pakistan, Jinnah dragged his creation to its feet. Millions of people lived in squalid camps where starvation and death were rife. The new state was broke: civil servants toiled in tents that served as ministries, using thorns as paper clips; ministers sat at desks fashioned from packing cases. Violent squabbles erupted over the ownership of Hindu and Sikh homes left behind by families who had fled to India. Jinnah had few foreign powers in his corner: Winston Churchill, his champion in London, was out of power and the United States was proving decidedly luke-warm towards Pakistan. When Jinnah requested a $2 billion loan in January 1948, Washington offered $10 million.

Pakistan's ruling Muslim League failed to inspire much confi-dence, dominated as it was by crusty stalwarts of the old order – feudal landlords, tribal chieftains and business tycoons – many of whom had supported Pakistan only at the last minute. 'A collection of gangs . . . with no soul to be damned and no body to be kicked,' judged one British diplomat. Muslim clerics, who had been sidelined in the partition negotiations, loomed in the wings, waiting for a chance to reassert their influence. The country's gangly geography portended trouble. Jinnah hoped to connect East Pakistan and West Pakistan with a land corridor that would slice through a thousand miles of Indian territory – a quixotic idea that was quickly forgotten after the outbreak of war with India.

The trigger was Kashmir – the 'K' in Pakistan – a land of stunning beauty, teeming with fruit orchards and fields of saffron, that was claimed by both countries. Kashmir was one of India's 565 princely states, whose rulers pledged loyalty to Britain but enjoyed a measure of independence. At independ-ence, they faced a choice: to join Pakistan or India. In most cases, the matter was dictated by location or majority religion;

by those terms, Kashmir should logically have gone to Pakistan. Its *maharaja*, Sir Hari Singh, was a Hindu, but most of his people were Muslims, and Kashmir sat on Pakistan's border. But Sir Hari was a weak leader and he came under pressure from Nehru, who had deep filial and sentimental ties to Kashmir. After a complicated sequence of events that is still hotly disputed, the *maharaja* acceded to India. Jinnah, furious, dispatched his military and a band of Pashtun tribal irregulars to Kashmir. The operation was an ignominious failure. The tribesmen paused to pillage Kashmiri villages along the way, and Pakistan's army suffered the first of several defeats at the hands of the largest Indian force. When it was over, Pakistan held about one-third of Kashmir, and India most of the rest. The short-lived 1948 war set the stage for one of the world's most intractable conflicts – one that, at several points in recent decades, has threatened to plunge South Asia into nuclear war.

But it was the ideological doubts that pressed hardest. Was Pakistan to be a theocratic state where the Qur'an dictated the law of the land? Or was it more a secular homeland, where Muslims could thrive and feel secure, yet where all religions were equal? At the eleventh hour, Jinnah declared his preference state. 'You are free; you are free to go to your temples, you are free to go to your mosques or to any other places of worship in this state of Pakistan,' he told the Constituent Assembly in Karachi on 11 August, three days before independence. 'You may belong to any religion or caste or creed – that has nothing to do with the business of the state.'

Finally, there was clarity: Pakistan would be a secular state. But was it too late?

For Jinnah himself, it was. The clues are there in the photo on my office wall, in his hollowed cheeks. Years of overwork, stress and a fifty-cigarette-a-day habit had exacted their toll; under the pressed white suit, cancer was rampant. Confined to Governor-General's House in Karachi, the seventy-one-year-old *Quaid* stretched out on a sofa, surrounded by stacks of papers and reams of telex tape, dictating orders. Guests noticed that he spent much of his time in bed.

In July 1948, Jinnah and his sister flew to Ziarat, a mountain retreat in western Balochistan Province, to convalesce at a summerhouse amid the cool, juniper-covered hills. After a brief respite, Jinnah's health plunged again, and when his weight hit thirty-five kilos (about seventy-seven pounds), doctors likened his emaciated frame to that of a starved prisoner-of-war. Ever loyal, Fatima stayed at her brother's side, reading aloud his papers. The Pakistani public was growing anxious, too. On 14 August, the first anniversary of independence, prayers rang out at mosques across the country for Jinnah, who was doing so poorly that an aide had to write the speech he delivered on state radio. Weeks later, pneumonia struck. The doctors rushed him back to Karachi.

Jinnah's secretive landing at the city airfield on 11 September contrasted with his triumphal arrival a year earlier. The ambulance that carried Jinnah from the airport broke down, slumping to a halt near a squalid refugee camp inhabited by Muslims who had fled India. With no back-up ambulance, the convoy had to wait an hour for a replacement to arrive. Fatima sat over her brother, fanning flies from his sweat-drenched face. Trucks and buses trundled past.

The convoy eventually reached Governor-General's House, where, late that night, Jinnah died.

Grief swept across Pakistan. At least one million mourners filled the streets of Karachi for Jinnah's funeral, including the boy Pervez Musharraf, whose family had moved into a modest house near the train station. So much was left unresolved: questions begging answers, ideological demons just starting to stir. In the thirteen months he ruled Pakistan, Jinnah failed to pull together the fraying fabric of his creation, held together by the thinnest of threads. Six decades later, they would be close to snapping.

Anwar Kamal Khan

4

Arithmetic on the Frontier

A Pashtun Takes On the Taliban

We rattled through the parched countryside, past fortress-like farmhouses and salt-flecked marshes, kicking up a cloud of dust. A village loomed ahead. As our jeep slowed, a gang of tribesmen stepped out, all long-locks and curly whiskers, brandishing Kalashnikovs with mobster panache. Some were smiling. They opened fire.

I crouched instinctively as the first bullets whipped overhead at a perilously low angle. My host, a burly sixty-one-year-old of martial bearing, was entirely undisturbed. Anwar Kamal Khan yanked open his door and strode purposefully towards the gunfire, waving cheerily. His bodyguard, a rakish-looking man with chipped teeth and a half-tied turban, trailed behind, cackling with delight as he, too, emptied his rifle into the sky.

Kamal was a veteran Pashtun politician. Over the course of a thirty-year career in Lakki Marwat, a dusty district along the northwestern frontier with Afghanistan, he had played many roles – lawyer and chieftain, landlord and warlord. On this occasion, he was a candidate. In previous elections, Kamal had notched up six straight victories; now he was canvassing his rambunctious constituents in search of a seventh.

A whistle sounded, the shooting stopped, and we were led into a small courtyard where the village elders were waiting: men with leathery faces and milky eyes, wrapped in wool shawls against the winter chill. A variety show kicked off. The gunmen took to the floor for the *attan*, a traditional dance that involved a kind of shuffle-step waltz, rifles swinging wildly. (I hoped they had engaged the safety catches; it seemed unlikely.) Next up were the volleyball aficionados – teenagers in baggy pants (no shorts) who tossed around a pink ball that jolted violently when it hit the rough ground, which was often. The spectators took the play seriously. When I stepped over a white scrawl in the soil, a gruff-looking man nudged me back with the barrel of his gun. 'Line,' he said.

After the game, Kamal, now garlanded with a Christmas-style tinsel necklace, posed for team photos and delivered a short speech over crackly speakers. I could make out just a few words – *electricity, money, America* – but the punters seemed to enjoy it, chortling at Kamal's gags and clapping vigorously at the climax. Finally, we were hustled into a long, low room where a feast had been spread out on a plastic floor mat: spicy chicken legs, chunks of juicy mango, sponge cake and sweet tea served in dainty china cups. As we knelt, Kamal turned to me. 'I hope you're enjoying yourself?' he asked. Of course I was.

❈

Even by the standards of Pakistani politics, Kamal was a larger-than-life figure. Theatrical, loquacious and utterly unapologetic, he struck me as a throwback to an earlier era – perhaps Harry Flashman, the roguish comic hero of George MacDonald Fraser's witty historical novels. His face was fleshy and pitted, dominated by a flamboyant moustache that swept from a centre part to twirled ends. He spoke slowly, floridly and expansively, in a raspy baritone that swelled on demand into a thunderous bellow – usually when addressing his fellow Marwat tribesmen. In private, he made for entertaining company, deploying a rascal's smile in the service of lurid tales of skulduggery and derring-do. He had a maddening disregard for precision. 'You see that man over there?' he would ask. 'He has killed six, seven, EIGHT men!' His idiosyncratic turn of phrase might have been charming if the ideas it expressed weren't so alarming.

'You see,' Kamal remarked casually as we drove away from the village, 'this murder and fighting business is very tricky.'

Murder and fighting, it turned out, were constant preoccupations in Lakki Marwat, an impoverished district that squatted on a sandy plain between the sluggish Indus River and the mountain wall of the tribal belt. I spent two days on the election trail with Kamal, jammed into the back of his jeep, for a dizzying whirl of rallies. We splashed through ponds of mud, weaved between stands of palm trees and stopped at high-walled compounds where weatherworn men gathered to listen earnestly. I didn't see a single woman. Guns, on the other hand, were everywhere – Soviet-design Kalashnikovs, old British Lee–Enfield rifles and Chinese pistols, usually festooned in rainbow-coloured beads. 'Carrying guns is a common fashion around here,' Kamal explained in his gravelly voice as we bumped along. 'Like a woman wears her necklace, this is our jewellery.' Few weapons were licensed, he admitted, but the authorities couldn't do much about it. He pointed to the rutted road. 'You see that strip of rubber? That is the only civilisation around here. Either side of it, the government does not exist.'

Kamal sweetened his electoral appeal with gifts – a wad of rupees here, an electrical transformer there – yet the voters seemed genuinely to love his devil-may-care style. 'All the wealth of Kabir Khan is not worth one hair from Anwar Kamal's moustache!' declared one village headman. Kamal grinned. Haji Kabir Khan was his political nemesis, a wealthy businessman with large reserves of hard cash – the key to electoral success in Pakistan – to splash around. The two men had once been allies. But if Khan had the voters' pockets, Kamal had won their hearts.

At one stop, villagers showed their appreciation by presenting him with a jet-black turban wrapped in thick, luxuriant folds; for good measure, they dropped one on my head too.

I noticed that most buildings – houses, gas stations, even mosques – were capped with a square tower, two or three stories high and studded with loopholes. This medieval-style fortification was called a *burj*, Kamal told me, and it served as both a home security system and a marker of status. The richer a man, the higher his *burj*; poor families made do by punching a few holes in a living-room wall. Their purpose was not to defend against an invading army but to ward off vengeful cousins or irate neighbours. Most Marwat families were embroiled in complex blood feuds, Kamal explained – disputes over murders, women or land that could drag on for decades, handed from father to son like cherished heirlooms. 'You never forgive,' he said. 'You may wait twenty, thirty, fifty years – and then you take revenge.' I realised why Kamal often held two rallies in the same village: a single gathering would risk a shoot-out among the voters.

The second day of campaigning took us into the southern part of Lakki Marwat, an area of stubbly hills, caves and shabbier houses. 'Bandit country,' Kamal said. Criminals found refuge here, as did the local jihadi fraternity – tribesmen who fought with the Taliban in Afghanistan during the 1990s, now returned home. Out of the car window, Kamal pointed to Shah Hassan Khel, a village said to have fallen under the spell of a radical pro-Taliban cleric. Kamal instructed his driver to keep going. 'We leave them alone and they don't touch us,' he said.

The light was fading as we rolled up to a whitewashed compound for the last rally of the day. The scene had a timeless quality. The first stars glittered overhead; a black camel, its back stacked with reeds, stood tethered in the corner; the low wail of infants drifted from the women's quarters. The village headman flourished a list. Kamal chuckled. In exchange for their votes, the villagers demanded a school, a connection to the electricity grid, and, rather ambitiously, a hospital. 'These people actually come from that village,' he said, pointing to dwellings a mile distant, 'but they migrated years ago due to an enmity. There have been five, six murders on each side. So now no man dares go outside without his gun.'

Inevitably we were presented with food: chicken, fruit, tea. My stomach clenched. It must have been our twentieth meal of the day; I couldn't face another bite. But the tribesmen were watching and Kamal, speaking sotto voce, issued a soft admonition. 'If you can eat, eat. If not, just touch it,' he muttered. 'These people get heavily annoyed if you don't take anything.'

I reached for a chicken leg.

❧

Warm hospitality, smouldering pride, cold and clinical revenge – thus it has always been among the Pashtuns. Their homeland straddles the border between Pakistan and Afghanistan, a thousand miles of rock, soil and sand stretching from the searing red deserts of Balochistan to the glistening peaks of the Hindu Kush. They number about thirty-three million people in Pakistan and fifteen million in Afghanistan. Theirs is a history of pride and dogged defiance against would-be conquerors – from Alexander the Great to the Mughals, the British Raj to the Soviet Union. Once, they were a nation. The Pashtun tribes united in 1747 under a king, Ahmed Shah Durrani, and formed a confederacy headquartered in Kandahar in present-day Afghanistan. Internecine conflict and a succession of invaders wrenched them apart. In the nineteenth century, the Pashtun faced down the marauding Sikh general, Maharaja Ranjit Singh, and then, from 1849, the British.

The capture of Peshawar that year drew the Pashtuns into the Great Game, the imperial contest for influence between the

British Raj and Tsarist Russia. Fearful of Russian expansion, the British viewed the Pashtun hinterlands, at the northern fringes of their Indian empire, as a crucial strategic buffer. Thus began the century-long occupation.

The British easily conquered the Pashtuns of the plains, but the men of the mountains proved stubbornly immune to the charms of empire. Armed tribesmen stormed from their jagged redoubts on horseback, raiding homes and snatching hostages before dashing back, booty in tow. The British countered with bribery, blandishments and violence. Colonial officers in pith helmets and pressed shorts wooed Pashtun chieftains with money and grandiose titles. When that lost its appeal, they resorted to 'punitive expeditions' – brutal sallies into the mountains, led by elephants pulling nine-pounder guns, that involved great bloodshed. Despite terrible losses, the Pashtun refused to bend. In his vivid account of the siege of the British garrison at Malakand in 1897, the young officer Winston Churchill described his tribal opponents as vengeful fanatics. 'Every influence, every motive, that provokes the spirit of murder among men, impels these mountaineers to deeds of treachery and violence,' he wrote.

The last Pashtun uprising, in the waning years of British empire, was led by the Faqir of Ipi, a Sufi cleric with a cult-like following. From 1936, the Faqir's tribal followers harried the British in Waziristan, ambushing their convoys and even stealing the bodies of fallen soldiers from graveyards, to be ransomed later. The British deployed their latest military technology – Audax and Wapiti airplanes – to hunt the Faqir, and Nazi spies based in nearby Kabul sought him out in a vain attempt to recruit him to their cause. Yet he eluded them all, hiding in caves and protected by followers who believed he possessed superhuman powers. The London press dubbed him 'The Scarlet Pimpernel of Waziristan', and when the British army finally quit India in

1947, the Faqir remained at large. He died thirteen years later, peacefully, in his own bed.

Still today, the colonists exert a powerful, and largely unwarranted, influence over our understanding of Pashtun society. As the Taliban insurgency in Afghanistan worsened from 2004, British ministers and American generals invoked Churchill's dispatches, or the faded diaries of other colonial officers, in an effort to penetrate the psychology of their turbaned foes. Some turned to the verse of Rudyard Kipling, whose poem 'Arithmetic on the Frontier' captured the clinical savagery of colonial efforts to contain the mountain warriors.

With home-bred hordes the hillsides teem,
The troop-ships bring us one by one,
At vast expense of time and steam,
To slay Afridis where they run.

Others wrote with a more sentimental, even misty-eyed pen. 'The weft and warp of this tapestry is woven into the souls and bodies of the men who move before it,' wrote Sir Olaf Caroe, the last British governor of North-West Frontier Province, in his book *The Pathans*: 'Much is harsh, but all is drawn in strong tones that catch the breath, and at times bring tears, almost of pain.'

In truth, the most enduring colonial bequest was cartographic. In 1893 a British diplomat named Sir Mortimer Durand signed a treaty with the Afghan emir, Abdur Rahman Khan, that created a 1,600-mile boundary through the Hindu Kush, separating the northern reaches of British India (present-day Pakistan) from Afghanistan. The Durand Line, as the border is known, split the Pashtun nation in two, and since 1947 has been a source of interminable argument and periodic warfare between Pakistan and Afghanistan. The Afghans refuse to recognise the border, insisting the emir agreed to it under duress, and formally lay claim to a swath of northwestern Pakistan that stretches down to the Indus River. The Pakistanis vehemently reject those claims. Since the 1950s, both countries have pressed their argument with underhand tactics, economic blockades or support to guerrilla movements in the rival country. After the attacks of 2001, the Durand Line became a Western preoccupation, a gun-toting corridor teeming with smugglers, spies and jihadis. The Pashtuns, as ever, found themselves caught in the middle.

❧

The 'frontier', as it is widely known, is composed of Khyber Pakhtunkhwa, the smallest of Pakistan's four provinces (called North-West Frontier Province until 2010), and the adjoining tribal belt, a constellation of seven tribal agencies clustered along the Afghan border. For a century, the difference was legal. While Khyber Pakhtunkhwa was ruled like every other province, the tribal belt fell under the Frontier Crimes Regulations, a draconian colonial-era law that outlawed political parties, provided for collective punishment and was offensive to just about every tenet of modern governance. (The government formally abolished the FCR in 2018, hoping to fold the tribal belt into the 'settled areas.' But the reforms were half-hearted and the area remains in limbo.)

Getting to the frontier is deceptively easy. The old route curled through Attock, where a centuries-old Mughal fortress towers over the swirling confluence of the Kabul and Indus Rivers (the same fortress where Musharraf imprisoned the ousted prime minister, Nawaz Sharif, in 1999). Today, visitors sweep in on a six-lane motorway from Islamabad, racing along a smooth road that passes houses with mirrored, Dubai-style windows – a sign of the remittances from Pashtun migrants in the Middle East and Karachi that, as much as anything else, keep the local economy afloat.

The provincial capital, Peshawar – the name is said to come from the Sanskrit for 'City of Men' – squats at the foot of the Khyber Pass, thrumming with nervous energy. Parts of the city retain the romantic exoticism of Kipling's verse. Blind beggars roam the spice bazaar; veiled women dart among sparkling jewellery shops; peacocks strut on the silky lawns of the governor's colonial-era mansion. Everywhere else are garish splashes of modernity – chromed plazas selling mobile phones; tacky American fast-food joints; giant billboards advertising remedies for male baldness; and 'slimming academies' for women. Cheap Chinese rickshaws worm through the raucous traffic.

Peshawar changed beyond recognition in the 1980s, when it was the cockpit of the *jihad* against the Soviet occupation of Afghanistan. The leaders of the seven *mujahideen* factions were based in Peshawar; so were the American and Saudi intelligence officers who supplied them with guns, missiles and bags of cash. The city had a Wild West air, romantic and seedy, its streets seething with Afghan refugees, Western spies and adventurers of all kinds. Osama bin Laden rented a pine-shaded house in the upmarket University Town neighbourhood, where, in a tailored *shalwar kameez* and handmade leather boots, he distributed funds and guns to Arab volunteers. (Towards the end of the war, he founded al Qaeda here.) The writer Doris Lessing, visiting in 1986, felt that Peshawar would make a good setting for a Humphrey Bogart film.

The 9/11 attacks turned the city inward. When I first visited in 2004, the only trace of foreigners to be found was in the smugglers' bazaar, where traders sold boxes of counterfeit Viagra that featured pictures of bare-breasted women, recordings of bin Laden's greatest speeches and American military uniforms stolen from NATO supply convoys as they trundled up the Khyber Pass. The Americans had retreated into their consulate, a prison-like compound that housed a major

CIA substation and a National Security Agency listening post. Desperate for any sign of the fugitive bin Laden, the Americans courted local journalists. One told me how a friendly diplomat offered him an unusual watch that he was to wear on his next trip to the tribal belt. The journalist declined to say whether he accepted it.

The provincial government was controlled by a coalition of religious parties that the ISI had boosted into power in an effort to broaden Musharraf's political base. I found one of its leaders at the city's Mohabbat Khan Mosque, an exquisite, white-marbled building. Muhammad Yousuf Qureshi was a jolly man with bright eyes and a henna-stained beard who was famed for his venomous anti-Western sermons. He welcomed me with warm, pillowy hands, and proceeded to explain his unhappiness with local movie theatres that tried to open on the Prophet Muhammad's birthday. 'We told them, "If you show the films on that day, we will burn your cinemas,"' he explained. 'So they closed them.' Still, he wasn't entirely averse to the West: three of his sons lived in the United States; until 9/11, he visited them regularly. That was no longer possible, because the United States refused to issue him a visa. He seemed hurt by the rejection. I made my excuses and headed for dinner.

I had been invited to a house in the old city by a friend who was hosting half a dozen college buddies – bankers, aid workers, civil servants, all in their thirties. We sat in a circle, legs crossed, in his garden. To my right was a pudgy *malik*, or tribal elder, from Darra Adam Khel, a lawless town of gunsmiths famed for their knockoff AK-47s. To my left was a shy man with a long beard, whom the others teasingly called 'Mullah Omar', after the Taliban leader. He was in charge of rolling the joints. The promised meal never materialised; instead, we drank and smoked. Bottles of cheap whisky circled in one direction; the hashish went in the other. The conversation was loud and raucous, full of politics and rude jokes, and after a few hours my head was spinning. I felt something: the *malik* had nudged his foot against mine and was stroking my toes. Unsure whether this was a sign of friendship or something more purposeful – jokes about the homosexual preferences of Pashtun men were rife – I discreetly curled my toes inward, safely out of stroking distance.

Finally, at midnight, the call went up: food. We piled drunkenly into three tiny cars and made a dash into downtown Peshawar, roaring and cheering like teenage joyriders. In my vehicle, a dashboard screen showed a bikini-clad dancer writhing to a Bollywood soundtrack; veiled female shoppers blurred past in the street outside. At the restaurant, we wolfed down plates of chicken with minimum ceremony and then parted ways: my new friends back to their homes and me to my guesthouse, where I flopped on the bed – exhausted, inebriated and exhilarated.

The origins of the Pashtun have long since melted into a genealogical fog. Some speculate they are 'lost Jews' descended from Saul, king of the Israelites – an odd theory, given the anti-Semitism of many Pakistanis. Others trace their roots to the invading armies that passed through, led by Arabs, Persians, Central Asians and Greeks. Simply being a Pashtun is a less complicated matter. Traditionally, there are two requirements: to speak Pashto, an ergative language considered harder to learn than Urdu, and to observe *Pashtunwali*, the Pashtun code of conduct – literally, 'the way of the Pashtun'. The bedrock of *Pashtunwali* is *nang*, or honour. *Nang* faces a multitude of threats – a murdered relative, a cheating wife, a casual insult – and is most simply remedied with *badal*, revenge. Hence the profusion of feuds in places like Lakki Marwat. But *Pashtunwali* also has many peaceful obligations – such as *melmastia*, hospitality to a stranger, and *nanawatai*, sanctuary to a fugitive – that must be equally fastidiously observed.

My usual driver on trips to the frontier was Ismail Jan, a burly Pashtun from Takht Bhai, a small town famous for its tasty kebabs. He set up a small car-rental company with the proceeds of a stint working as a labourer in Saudi Arabia. He was a staunch Musharraf supporter – keen to get ahead, sceptical about dynastic politics – and an indefatigable, unflappable companion. Once, as I interviewed a group of tribal rogues in Dera Ismail Khan, Ismail realised they were mulling over whether to kidnap me for ransom. Without explanation, he ended the interview, made our excuses and spirited me away. Ismail called me *brother* and treated me like one.

Talk of *Pashtunwali* irks many Pashtuns, who consider the image of the trigger-happy tribesman, tethered to tradition and a blind belief in violence, as an orientalist cliché. 'You cannot understand twenty-first-century Pashtuns through nineteenth-century colonial prisms,' writes Abubakar Siddique, a native of Waziristan. He has a point. Many tribal societies, like the Bedouin of Sinai, have similar codes; Pashtunwali's violent aspects have been romanticised by foreigners whose writings have stereotyped Pashtuns, and obscured those with modern lives. There are Pashtun pilots and pop stars, generals and ambassadors; Pashtun women stand for election, even in conservative areas; and for a while, the national cricket team was captained by Shahid Afridi, a showy batsman from Khyber nicknamed 'Boom Boom' for his ability to lash the ball into the stands.

Moreover, Pashtun politics has a noble tradition of pacifism. In the early part of the twentieth century, a movement arose led by Abdul Ghaffar Khan, known as the 'Frontier Gandhi', that challenged British rule with tactics of non-violent resistance. In a notorious incident, in 1930, British troops massacred hundreds of Khan's unarmed supporters at Peshawar's Storytellers Bazaar. The Awami National Party, the inheritor of Khan's legacy, swept the provincial elections in 2008.

Pashtunwali has evolved. These days most Pashtuns live in the cities, where a shoot-out with the neighbours is considered a drain on one's time. Yet in the more far-flung corners of the frontier, tradition retains its grip. Here, tribesmen observe the laws of Islamabad in the breach — a state of affairs that can place unusual demands on their elected representatives.

※

There were, by his own admission, two Anwar Kamals. One was the 'polished gent' of Peshawar, a leading member of the Pashtun elite with a taste for frontier bling. His pied-à-terre was a spacious house in Hayatabad, the city's most exclusive suburb, where he frequently dined with his three university-educated sons. His imposing four-wheel-drive had a dashboard television and a prayer counter for Islamic recitations. He kept a small plane at the local airfield and owned a pair of greyhounds, imported from England, to hunt boar on the family lands. His father, Khan Habibullah Khan, had been a high-court judge who, for a brief period in the 1970s, was acting president of Pakistan. Kamal's political career was less glittering yet also distinguished: he had been a provincial minister and a senator, and on one occasion addressed the United Nations General Assembly in New York, where he stayed at the Roosevelt Hotel in midtown Manhattan.

The second Anwar Kamal emerged when he jumped into his jeep and headed for Lakki Marwat, a bumpy four-hour ride to the south. Lakki was not only his constituency but also his land, his power, his identity. Here, Kamal slept with a rocket launcher under his bed in a draughty fortress guarded by dozens of tribesmen, spent his time in lengthy confabulations with bearded elders, and generally acted in a manner that seemed to contradict everything the first Anwar Kamal stood for.

I got a first glimpse of this second persona from a Kodak album that I found on a table in his Peshawar living room. In one photograph, Kamal posed with a group of rough-hewn, heavily armed tribesmen, grinning widely; in another, he sat at the helm of an imposing, if rather vintage-looking gun – an *ack-ack*, he informed me, of the kind used to shoot down German bombers in World War II. A most satisfying weapon, he added, recounting its most recent use. 'You see, we were being fired on from three sides by some individuals who were hiding in a *burj*,' he said in his gravelly voice. 'So, I called up my driver, Akhtar' – a smiling young chap I'd met earlier – 'and I said, "Bastard! Get that *ack-ack* and fire back!" So he grabbed it and gave it a burst of seven or eight rounds. What a noise – the whole ground started shaking! The bullets went right through that *burj*, killing two of those individuals who were sitting there.'

Kamal chuckled. 'Within a split second there was absolute silence. Everyone was calm and cool.'

He was describing a dispute between the Marwats and the Bhittanis, their nearest neighbours and oldest rivals. For years, hotheads from both tribes had needled each other with the usual tactics: shootings, hostage-taking and so on. But then the Bhittanis kidnapped two Marwat women, which Kamal considered provocative. 'Kidnapping men we don't mind,' he said. 'But taking our ladies – that was totally unprecedented!'

To even the score, the Marwats abducted several Bhittani women and children from a passing bus, then mustered an armed posse, known as a *lashkar*, with the intention of sallying into Bhittani territory and retrieving the Marwat hostages. Kamal led from the front, binoculars in one hand and pistol in the other. By several accounts, it was a messy business. The fighting was sporadic, indecisive and failed to achieve its goal. One of the Marwat women was burned alive in disputed circumstances; the other was spirited away to a hiding place deep in the tribal belt. She was finally released, a year later, but at a cost: a tribal council ordered the Marwats to pay sixteen million rupees (about

$260,000) in blood money for the Bhittanis they had killed. That was expensive, Kamal conceded, but worth every rupee. 'It's not about money,' he said. 'The question is: "Did you restore your honour?" And we did.'

I stayed in Kamal's guest quarters that night, and found him after dawn the next morning, watching the National Geographic channel alone in his bedroom, an AK-47 propped against his bed. His wife, who suffered from hepatitis, had died tragically a year earlier when a trip to China, for a liver transplant, went wrong. Kamal flew home alone, with her body. It pained him to talk about it. After a breakfast of eggs and greasy *paratha*, an oily flatbread, we plunged into the Peshawar traffic, headed south towards Lakki.

Politically, Kamal was a member of Nawaz Sharif's Muslim League, which seemed an odd choice because it was rooted in Punjab and had limited appeal to Pashtuns. But the alternatives – Pashtun nationalists, liberals and mullahs – were not to Kamal's taste. He reserved particular scorn for Maulana Fazlur Rehman, one of the country's leading cleric-cum-politicians, who hailed from a neighbouring district. Rehman accepted Saudi funding and supported the Taliban, yet also stood for election and, according to occasional rumours, would make any concession to make money. Kamal was sceptical about both his piety and the source of his considerable wealth. 'His father was a great Islamic scholar, but their family lived in a small muddy house with donkey carts in the yard,' he said. 'Now Maulana Fazlur Rehman is one of the richest men in the province. You tell me: where does the money come from?'

Like any Pakistani politician worth his salt, Kamal had suffered a few brushes with the law. He served a short jail term in 1993, on political charges, although the authorities alleviated his hardship by permitting his cook and a manservant to accompany him into the cells. Earlier that year, he had led a convoy of supporters to Islamabad Airport, where they were due to welcome Nawaz Sharif back from exile. They never made it. On the way, the Marwats clashed with the police, sacked a constabulary and took hostage seven officers – events that led the police to charge Kamal with kidnapping and banditry. He laid low for a while, to avoid arrest. The charges were eventually dropped.

For all his loyalty to Sharif, Kamal could also be sharply critical of his leader – 'Frankly, I find him to be a mediocrity' – and his rustic, shoot-from-the-hip style didn't always sit well with the urbane Punjabis who ran Sharif's party. 'Sometimes,' he said in a moment of exasperation, 'I think I am the only straightforward man in my party.'

After four hours of driving, we reached Lakki Marwat. A reception committee was waiting on the town's outskirts: a dozen tribesmen leaning against a pair of seventies-model Datsun cars with red velvet curtains across their rear windows. A sign peppered with buckshot read: KARACHI, 1,400 KILOMETRES. The tribesmen hugged Kamal warmly, served him a glass of soda and led the way, their gun barrels poking out of the car windows.

The Marwats are not among the celebrated tribes of the frontier like the smuggler Afridis of Khyber or the rebellious Yusufzais of Swat. Farmers by nature, they migrated from southern Afghanistan perhaps 500 years ago. When British colonists arrived in 1850, bringing bureaucracy, trains and a smidgen of development, they grew to like the Marwats. 'In person, they are tall and muscular; in bearing, frank and open. Almost every officer who has administered the District has left on record a favourable mention of them,' observed the *Imperial Gazetteer of India*, a British colonial record, in 1909, when the area numbered 52,000 people.

Now the population had swelled to more than 700,000 – as Kamal put it, 'Sexual intercourse is appealing to everyone. Everyone!' – and Lakki town had a sparse, dust-blown feel.

Traders squatted in boxy stores before gunnysacks of grain and sugar. Camel-drawn carts bumped along the main street.

The local bigwigs were the Saifullahs, one of the richest clans in Pakistan. They owned textile mills, power plants and a fancy hospital in Islamabad; one of the older brothers, Salim Saifullah, supported Kamal and accompanied him to election rallies wearing a pair of soft Gucci loafers. Salim's main residence was in Islamabad, where I had befriended his son, an American-educated lawyer with a sideline as a techno DJ, and his son's wife, a fashion guru who published the local edition of *Hello!* magazine. That was a world away from Lakki, where the land was so parched that well diggers frequently bore down 700 feet before striking water. A Saifullah-owned cement factory provided some jobs, as did a secretive government-run uranium mine that extracted 'yellow cake', used to manufacture nuclear weapons. But most families got by on remittances from young relatives who worked in menial jobs in Karachi or Dubai.

The Marwats had a feeble attachment to the state. Few paid income tax, smuggled vehicles plied the roads and electricity theft was rampant. The government gave them little reason to change: schools were dilapidated, the local hospital offered rudimentary care, and just 12 per cent of women could read or write – predictable, given how seldom they were permitted to leave their homes, but literacy rates were even shockingly low among men. Kamal offered a dispiriting explanation. 'To his father, a crude man is an asset. You tell him to plough the land, or kill another man, and he will do it. But if the son is educated, he will say, "I am too good for that." And if he cannot find a job, he will get frustrated. So the father prefers a crude man.'

In this Bermuda Triangle of governance, the one constant was tradition. Kamal spent much of his time on *jirgas*, the councils of tribal elders who mediated disputes. Most frequently, they resolved murder cases through the payment of blood money.

That was not a cheap solution, Kamal noted. It could cost $1,000 to settle a murder charge, and he had seen poor families driven to the wall to end a feud, forced to sell their houses or pawn their possessions. Still, there were loopholes. A man guilty of multiple murders, Kamal continued, may delay *jirga* justice until his enemies have bumped off an equal number of his own relatives, thereby evening up the score. He called this 'a trick of the trade'.

Another solution was to give a daughter in marriage to the son of an opponent. Such exchanges generally produced the most durable settlements but represented a raw deal for the women, who were treated little better than chattels. Even so, neither side forgot that blood had been spilled. 'The enmity and sense of insecurity are always there,' said Kamal. He picked up a glass. 'It's like that glass. You might break it and mend it, but the crack is always there. So, you have to be careful, for the rest of your life.'

One evening, Kamal took me to see Saadullah Khan, a notorious local brigand. We were guided into a sparsely furnished room where ten men, brothers and cousins, waited. Several were cross-eyed. It was ferociously hot, so a young tribesman was deputed to fan Kamal and me by hand. 'A very dashing group,' Kamal whispered in my ear. 'They must have killed eighteen or nineteen people. Very hotheaded, always in trouble.' In the corner, a toothless old man sat silently in a chair. This was Saadullah Khan. The police had been trying to arrest him for years, but every time it resulted in a gunfight with his sons, who usually won. Saadullah spoke up. He wanted Kamal to get jobs for his sons as guards at the local primary school – a sinecure. Kamal nodded his assent.

Over supper that night, in Kamal's gloomy dining room, I asked about the contradictions in his life. Was it not odd for an elected official to spend his time shielding outlaws, pardoning murderers and leading his constituents into battle? People often asked that, he replied. 'They say, "You are a law graduate. You consider yourself to be a polished man. So why do you act like a barbarian?" But that is not the point. Certain things are our compulsion. To me, my customs and my traditions are more holy than the law of my country. You live with them and you die with them, whether you like it or not.' In other areas, he added, the *khans* – Pashtun chieftains – had lost touch with their people. But the Marwats, for all their desperate poverty, remained a 'compact' tribe, united behind their chief. In his hour of need, rogues like Saadullah Khan would stick by him.

As a religious man, Kamal conceded, this was problematic. Islam did not sit easily with *Pashtunwali*'s obligations of bloody revenge. 'Belief relates to your heart, your prayers; *Pashtunwali* is about traditions, culture, life,' he explained. When the two clashed, *Pashtunwali* usually won. Kamal posed a practical dilemma. 'Suppose your wife elopes with someone else; you are the most disgraced man in society. Can you leave it to Allah that the man will be punished at death? How can you live in society until then?' He shrugged. 'Pashtuns are Pashtuns.'

❈

If the Pakistani state was no competition for the magnetic lure of Pashtun tradition, a potent rival was rising in the nearby tribal belt.

I saw the first signs of it in early 2006 when a Pashtun friend arrived with a video purchased from a Peshawar bazaar. 'You need to see this,' he said. It had been filmed in North Waziristan, the lawless tribal agency once home to the redoubtable Faqir of Ipi. The opening scene showed three bodies hanging from electricity poles, while a fourth lay slumped on the ground. A whisky bottle had been posed on the dead man's lap, and his mouth was stuffed with banknotes – elementary symbols of decadence and disgrace. A long-haired gunman announced their crimes: kidnapping, banditry and 'forcing women to remove their veils'. Hundreds of townspeople watched silently. The video ended with a pick-up truck dragging three corpses through the streets, yahooing gunmen hanging off its back. 'This is reality, not fiction,' read the caption. 'Come and wage *jihad* or you will miss the caravan.'

I called the spokesman for the Pakistani army, who downplayed the recording as the chronicle of a tribal dispute. But more canny observers saw it for something else: the seeds of Pakistan's home-grown Taliban insurgency.

The word *talib* means student; the original Taliban were born in the chaos of the Afghan civil war that followed the defeat of the Soviet occupiers. In 1994, a group of righteous Pashtun students rose from the countryside around Kandahar to challenge the predatory warlords then ripping Afghanistan apart. Led by Mullah Muhammad Omar, an enigmatic, one-eyed cleric who refused to be photographed, they announced themselves by hanging an accused rapist from the barrel of a tank. Such savage theatrics would become the Taliban's hallmark as they fought their way to power in Kabul. Kite-flying, shaving and music were banned; accused adulterers were stoned to death; in 2001, they gained global infamy for blowing up the ancient Buddha statues at Bamiyan. Pakistan's ISI provided discreet support, viewing the Taliban as a useful proxy in its longstanding struggle for supremacy along the Durand Line.

Pakistan's Taliban, on the other hand, was born of the tumult that followed the September 2001 attacks. As American warplanes bombed the mountains of Tora Bora, hundreds of al Qaeda jihadis who had been sheltering under the Taliban in Afghanistan – Arabs, Uzbeks and Chechens, mostly – fled across the border into Pakistan's tribal areas. Most ended up in North Waziristan and South Waziristan, where local Pashtun tribesmen flung open their doors in a warm welcome – partly out of *nanawatai*, *Pashtunwali*'s obligation of sanctuary to needy strangers, and partly out of more earthly considerations: bin Laden's Arab disciples paid for their bed-and-breakfast with thick wads of American dollars.

The Americans, realising that their al Qaeda foe – the very reason they invaded Afghanistan – had slipped the net, pressured the Pakistani leader Pervez Musharraf to deploy troops to Waziristan. The operation quickly turned to disaster. Pashtun tribesmen, enraged by the intervention, defended their guests with gunfire. Dozens of Pakistani soldiers were killed. A revolt stirred.

Gangs of tribal militants seized control of Waziristan and imposed a new order. Video stores were torched and barbers were forbidden to shave men's beards. Disputes were no longer settled in *jirgas* but in Saudi-style *sharia* courts. The *maliks* – pro-government elders who upheld the old social order – were assassinated or forced to flee. Many of the rebels hailed from the tribal underclass: barbers, small farmers and day labourers who had grown up in penury watching corrupt neighbours grow rich through government connections. Now, thanks to al Qaeda funding, they were being paid five times more than the military-run Frontier Corps. Young tribesmen joined in droves.

The army's ability to suppress this incipient insurgency was compromised by its own double games. For decades, the military had coddled jihadis to fight its wars in Afghanistan or Kashmir, and even now it maintained ties to some groups in Waziristan. Many officers were deeply ambivalent about following orders that effectively came from Washington.

The Red Mosque siege, in July 2007, catapulted the insurgency onto the national stage. Militant factions spread up in all seven tribal agencies; one, the Ghazi brigade, was named after Abdul Rashid Ghazi. They grew in strength and, by the end of that year, had coalesced into a single movement that formally announced itself as *Tehrik-i-Taliban Pakistan*: the Pakistani Taliban.

The insurgency oozed across the frontier with a viral intensity. Inevitably, it reached Lakki Marwat.

❦

Three months after the 2008 election, Anwar Kamal walked through my front door. A thunderstorm had just passed, and it was one of those rare balmy summer evenings in Islamabad, when the air is fresh and the streets gleam with a fresh slick of rain. The atmosphere was tense. A day earlier, an al Qaeda suicide bomber had rammed his vehicle into the Danish Embassy, about a mile from my house, killing five people. Plainclothes security men loitered on street corners toting Kalashnikovs. Fresh concrete barriers were being erected.

To my surprise, Kamal had lost his seat in Parliament – nudged out by just forty-four votes, he grumbled, after 200 dead voters apparently rose from their graves to vote for a candidate sponsored by his old rival, Haji Kabir Khan. But that wasn't what was bothering him. Kamal pulled out his phone and played a video. It showed a young man with Central Asian features, blood trickling from his temple, lying motionless on the ground. The camera zoomed in to show a wispy moustache that suggested a teenager. 'He's an Uzbek,' said Kamal. 'We killed him last week.'

The Taliban were banging on the gates of Lakki Marwat. Raiders were spilling out of Waziristan, kidnapping people for ransom. A mobile phone company paid out $50,000 to free two of its engineers. Then six militants snatched the town mayor of Lakki, triggering a series of events that led to the gory video. Kamal's gunmen caught up with them as they raced back towards the mountains. Several were hit by a rocket-propelled grenade fired by Kamal's driver, Akhtar, now sipping tea in my kitchen with Mazloom. 'He's a dead shot, you see,' Kamal said. Others, including the teenage Uzbek, were executed on the roadside.

The other danger came from within. Shah Hassan Khel, the village we skirted during the election campaign, had become a Taliban stronghold. The militants' leader, a smooth-talking young cleric named Maulvi Ashraf Ali, had banned sport, shuttered the girls' school and teamed up with local bandits to rob trucks on the Indus Highway. Kamal worried they might link up with the larger Taliban group in Waziristan. 'This is a war of nerves,' he said.

A *qaumi jirga* – a grand meeting of the Marwat sub-tribes – was convened. On a sweltering summer morning, 300 tribesmen gathered under a stand of trees, having agreed to put aside their web of internecine feuds. Kamal addressed them. 'If the government will do nothing, then we must take matters into our own hands,' he thundered, turning on his heel as he jabbed the air. 'Now is the time for action!' The tribesmen roared their approval.

After the meeting, as Kamal and other elders met in a nearby room, a young man in a glinting prayer cap appeared at the door. A pistol was tucked into his belt. After greeting the elders respectfully – and pointedly refusing to shake my hand – he announced himself as a member of the local Taliban. He had come to deliver a message. The militants had no beef with the Marwats, he declared; their goal was to fight the Americans across the border in Afghanistan. He repectfully made his excuses and left.

Across the frontier, the old Pashtun order was coming under unstinting assault. In Swat, a picturesque valley at the northern end of the Pashtun belt, once beloved of Pakistani honeymooners, fighters torched girls' schools and hanged the area's most famous 'dancing girl' – a woman who performed at weddings and parties – from a pole in the main square. In Orakzai tribal agency, a suicide bomber killed one hundred and ten people at a meeting of tribal elders. A Polish geologist, Piotr Stańczak, was kidnapped and beheaded. Suicide bombers twice attacked Musharraf's snowy-haired interior minister, Aftab Ahmad Sherpao, missing their target but killing seventy-nine other people.

The upheaval began to impact Kamal's life. An eruption of fighting in Dara Adam Khel, the city of gunsmiths, forced him to take a circuitous detour to reach Lakki. His aeroplane remained locked in its hangar out of fear it might be attacked if he landed in Lakki. One evening, after failing to appear in Islamabad for supper, he sent me a text message: 'Sorry. On my way to Peshawar. One of my friends died in a suicide attack today.'

Like many Pakistanis, Kamal sympathised with the Afghan Taliban, who, as far as he was concerned, were fighting a legitimate war of resistance against American occupiers. But he vehemently opposed their Pakistani cousins and al Qaeda allies. 'Killing women and children, committing suicide in the mosques – that is something they cannot explain,' he said. 'No individual is allowed to wage a holy war. Who the hell is Osama to start one?' He organised armed patrols to fend off the raids from Waziristan, and sent a message to the militants in Shah Hassan Khel. 'If I bleed, then so will you,' he told them.

The Taliban *emir*, or leader, was Baitullah Mehsud, a high-school dropout and one-time bodybuilder from South Waziristan. Like his mentor Mullah Omar, Mehsud cultivated his image by shunning photographs, and proved a formidable guerrilla organiser, establishing suicide-bomber academies that churned out hundreds of brainwashed, frequently drug-addled, teenage recruits. His weakness was his health: Mehsud suffered from kidney disease and required regular medical attention.

The Taliban leader did not take kindly to Kamal's defiance, and demanded a meeting with the tribesmen who dared challenge his advance. After some nervous procrastination, Kamal agreed.

One night in January 2009, Kamal led a delegation of elders and dozens of Marwat fighters into Jandola, on the border with Waziristan, to an appointed meeting place. A Taliban force of equal size was waiting for them. Guided by the light of their mobile phones, the Marwat elders stumbled up a remote mountain slope. They found Mehsud perched against a rock, being tended to by a doctor. A Thermos flask with tea and a packet of biscuits were produced. The two sides sat in a circle and began to talk.

It was a polite, if forthright, conversation. Mehsud complained that the Marwats' obstinate resistance was preventing him from expanding out of Waziristan. 'I am at war with the government,' he said. Kamal parried that the Taliban's targets – police officers, health workers and teachers – were also Marwat tribesmen. Should they be killed or kidnapped, *Pashtunwali* obliged Kamal to retaliate. 'You have your compulsions, I have mine,' Kamal said. 'As a Pashtun, I cannot deviate from my tradition.'

It was effectively a debate between two visions of the frontier – Kamal representing the old ways, Mehsud as the harbinger of a new order that justified its violence with a lumpen version of *sharia* law. There could be no agreement. 'It's very simple,' Kamal told the Taliban leader. 'You kill two of my people, I will kill ten of yours.'

A few hours later they rose, shook hands and parted ways. Kamal returned to the sandy plains of Lakki, where his tribesmen would redouble their fortifications; Mehsud slunk back into the inky mountains of Waziristan.

❧

I was on vacation in Ireland on New Year's Day in 2010 when the radio brought news of another bombing in Pakistan. Of itself, it was nothing new: almost 2,500 people had died in militant attacks in northwest Pakistan over the previous twelve months, many in suicide attacks. Then the newscaster uttered a name that made me sit up: Lakki Marwat.

I phoned Kamal. A Taliban militant had driven a vehicle loaded with explosives into the crowd at a volleyball game to celebrate the New Year, he said. Ninety-seven people had been slain: children, adults, volleyball players. The attack took place, he added, in Shah Hassan Khel.

Weeks later, I drove down to Lakki with Kamal in his four-wheel drive. He was uncharacteristically jittery. As we entered the district, we passed a blackish spot that marked a roadside bombing that had killed the deputy police chief. Further along, a *madrassa* suspected of having Taliban links had been destroyed by the army. When a car with a single occupant passed our convoy twice, the tension in our vehicle spiked: Kamal's bodyguards discussed shooting the driver, fearing he might be a suicide bomber. The car drove off.

Lakki town had an air of siege. Kamal's house had been fortified with extra concrete barriers and guards. The police chief quit his job after the Taliban threatened to behead his children. 'The man got shit-scared,' Kamal said. 'Once that happens, you can't expect him to do any good.' The new police chief came for supper, arriving in civilian clothes in an unmarked car. After the meal, two men with pinched faces joined us: Lakki's two most notorious outlaws, responsible for a string of robberies and murders, who had struck a deal with the police chief. In return for amnesty from arrest, their men would join the anti-Taliban effort. 'Sometimes you need criminals like this,' Kamal whispered to me in English. 'They know where a Talib gets his food, where he sleeps, who are his friends.' The police chief nodded in agreement.

The next morning, a delegation of grim-faced elders from Shah Hassan Khel trooped into Kamal's courtyard, still mourning their dead. Their leader was Mushtaq Ahmed, a bony-faced man with quivering hands, who recounted the events leading up to the volleyball bombing. At first, he said, the rebel cleric Maulvi Ashraf Ali enjoyed popular support, especially from youngsters entranced by his flowery speeches and dramatic accounts of fighting the Americans in Afghanistan. But then the Taliban banned girls' education, television and sport, and their popularity waned. 'Ashraf Ali talked about *sharia*,' Ahmed said. 'What he really wanted was power.'

The villagers got some relief when the army arrived in Shah Hassan Khel, pushing out the Taliban with artillery and helicopter gunships. The militants fled to Waziristan where, months later, seventeen of them were killed in a CIA drone strike. On New Year's Eve, they struck back. Mushtaq Ahmed's face darkened. The explosive-laden car that drove into the crowd at the volleyball match, he said, was driven by a local boy who had fallen under the Taliban's spell. The blast left a mound of charred bodies that included members of every family in the tight-knit village – even the bomber himself, whose stepbrother was among the dead. It was a blood feud of gargantuan proportions.

'We are Pashtun and we want revenge,' Ahmed said in a quiet, cool voice. 'We will track them down. We will capture them. And we will kill them, one by one.'

Kamal huddled with the elders as they drew up plans for fighters to slip into Waziristan in search of Ashraf Ali. It seemed a quixotic mission: a small band of Marwat vigilantes in an area crawling with ruthless Taliban. And the Taliban had already won a symbolic victory: with so many people dead, the volleyball court in Shah Hassan Khel now stood empty.

As we drove back to Peshawar, though, Kamal insisted that the Taliban would never prevail. They were the 'rejected people', he said, the dregs of Pashtun society. Their nihilistic violence had alienated tribesmen who had seen through their hollow promises. Marxist revolutionaries they were not. 'We have a saying,' he said in his gravelly voice, as Lakki disappeared into the dust behind us: 'If a man with a bald head grows nails, then tomorrow he will injure himself.' In other words: give power to the foolish and they will eventually implode.

❧

By the time Kamal died in 2012, of a heart attack, there were signs he had been right. A Pakistan army counter-offensive had driven the militants from their stronghold in Swat. CIA drones thinned the ranks of their leaders. Baitullah Mehsud had been assassinated as he lay on the rooftop of his wife's family home, receiving treatment for his kidney ailment. The last image of him, before a Hellfire missile struck, showed a sick man stretched out on a rope bed and hooked up to a drip.

Yet there was no denying that the Taliban revolt had shaken Pashtun society to its core. The firestorm of violence unleashed by the militants had exposed the chronic weakness of the Pakistani state in the northwest. It laid bare other failings too: the foolish policies of a military ruler; the deep inequalities in Pashtun society; and perhaps even the limitations of the centuries-old system of *Pashtunwali* itself. The arithmetic of the frontier had changed, for ever.

Asma Jahangir

5

The Fabulous Senorita

A Human Rights Heroine Versus the Generals

A winter fog laced Lahore, shrouding the city in milky hues. The car barrelled down the Mall, the grand colonial-era boulevard, then turned into Gulberg, an expensive neighbourhood of spacious villas. We halted outside one of them – a handsome sixties-era house with palm trees, a tropical garden and a swimming pool. A pair of policemen came to the gate, in mustard slacks and wool sweaters, wielding Kalashnikovs. I tensed. A young woman in the back seat beside me issued whispered instructions. 'I'll do the talking, okay? You just keep quiet and follow.'

It was November 2007, and President Pervez Musharraf, after eight years of seemingly unassailable rule, was suddenly tottering. Rowdy protests filled the streets, calling for his adversary. Benazir Bhutto, his most potent political rival, had finally returned from exile and planned to stand against him in a forthcoming election. His own generals were growing nervous and the Americans, sensing the changing wind, were turning tail. Condoleezza Rice, the US secretary of state, had called Musharraf the previous August to warn him against 'doing something stupid' like imposing emergency rule. Now, with power slipping through his fingers, Musharraf panicked and did it anyway. Appearing on state television, Musharraf announced that he was suspending the constitution and imposing *de facto* martial law. Television stations were yanked off air, the entire bench of the Supreme Court was dismissed and his loudest critics were rounded up and flung into jail. First among them was the lawyer Asma Jahangir, doyenne of Pakistan's human rights movement, who had been placed under house arrest. The government designated her Lahore home, where I had just arrived, as a 'sub-jail'. I was hoping to break in.

My accomplice was Jahangir's thirty-year-old daughter, Munizae. The car pulled up to a door where two female wardens huddled over a gas fire. Munizae, a journalist, leaped out and signed me into the visitors' register as 'Adam Ullah Hassan', supposedly a family friend from Peshawar. It seemed a dubious plan: although I was wearing baggy *shalwar kameez*, I hardly resembled your typical Pashtun, so I tapped aimlessly on my phone, hoping to avoid eye contact. Somehow it worked. A moment later, I was trotting up a staircase to the lounge where the prisoner was waiting.

Asma Jahangir sat curled up in front of the TV, flicking through the channels that were still on air. Her husband, Tahir, a bow tie slung around his neck, hovered behind her, nursing a glass of Scotch. At five feet tall, Jahangir, who was fifty-five, was physically unimposing but crackled with restless energy. She sprang from her seat, strode to the window, whipped shut the curtains and sat down again. She'd been stuck in here for a week, she said – chain-smoking, smouldering, firing off indignant emails. 'He's finally lost his marbles,' she said of Musharraf.

To relieve the boredom, she sometimes went downstairs to the wardens to share an ear of roasted corn and talked politics and literature. Jahangir recommended a book of leftist poetry and got sucked into their personal dramas. Earlier that day, the male police officers had blocked a male visitor from reaching one of the female wardens. 'They said the man had no business coming here because the warden wasn't married,' Jahangir explained.

'She got really upset because this man was her boyfriend. She told me, "This is what you mean about women's rights."'

Jahangir spent her life fighting other people's battles. In a country famed for its anti-heroes – reckless nuclear proliferators, hawkish generals, thieving politicians and world-class terrorists – she was that rare individual: a cast-iron idealist. She didn't just stand on her principles, she waved them from the barricades, wielded them as a weapon and broadcast them with a megaphone. She defended Christians accused of blasphemy; women raped or burned by acid; Islamists who vanished into the military detention cells and torture chambers. She embraced the untouchable and advocated the unthinkable, leading indefatigable crusades to reform Pakistan's bigoted laws or to protect its most vulnerable minorities. And she publicly confronted Pakistan's most powerful men, the senior generals she accused of pushing the country towards ruin with their disastrous strategic double-games. 'Useless duffers,' she called them on television, her lip curled. This was dangerous work, facing down the extremists and jihadi generals, and foes had repeatedly tried to shoot her dead. Occasionally, she encouraged them. When the first anti-Musharraf protests erupted that year, she waded into the milky clouds of tear gas, glasses glinting in the spring sunshine, and yelled at the riot police: 'Come on, shoot me!'

The men – and they were always men – didn't like her much. Over the years, she had been beaten, spat on and jailed. Newspapers tarred her as a heretic and a home-wrecker; nationalists said she was an Indian spy; clerics branded her an apostate. After one contentious court hearing, extremists surrounded her car and pelted it with stones. Later, militants broke into her home on a mission to kill her. She was out, but the incident prompted her to send her teenage daughters, Munizae and Sulema, to boarding school in England. Jahangir stayed behind, impatiently dismissing anyone who suggested that she pipe down.

'There have been times I have been scared,' she said. 'There have been times that I have cried. But does that mean you give up in the face of brute force? No. Never!'

I first encountered Jahangir during a spirited episode of Pakistan's neverending culture wars. In the spring of 2005, stick-wielding Islamist thugs started to intimidate and sometimes assault women who participated in mixed-gender road races, which they deemed un-Islamic. Musharraf, who had been wooing Western audiences for years with talk of 'enlightened moderation', his homespun philosophy that purported to blend Islamic culture and Western values, might have been expected to stand up for the menaced women. But Musharraf relied on the religious right for political support, so he capitulated and banned mixed-sex races in Punjab. Infuriated, Jahangir organised her own race through central Lahore. The police broke it up, and during the melee ripped the shirt off her back – a shocking humiliation for a Pakistani woman. 'Teach the bitch a lesson,' a police commander ordered. A week later, Jahangir and her female runners were out again, and this time they passed without incident. They called it a 'mini-marathon' although in truth it wasn't much of a race: a few dozen middle-aged Lahoris, some in heels or slacks, shuffling down the street. When it was over, supporters hoisted Jahangir onto the bonnet of a police vehicle. 'We will not be cowed by Musharraf or the mullahs!' she declared.

Unlike some wealthy Pakistani women in public life, Jahangir spurned fancy clothes and expensive jewellery, instead commanding respect with a kind of high-voltage intensity. She spoke in rapid-fire sentences, flicking between plain English and legalese as she pulled on *beedis* – thin, hand-rolled cigarettes of a kind typically used by poor Pakistanis. She could be curt to the point of rudeness and often dismissed critics – or friends, when they irritated her – with an impatient snort. In court, she earned respect from her adversaries with calculated shows of aggression, spearing pompous lawyers with deadpan one-liners. Human rights groups across the world praised her courage and the United Nations hired her to investigate atrocities in countries such as Sri Lanka and Iran. At times, though, Jahangir seemed to relish the danger, to glory in her many brushes with authorities, even with death. She saw it as part of the job. 'Let me tell you one thing,' she told me. 'You can't be a self-respecting citizen in this country if you don't go to jail.'

Off camera, Jahangir cut a softer figure. An inveterate gossip, she loved to stay up with friends late into the night, swapping stories and sipping whisky. Irreverent and caustic, she had a tittering laugh and was known among friends as a professional-level mimic, sending them into howls of laughter with her imitations of cocky generals and preening society queens. Now and then, in gatherings of female friends, they sang *ghazals* – keening, Urdu-language ballads about love and loss.

A week into the emergency rule, Musharraf convened a meeting of Western ambassadors in Islamabad to justify his draconian crackdown. In what the American ambassador called 'a rambling monologue', he disparaged Jahangir as 'mentally unbalanced'. But by then it was clear that the military dictator was the one under strain.

Only a year earlier, Musharraf had been riding high. On a trip to the United States in 2006, he appeared on *The Daily Show with Jon Stewart*, where the two men swapped jokes and ate Twinkies (a small sponge cake), and he shamelessly plugged his new memoir, *In the Line of Fire*, in the middle of a press conference at the White House. '"Buy the book," is what he's saying,' President George W. Bush told bemused reporters. The cheeky commando ruthlessly exploited what the academic Fouad Ajami called Americans' 'weakness for dictators with charm and guile and a "modernist" veneer who rule exotic, dangerous lands.' But at home Musharraf's book received a sullen reception, which should have warned him of his coming troubles.

They started in March 2007 when Musharraf summoned the chief justice, Iftikhar Muhammad Chaudhry, to his official residence in Rawalpindi. Chaudhry was an idiosyncratic man who supported Musharraf after the 1999 coup, but then made trouble by demanding answers about the 'disappeared' – Islamists who vanished into ISI custody. At Army House, Musharraf gave the judge a dressing-down and then his marching orders. To the great surprise of all Pakistanis, not least Musharraf, Chaudhry refused point-blank to go. It was an astonishing moment – no judge had ever defied a military order in such brazen fashion – and the public's amazement turned to disquiet that night when the TV news showed a policeman grabbing the judge by his hair and shoving him into a car. Furious, black-clad lawyers surged onto the streets in support of the judge with calls that soon turned on their ruler. 'Go, Musharraf, go!' Many ordinary Pakistanis, weary of his high-handed rule, poured out of their homes to back the lawyers. A fire had been lit.

Musharraf's distress was evident in the rambling, tautology-laden speech that he delivered on state television to announce emergency rule. 'Extremism has become more extreme,' he declared at one point. People sniggered; as the writer Mohammed Hanif observed, Musharraf resembled a drunken uncle at a family gathering, nursing a bottle in the corner, desperate to be taken seriously.

Asma Jahangir considered the uproar a vindication. 'He's just a ruthless bully who believes his own lies,' she told me as we sat in her lounge. Pakistan's military rulers had never lasted much more than a decade, she continued; Musharraf was simply approaching his expiry date. Had he not done some good? He had, she conceded – a modest increase in the number of female parliamentarians, reforms that enfranchised religious minorities and softened the country's notoriously anti-woman laws. Extramarital sex, punishable by stoning to death under the Zia-era laws, was now subject to a lengthy prison sentence.

'Even Hitler made very good roads,' Jahangir snorted. 'That doesn't mean his system was the right one.'

The doorbell rang. Munizae popped her head in. 'It's the warden. They're getting suspicious.'

Jahangir lit another cigarette. 'Let's hurry up,' she said.

The revolutionary fervour gripping Pakistan that autumn promised exciting change – a gust of revolt to burst the long years of peremptory military rule. But some worried that it carried risks. Bearded Islamists calling for a return to 'rule of the prophet' stood in the streets behind the protesting lawyers; some foreign commentators saw parallels with pre-revolutionary Iran in 1979, when clerics hijacked a revolt against the Shah to impose theocracy. Could it happen in Pakistan? Jahangir scoffed. 'Believe me, there are no Khomeinis waiting in the wings here. People just need to believe in civil society – the lawyers, the journalists, the activists. The Americans, especially, need to believe in it. They've been blindly supporting Musharraf, and that doesn't help.'

The doorbell rang again; this time, her husband rose. 'He really should go,' he said, gesturing at me. 'Otherwise, you'll not be allowed more visitors.' Jahangir shot him an irritated glance, and they exchanged a few testy words in Urdu, but she conceded that he was right. She slipped my notebook between the pages of a magazine, handed it to Munizae and hustled us out into the night.

❃

For much of its history, Punjab, the province Jahangir called home, has oscillated between conquest and supplication.

In the seventeenth century, triumphant Mughal emperors rode warrior elephants through the majestic arches of Lahore

Fort, radiating an aura of power that extended thousands of miles. The British called Punjab 'the sword army of the Raj', the principal recruiting ground for the colonial army, prompting fanciful myths about Punjabis as a 'martial race'. Still today, the vast majority of the Pakistan army's officer corps come from a small area in northern Punjab that straddles the Grand Trunk Road, a chaotic highway that arcs across the province, through conservative country that is Pakistan's version of the Bible Belt. The legacy of Pakistan's bloody creation hangs heavy over the province. Sliced in two in 1947, Punjab was the stage for the most horrific atrocities of partition – trains filled with corpses, entire villages razed to the ground. Indian warplanes roared over the province in the 1965 war, dropping bombs on the suburbs of Lahore, and today Punjabis are the leading proponents of a brittle, army-centric brand of Pakistani nationalism. One Lahore-based media magnate, founder of the Pakistan Ideology Trust, hailed its nuclear weapons as 'shining swords' and fantasised in public about using them to lay waste to India. Size is a factor: Punjab accounts for just over half of Pakistan's 220 million people, making it more populous than the largest country in Europe. Other Pakistanis resent this dominance. After the Supreme Court ruled in favour of Musharraf, during his battle with the lawyers, a text-message joke denigrated the judges: 'One Hindu, two Pathans and six fucking Punjabis.'

Punjab's wealth rises from the countryside, a rich land of perfumed citrus groves and lush rice paddies, nourished by canals fed from the Indus. Its popular culture, especially Punjabi cinema, is filled with lurid tales of honour and larger-than-life rascals. In the 1980s, the dominant Punjabi movie character was Maula Jatt, a swaggering beefcake who roamed the Punjabi countryside, picking fights and rescuing forlorn womenfolk. Jatt's creator boasted that, in helping to purge Pakistan of Indian and Hollywood influences, his films represented 'the true culture of Pakistan'.

❦

Asma Jahangir was born in 1953 in Montgomery, a farming town ninety miles west of Lahore now known as Sahiwal. Her grandfather was a landowner who bred horses for the British Indian army; her father, Malik Ghulam Jilani, was a senior civil servant. Jahangir spent her childhood amid swaying fields of cotton and tobacco, chauffeured around in a horse and tonga, or parked before the family's movie projector. She remembered that it played the same film, *The Fabulous Senorita*, over and over again.

Pakistan's first military coup, in 1958, shattered the idyll. Her father, a fierce advocate of civilian rule, moved the family to Lahore, where the Jilani house became a kind of opposition salon. The regime didn't take kindly to it. When Asma was thirteen, shooting erupted outside their front gate, killing two men – a journalist, who died instantly, and a politician, whom she helped cart to the hospital. 'We came out and found him bleeding profusely,' she recalled. 'That was the first time I saw human bloodshed.'

She spent much of her teenage years attending court hearings for her father, who flitted in and out of jail. It drew her to the world of the law, with its theatrical speeches, horsehair wigs and promises of justice. 'The court was a place where you dressed up to meet your father,' she said. 'It had a very nice feeling to it.' She got her first case in 1971, when the military detained Malik Jilani yet again, and Jahangir launched a petition to set him free. A year later it succeeded, making Pakistani legal history. She was nineteen.

For the next decade, she took a detour through marriage, which was less satisfying. She had married Tahir, the boy next door and the scion of a family of conservative textile-mill owners. Their early years were hard. The couple moved in with Tahir's parents, who prized formality and expected filial respect. A young wife was expected to listen silently to her elders – a far cry from the raucous dinner-table debates at home – and her in-laws seemed disappointed that their son had not married a society beauty. 'They wanted an ideal wife for the only son,' she recalled later. 'I didn't want that.' After giving birth to a second daughter, dismayed to have put on weight, she looked in a mirror and imagined a life spent 'going to all the coffee parties in the world, and ending up looking like a pumpkin, and feeling and thinking like one'.

Jahangir went back to college, enrolling for law classes by night at the University of the Punjab. She graduated in 1978, just in time for some of the darkest changes in Pakistani society for decades.

General Zia, who seized power a year earlier, had embarked on his Islamisation drive with draconian new laws, known as the Hudood Ordinances, that squarely targeted women. Asma, her sister Hina and two other women founded Pakistan's first all-female firm, named AGHS after their initials. Chauvinists dubbed it 'HAGS'. They moved into a cramped, one-room office over a radio shop and took turns answering the phone and pretending to be the secretary. Sceptics derided the firm as a novelty; in fact, there was huge pent-up demand for its services. Although women were not stoned to death for having sex outside marriage, as Zia's new laws prescribed, plenty were thrown in prison. Case files piled up around Jahangir and her colleagues, who toiled in the summer heat under whirring fans as the telephone trilled. They also took to the streets, forming a women's collective that led rowdy protests against Zia's anti-woman laws. Jahangir and her friends would clash with the riot police amid billowing clouds of tear gas, then dash back into her offices to splash water in their eyes. Although small, the significance of the protests lay in their composition: for the first time, Pakistan's elite revolted against a military dictator.

A short stint in jail provided Jahangir's first big case. In the cells, she met a thirteen-year-old domestic worker who had been raped by her employer, a powerful man, and fallen pregnant. But instead of receiving justice, the girl was convicted on charges of *zina*, fornication, and sentenced to three years imprisonment and fifteen lashes of a whip. After her release from jail, Jahangir took on the girl's case, and won – an early blow against Zia's misogyny.

Two other cases attracted international attention. In 1993, Jahangir defended two Christian teenagers who faced the death penalty on charges of blasphemy – insulting Islam. Muslim neighbours accused the boys of scrawling the insults on the wall of their local mosque – an unlikely crime, it turned out, when Jahangir proved that one of them, who was eleven, was illiterate. A third defendant was shot dead by a vigilante during one hearing; after another hearing, a mob stoned Jahangir's car. The Christians were eventually acquitted, but it was a qualified triumph. Unsafe in Pakistan, they had to flee Pakistan for Germany, never to return.

The second famous case was an unmitigated disaster. In 1999, a woman named Samia Sarwar arrived at the women's shelter operated by Jahangir and asked for help. Sarwar, who was twenty-eight and from Peshawar, was fleeing her own parents. She had left an abusive marriage and wanted to marry an army officer she'd fallen in love with. But her parents refused their permission (required by law), saying it would dishonour the clan. Weeks later, there appeared to be a breakthrough: Samia's mother, Sultana, came to Jahangir's office, accompanied by a man, offering a truce. When they sat down, the man pulled out a pistol and shot Sarwar in the head. Then he and Sultana, who was in on the plot, fled out of the door.

The killing was a stark example of how 'honour' killings were prevalent even in the most educated families. Samia's father headed the Peshawar Chamber of Commerce; Sultana was a trained gynaecologist. Yet they were willing to kill their own daughter. 'I am not in a position to change society,' her father said. 'Everyone must have honour.'

Thinking of this case, and others, such as that of Malala Yousafzai, who was shot for daring to advocate girls' education, I once asked Jahangir why Pakistan was such a heartless place for women. 'Look, many of these things are crimes, and crime takes place in every country,' she replied. 'They only become human rights abuses when the state fails to respond to them. That is the shocking part of it.'

Still, such savage cruelties defined Pakistan's image abroad, and I found it hard to square them with the permissiveness I saw in other parts of society. The rich, for the most part, did as they pleased: lavish, boozy parties inside high walls (and, later, a lot of cocaine consumption). At a ball on New Year's Eve, women in slinky dresses weaved between the tables as inebriated men traded sloppy punches on the dance floors and the bouncers watched helplessly, apparently afraid to intervene in rich-on-rich action. At the opening of a Porsche dealership, revellers drank from an open bar while a troupe of showgirls, flown in from Eastern Europe, kicked their heels on stage. The poor also knew how to party: one year during *Basant*, the spring festival, I ended up on the rooftop of a poor man's house, where he offered me a drag on a joint as he fired a few celebratory shots from a pistol. Later he took me down to the local Sufi shrine, where a handful of traditional wrestlers pinned each other to the ground, cheered on by dope-smoking spectators.

Jahangir recognised the contradictions of a culture that glorified and punished transgression in equal measure. 'Our folklore is about passionate love, and how the man who stops two lovers from meeting is considered to be evil,' she said. 'Yet when a woman wants to marry the man she loves, her family might take her to court or kill her. It's very strange.'

Some of Jahangir's peers saw her as a class traitor. Well-bred Lahori women became fashion designers or took over the family business, and they appeared in public at weddings, art openings and in the pages of the society magazines. They did not rush through the streets hurling abuse at the military or inflaming the passions of the poor. As a child, Munizae told me, the parents of her friends openly disapproved of her mother's activism, and in one instance called her a 'home-breaker'. Pakistan's elites were not famed for their sense of civic responsibility. Certainly, many donated to charity. But wealthy Pakistanis were also South Asia's worst tax-evaders, not to mention enthusiastic supporters of military rule. The gulf between rich and poor had narrowed since the 1960s, when the country's wealth was estimated to be concentrated in the hands of twenty-two families. Still, there was far to go. In a light-hearted feature for a Sunday magazine, a fashion designer from one super-wealthy clan told of how she wept when her tailors formed a union, 'and I had no choice but to fire them all'. She added: 'I wish I wasn't such a push-over.'

Even Jahangir's husband could be unenthusiastic about her work. Chairman of the Towel Manufacturers Association of Pakistan, Tahir Jahangir – or T. J., as he was known to friends – liked to hike, socialise at the elite Punjab Club (a holdover from the colonial era) and write newspaper articles about Lahore's Mughal history. He did not share his wife's passion for social activism. They argued fiercely in the early days of their marriage, she recalled. 'He would say "My God, what is happening? This is not my wife. Stop it! Stop her!"' An unspoken arrangement evolved – he avoided her protests and she didn't read his articles. Even so, ambivalence lingered. Tahir, she told an interviewer, was 'sometimes proud; sometimes resentful; and sometimes I wonder if he even knows me any more'.

Jahangir did not, however, view her privileged background as an obstacle to her activism; on the contrary, she saw it as a key to her success. 'I have less to lose,' she said. 'I am more protected than ordinary people.' Despite her trenchant views, she cultivated friendships across the social and political spectrum – conservative mullahs were invited to her children's weddings; she retained a schooldays friendship with Shireen Mazari, a right-wing nationalist firebrand. Although conservatives liked to portray Jahangir as a Westernised woman of questionable morals – and the wife of an Ahmadi to boot – she ran a socially conventional South Asian household. Her mother and sister lived next door, she shunned affairs that some friends indulged in, and she shamelessly meddled in her daughters' lives, at one point clashing with Munizae over her taste in boyfriends. She confessed to feeling guilty about the lengthy, work-induced absences that caused her only son to be raised by a nanny. 'I missed him, and he missed me,' she said years later.

But like her father, it was Jahangir's implacable opposition to the military 'Deep State' – the semi-visible iceberg of army garrisons, military spies and their political satraps, which had dominated Pakistan for decades – that steered her into the most perilous waters. She passionately believed that the Deep State was responsible for Pakistan's greatest woes. It rigged elections, intimidated or bought off journalists, made bad laws and broke the good ones, and of course relentlessly instrumentalised Islam by coddling violent extremists – all in the service of the military's ultimate goal, as Jahangir saw it, of maintaining its grip on power. The army swallowed at least one-third of the government's budget but accounted for barely a penny. Its generals presided over an empire of private business interests in everything from insurance to cornflakes and airlines, while doling out vast amounts of public land as gifts to senior officers, many of whom became property tycoons upon retirement. Around that time, a courageous researcher named Ayesha Siddiqa published a book, *Military Inc.*, detailing these commercial interests. Its publication so irked the military that it prevented every hotel in Islamabad from hosting the launch party. Siddiqa hosted the event at her home.

To the generals, Jahangir and her ilk embodied everything that was wrong with Pakistan's dissolute, unpatriotic civilian leadership. Pakistanis were not ready for Western-style democracy, they insisted, because the political class was unfit for rule. 'These politicians,' croaked Niaz Ahmed, a retired brigadier who advised Musharraf, when I went to see him one day. 'To deal with them you have to be a liar, a thief and a hypocrite. Am I right?' There was nothing wrong with democracy per se, he continued − 'it's the best system, I agree' − but was Pakistan ready for it? Half the people were illiterate, and at election time, feudal landlords drove their tenants to polling stations in trucks, or lured them to vote for a favoured candidate with promises of free chicken *biryani*. Niaz lit his cigar. 'Is that democracy? You take a plant and put it in the desert − it cannot grow.'

Brigadier Ahmed had done well under military rule − his palatial Islamabad mansion had been funded by the arms deals he brokered for the military. Jahangir harrumphed at what she perceived as the hypocrisy of such men, and she fought them at every turn. She probed the generals' human rights abuses, scorned their battlefield failures and mocked their brazen money-making schemes. That issue, the never-ending battle for supremacy between military and civilian leaders, was the biggest fight you could pick in Pakistan. It was also the most dangerous one.

❀

The imposition of emergency rule in November 2007 had been set in motion by a chain of dramatic events that started a month earlier, on the tarmac of Dubai International Airport.

Emirates Flight 606 from Dubai to Karachi was preparing to take off amid chaotic scenes. Chubby men in ill-fitting suits swarmed through the aisles, swinging cheap briefcases and jockeying for the best seats. Imperious women in sunglasses, clutching leather handbags in ring-studded hands, shoved aside journalists who, in turn, clambered over the seats. At the rear of the plane, a contingent from London, well oiled after a long stop at the hotel bar, burst into song. A delicate-looking Japanese flight attendant pleaded for calm. Other passengers looked on in horror.

The focus of this commotion, Benazir Bhutto, was safely ensconced in business class. Eight years of lonely, peripatetic exile were drawing to an end: winters in Dubai, where she raised her three children, and summers in London, where she strolled in Hyde Park and huddled with confidants at the coffee shop in Harrods, plotting a return that never seemed to come. The odour of corruption haunted her. In London, the Foreign Office sent a lowly minion to meet her; in Washington, she couldn't even get an appointment with the State Department. It was humiliating.

Now, finally, she was going home. As the Emirates jetliner took off, exuberant chants filled the cabin. A portly man in a striped pink shirt sprang into the aisle and launched into a haka dance, shaking his hips and punching the air. 'Jiiii-yayyyy Bhutto!' he cried.

'Long Live Bhutto!' the others shouted back.

Like Jahangir, Bhutto's life had been framed by a private war with the Pakistani Deep State. The execution of her father in 1979 redefined the parameters of the decades-old struggle between civilians and generals. 'The bastard's dead!' General Zia declared jubilantly after learning that Zulfikar Ali Bhutto was dead. Now every politician knew how far the generals were willing to go. In the early 1980s, the military cast Benazir into a cockroach-infested cell in Sukkur, a town in Sindh, where she slept on a concrete floor in blistering temperatures beside a stinking hole that served as a toilet. The tables were turned in 1988 with the mysterious plane crash that killed General Zia, when Al Zulfikar, the militant outfit founded by Benazir's brothers, Murtaza and Shahnawaz, came into the frame as potential saboteurs – but then so did the Russians, Americans and Indians, not to mention several of Zia's generals. Through the late 1980s and 1990s, Benazir's two terms as prime minister were blighted by her hidden tussles with the ISI, which devoted considerable resources to undermining or ousting her. In one election, the spy agency distributed photos that purported to show Benazir in a bikini; for the next one, they pumped millions of dollars into a slush fund to boost her rivals. 'I thought it would be better if the lady did not come to power,' Asad Durrani, the ISI chief in 1993, admitted in court two decades later.

On the flight to Karachi, Benazir hoped to put all that behind her. Weeks earlier, in Washington, she publicly acknowledged errors from her previous stint in power, such as her government's support for the Afghan Taliban. She spoke with urgency about the need to confront the radical forces now rising inside Pakistan. Conspicuously, she left her controversial husband, Asif Ali Zardari, at the gate in Dubai airport – an attempt to signal a new start. Cynics saw in those gestures yet another shameless grasp for power, but friends insisted that Benazir had changed – that she was returning to Pakistan with an air of purpose and mission, perhaps even seeking redemption.

But the price of that return was an unsavoury deal with the hawkish military she had spent a lifetime fighting.

British and American diplomats, alarmed at Musharraf's crumbling authority, had brokered a power-sharing deal with Benazir. The terms were simple enough: if Musharraf quashed the outstanding corruption charges against Benazir, and allowed her to contest the election, Musharraf could stay on as president. To the West, it was a dream ticket: they would retain a strongman ally while easing Pakistan towards democracy. But inside Pakistan, the pact was wildly unpopular. To Musharraf, Benazir embodied the kleptocratic politics that the army resented, and posed a direct threat to his power. Benazir saw Musharraf as the incarnation of the ruthless military establishment that had hanged her father. Both faced stiff opposition from their supporters – and on a personal level, they couldn't stand each other. How would they share power?

On the flight to Karachi, Benazir feigned easy confidence. 'I'm not nervous,' she told reporters. But her stomach was churning. Weeks earlier, during her trip to Washington, Musharraf had phoned her. Once she landed back on Pakistani soil, he told her pointedly, 'Your security is a function of your relationship with me.' Bhutto took it as a threat. She called the American vice-president, Dick Cheney, to request the same security detail provided for American diplomats. The Americans proposed a defence contractor, Dyncorp, which Musharraf refused point-blank. As she waited to take off at Dubai, Benazir phoned Adam Thomson, a senior British diplomat who had helped broker the arrangement with Musharraf. Benazir told Thomson she had learned of a plot to kill her that had been hatched by powerful 'Deep State' figures including Hamid Gul, a former ISI chief with a longstanding anti-Bhutto animus, and Qari Saifullah Akhtar, a legendary jihadi commander who had once been part of a failed plot to overthrow her. Benazir told Thomson she was considering cancelling the trip.

Thomson replied that Musharraf had been considering shutting down Karachi Airport to prevent her plane from landing. If she backed out, he advised, the window to return to Pakistan might close.

'So,' he said, 'get going.'

Any doubts about Benazir's popularity evaporated the instant she landed in Karachi. A sea of supporters filled the streets for a euphoric celebration. Boys clung to trees over the crowd, flinging rose petals; scratchy disco music filled the air, and the homecoming queen rode a double-decker bus that inched through the throng. It went on for hours, and before leaving I managed to clamber onto the top deck where I found Benazir standing behind a bulletproof shield, still waving at her supporters. 'It's really overwhelming,' she said.

The procession was scheduled to culminate, in the wee hours of the morning, at the marble tomb of Muhammad Ali Jinnah, where Benazir would address the adoring crowd. But just after midnight, as I filed a story in my hotel room, an orange flash filled the television screen. Seconds later, another explosion. Blood, smoke and body parts came into view.

A pair of suicide bombers had struck, killing 149 people and wounding more than 400, one of the deadliest terrorist attacks in Pakistan's history. Benazir escaped unscathed. Moments before the blasts, she had repaired to a secure compartment inside the bus to rest her swollen feet. But when the cameras showed her being pulled from the wreckage, there was an unmistakable glint of terror in her eyes.

In November 2007, facing a swelling drumbeat of international criticism, Musharraf was forced to end his emergency rule. In Lahore, Bhutto and Jahangir were released from house arrest. That night, Bhutto drove across the city to Jahangir's Gulberg mansion.

They were probably the two most famous women in Pakistan – not exactly friends, not exactly allies, but joined, as Jahangir put it, 'by a strange connection'. In the 1960s their parents were comrades in the early struggle against military rule. Zulfikar Ali Bhutto founded the Pakistan Peoples Party (PPP) in Lahore in 1967, and a year later landed in jail there. During his trial, Bhutto's wife and children moved into Malik Jilani's house, where Jilani held court in his bedroom, smoking and chatting while a servant massaged his feet. Bhutto's eldest daughter, Benazir, visited from boarding school at weekends.

That friendship collapsed spectacularly after Bhutto came to power in 1971, when old friends who criticised him were sidelined or imprisoned, among them Malik Jilani. Yet after Bhutto was ousted in 1977 and later sentenced to death, Jilani 'went from pillar to post' in a frantic effort to secure his release. His daughter, Asma, was puzzled. 'I thought: "What kind of friendship is this, that he can try to save someone who put him in prison?"' she said. When Bhutto was executed in 1979, Malik Jilani wept bitterly.

For Asma Jilani Jahangir, it was an object lesson in Pakistani politics: faced with the crushing might of the military, you couldn't afford to be choosy about your allies. 'You stand for your principles,' she told me. 'You do not support or de-friend people because they treated you a certain way.'

When Benazir Bhutto came to power in the late 1980s and again in the mid-1990s, Jahangir and Benazir Bhutto were both allies and enemies. They had a common foe in the Pakistani military, yet took different roads to fighting it – one uncompromising and principled, the other hardnosed and pragmatic. Jahangir attacked Benazir for the many failings over her governments – a rash of police killings in Karachi; her inability to reform Zia's hated Hudood Ordinances; and her government's support for the odious Taliban regime in Kabul. Benazir bristled indignantly at the criticism. 'I'm running a country, not a human rights organisation,' she snapped.

Jahangir sneered at the sordid deals that politicians like Bhutto did to stay in power. Bhutto countered that power was a prerequisite to delivering change, and if she had to make unsavoury alliances with unlikely allies, such as the religious parties she occasionally partnered with to get votes through Parliament, then so be it.

At the same time, the two women privately collaborated. Benazir ensured Jahangir got airtime on state media, intervened to help a group of persecuted Christians – Jahangir's clients – reach safety, and quietly ordered bureaucrats to ensure the success of Jahangir's campaign for the elimination of bonded labour on feudal farms. Both women came to an appreciation of the other's limits. Jahangir's noisy activism highlighted issues that Bhutto sympathised with but felt powerless to change, owing to her weak parliamentary support or the military's ceaseless efforts to undermine her. Jahangir, for her part, recognised that Bhutto was no Mother Teresa or Che Guevara, but that she also had the right instincts and the ability to convert popularity into the kind of the power that could make a real difference.

And both women recognised that the struggle for civilian supremacy necessitated strange alliances, occasionally jarring stances. In 1999, Jahangir had even welcomed the coup that brought Musharraf to power, as a solution to the increasingly authoritarian rule of the elected prime minister Nawaz Sharif. A decade later, Jahangir would ally with Sharif, even becoming a discreet confidante, in their mutual struggle against the generals.

Jahangir's sympathy for the prime minister was not widely shared among elite Pakistanis, many of whom viewed Bhutto with abiding suspicion. Some focused on the tales of corruption – on grounds of taste, as much as anything else, because they viewed her husband as a gauche arriviste – while others were still embittered by Zulfikar Ali Bhutto's nationalisation programme in the 1970s, when he stripped powerful families of their assets. One night, at a dinner party in Islamabad, a young woman at the table launched into an extended tirade against Benazir. 'Look at me,' said the woman, whose father was a senior diplomat. 'I'm secular, I'm liberal, I'm a woman. And I hate her.' Other guests objected loudly, triggering an escalating argument in which the woman called Benazir a 'whore'. When things had calmed down, I asked her why she felt so strongly about Benazir.

'We hate her,' she said, 'because she is like us.'

It pointed to the difficulty of succeeding as a woman in Pakistani public life. Sure, there were more women than ever in politics, the media, even the military; yet they seemed to be constantly judged in terms set by men: family honour, patriotism, religious virtue. After the schoolgirl Malala Yousafzai was shot in the head by a Taliban gunman on a school bus in the Swat Valley in 2012, she was hailed across the globe as an anti-extremism heroine, and later admitted to Oxford University and awarded the Nobel Peace Prize. At home, she became a pariah, attacked by conspiracy theorists who derided her as a CIA agent who orchestrated the shooting for personal gain. A chain of schools refused to handle Malala's best-selling book; she was even shunned by some fellow pupils in Mingora, her hometown in Swat. A familiar impulse lay behind the accusations: that, in being lauded by the West, this girl was bringing shame on Pakistan.

In stark contrast, Aafia Siddiqui, an al Qaeda supporter who languished in an American penitentiary, had become a national cause célèbre. Siddiqui, a mother-of-three from Karachi who had been radicalised and married an al Qaeda terrorist, was arrested in Afghanistan on a mission apparently to plant bombs. During her interrogation, she seized an American soldier's weapon and tried to shoot him; at her trial in New York, she made regular outbursts about a 'Jewish conspiracy'. The court sentenced her to eighty-six years in prison. Despite all that, in Pakistan, her case was taken up at the highest level. Ministers petitioned the Americans to set Siddiqui free; mass protests in her support filled the streets; the newspapers called her 'Qaum ki Beti' – 'The Daughter of the Nation'.

Pakistani men in public life flaunted their wealth, dodged their taxes and even fathered children out of wedlock. Yet a woman could be a hero, it seemed, only if she adhered to rigid standards of piety, virtue or nationalism on terms set by men.

On the night in November 2007 when Benazir visited Jahangir at her home in Gulberg, it was more than a social call. Jahangir had gathered dozens of civil-society leaders – lawyers, editors, pro-democracy campaigners and suchlike – to hear Benazir's pitch for a return to power. Many distrusted her since her last time in power, or were sceptical of the deal with Musharraf. They gathered around Jahangir's dinner table, peppering Benazir with questions that she answered patiently. Some doubters said they left reassured, even charmed.

Jahangir, however, had a dark secret she needed to air. Some time earlier, Jahangir's father, on his deathbed, revealed that he had been badly tortured in prison under Zulfikar Ali Bhutto in the 1970s. Delirious with cancer drugs, he blurted out his hidden agonies. At first stunned, then filled with rage, Jahangir wanted to confront Benazir about this ugly episode between their families.

After the meeting around the dinner table, when the guests had left, the two women sat quietly in private again. Jahangir confronted Benazir, who apologised. They moved on.

Despite her political bravado, Benazir was still traumatised by the horrific attack in Karachi. She told Jahangir she had identified several Deep State plotters, including the jihadi Qari Saifullah Akhtar and a former ISI chief, whom she had learned were plotting to kill her. She had given the names to a CNN journalist, for publication in the event of her death. Would her unseen enemies strike again?

Benazir left for Dubai to spend time with her family. During that time, Jahangir obtained information about a new threat to Benazir's life. 'Don't come back,' she messaged Benazir. 'They have laid a trap for you.'

Days later, Benazir flew back to Pakistan, and resumed the election campaign.

On 27 December, 2007, Benazir drove out to Rawalpindi to address an election rally at Liaquat Bagh, a public park that was heavy with history. In 1951, Pakistan's first prime minister, Liaquat Ali Khan, was shot dead here by an Afghan gunman, the first of many unsolved political assassinations in Pakistan. A few miles away lay the military's General Headquarters, where successive generations of Pakistani generals had schemed against the Bhuttos; her father, Zulfikar, had been hanged at nearby Adiala Jail.

Benazir, though, was in a buoyant mood. Under international pressure, Musharraf had been forced to allow her to campaign in the election that was now weeks away. With no serious opponent, she seemed likely to become prime minister for a third time. That morning, she had a friendly meeting with the president of Afghanistan, Hamid Karzai, in the Serena Hotel, where they joked about his stylish cloak. At the rally in Rawalpindi, she addressed her supporters with passion and urgency. 'Wake up, my brothers!' she urged, stabbing a finger in the air. 'Pakistan is in grave danger. This is your country, my country. We must save it!' The crowd roared back: 'Benazir, prime minister!'

Around her, strange things started to happen. Under the stage, a security guard named Khalid Shahenshah rolled his eyes toward Benazir, in an exaggerated fashion, as if signalling to someone in the crowd. He pulled his finger across his throat in a slicing motion. In the crowd, a teenager named Bilal pushed forward. He wore dark glasses and a dark leather jacket that made him look older than his fifteen years; under the jacket, he wore a vest packed with explosives. After the speech, Bhutto climbed into her armoured Toyota Land Cruiser, but she insisted on standing through a hatch in the roof to wave at supporters who crowded around the vehicle. Bilal stepped forward, raised a pistol and fired three shots. As Benazir collapsed into the vehicle, Bilal dropped his chin and detonated his vest, triggering an explosion that ripped his body apart and caused Benazir to slump into the lap of her assistant. Blood poured from a large gash in her head. Bhutto's security team panicked and, inexplicably, drove off to Islamabad, leaving her crippled vehicle to hobble towards the nearest hospital on blown-out tyres. An hour later, after an open heart massage, Benazir was pronounced dead.

In an eerie coincidence, the man who tried to save her was the son of the doctor who had tried to revive the fatally injured prime minister Liaquat Ali Khan in 1951.

As these events were unfolding, I was on a flight to Karachi. By the time I landed, the city had plunged into chaos. Beyond the airport gates, protesters burned tyres and pelted the police with stones; in Sindh Province, ancestral home of the Bhuttos, vehicles were being torched and prisoners broke out of jail. I spent the night in a packed airport restaurant, punching out a story on the corner of a table, surrounded by stranded passengers who, like me, wondered what was coming next.

The following morning, I managed to get a seat on a chartered flight to Sukkur, 200 miles to the northeast, where Bhutto was being buried. A sea of male hands bore Benazir's coffin, draped in her party's flag, from the family residence in Naudero. Anguished wails rang out from the women's enclosure. The cortege trundled down a country lane, past silver-barked euca-lyptus trees and pools of bathing water buffalo: thousands of stone-faced men lined the route, some weeping openly and others gently pounding their chests. We passed a deserted train station where the charred remains of a burned-out train stood at the platform, pouring smoke.

I was being driven by Zulfikar Mirza, a former provincial minister, who had a large gun tucked beside his seat. 'This is civil war,' he said.

At the Bhutto family mausoleum, an ornate building with onion-shaped domes, an ambulance ferried Bhutto's coffin into a cavernous hall. A shaft of light fell from the roof. Asif Ali Zardari stood by his wife's grave, his black *shalwar kameez* smeared with dust, beside their nineteen-year-old son, Bilawal, who had completed his first term at Oxford. Nearby tombs housed Benazir's father and her two brothers, all of whom died prematurely. Now she joined them. Zardari dropped to his knees, casting fistfuls of soil onto his wife's coffin. Bilawal's face creased in pain.

Celebrations rang out in Waziristan, where Benazir's assassin, a fifteen-year-old Taliban suicide bomber named Bilal, had been trained. The attack seemed to reflect Pakistan's brewing jihadi storm: Bilal had spent his last night at the Darul Uloom Haqqania, the *madrassa* run by Maulana Sami ul Haq; the Taliban leader Baitullah Mehsud took credit for the operation. 'A spectacular job,' he said in an intercepted conversation that was later released by Musharraf's government, and verified by the CIA. 'They were really brave boys who killed her.'

But if the Taliban pulled the trigger, who gave the order? Within hours of Bhutto's death, there were suggestions of a cover-up. A three-star army general ordered fire officers to hose down the crime scene, washing away valuable evidence. Benazir's damaged vehicle was thoroughly cleaned before forensics experts could examine it. Police investigators collected only twenty-three pieces of evidence. Powerful officials, it seemed, were uninterested in the truth.

Asma Jahangir had little doubt who was responsible. She had been on a television set in Karachi to record *Enter the Prime Minister* — a light-hearted show that crossed *American Idol* with Pakistani politics — when news of Benazir's death came through. Hours later, she publicly accused the military. 'Everyone is saying that this army has killed Benazir,' she said on television. 'Will the world finally wake up?'

Later that night, Jahangir sobbed for her dead friend. 'I want this damn army out of our lives,' she told an Indian journalist. 'They won't go away without killing all of us.'

✤

Pervez Musharraf's moment of reckoning came during the summer following Bhutto's death. In August 2008, he hosted a party to mark Independence Day at Aiwan-e-Sadr, the Presidential Palace, a building designed by the American architect Edward Durell Stone that commands a hill over Islamabad. Musharraf's supporters filed into the ballroom, a vast chamber of chandeliers and oil paintings, for a concert. Performers included jaunty pop minstrels, a bedraggled Sufi singer and a plump classical singer whose delicate *ghazals* made the crowd cry, 'Wah! Wah!' in appreciation. Musharraf sat in the front row: hair buffed, shirt open and a smile plastered to his face, nursing a cigar in one hand and a crystal tumbler in the other.

But something was off. At the back of the hall, I sat among dozens of empty seats, indicating guests who had quietly declined their invitations. And although the musicians of the state orchestra appeared to be vigorously thrashing their instruments, the music was coming from a recorded soundtrack. It seemed an apt coda to the Musharraf years: the ship was going down, the deckchairs were empty and the band was only pretending to play.

Five days later, Musharraf went on television and resigned. Another bout of army rule juddered to an ignominious end. But the bigger battle for supremacy, between Pakistan's civilian and military leaders, had merely shifted gear.

Musharraf was succeeded as president by Bhutto's widower, Asif Ali Zardari, after his party swept the general election. The position had been stripped of much of its executive powers, and Zardari's reputation as 'Mister Ten Per Cent' doggedly followed him. But as the head of the Pakistan People's Party, Zardari was the most powerful politician in the country, which propelled him into endless battles with the military. The new army chief was General Ashfaq Parvez Kayani – a taciturn, chain-smoking man who previously headed the ISI. The president and army chief circled one another endlessly, negotiating quietly over matters of state even as they manoeuvred against each other, wary and suspicious. Zardari told visitors to the presidential palace that 'the walls were listening' – the ISI was monitoring his conversations, and perhaps even wished him ill. At the height of one crisis, he summoned a senior reporter to his quarters to tell him that he believed the military was plotting to kill him. They would make it look like suicide, he said, pulled out the gun he said he would use to defend himself. Days later, Zardari flew to Dubai where he was hospitalised for stress.

Asma Jahangir, worried that the return to democracy could be overturned at any moment, continued to criticise the army. A golden opportunity presented itself in May 2011, in the aftermath of the American commando raid that killed Osama bin Laden in Abbottabad, a few hours drive north of Islamabad. A tide of anger and confusion washed across Pakistan. How did the world's most-wanted fugitive remain undetected for so long? How come he was living in a house one mile from a major military training academy, Pakistan's version of West Point? Most of all, how could Pakistan's proud army allow American helicopters to get into the country undetected, engage in a major gunfight, and then slip back over the border into Afghanistan? Incompetence or collusion – or both?

On television, Jahangir lacerated the army for its role in the fiasco, and pressed her demands for reform. She upgraded her epithets – the 'useless duffers' had become 'dangerous duffers,' she declared – and accused the generals of being more interested in running wedding halls, a reference to the army's vast commercial interests, than in defending borders. She called for the establishment of a judicial commission to determine the truth about Abbottabad, an increase in parliamentary scrutiny of the ISI, and a debate about the military's voluminous spending. Did Pakistan really need such a large army?

The risks of such a provocative stance were evident. Four weeks after bin Laden's death, an investigative journalist named Saleem Shahzad vanished as he drove to a TV studio in Islamabad. His body was found floating in a rural canal a day later, bearing signs of a severe beating. Months earlier, it transpired, the ISI had warned Shahzad to stop writing stories that embarrassed the agency. After his death, the ISI abjured any role in his death, which it termed 'unfortunate and tragic'.

Three days after Shahzad's body was found, an NPR journalist asked Jahangir about her trenchant criticism of Pakistan's army. 'Is it dangerous to speak like that?' he asked. 'I'm sure it is,' she replied, 'but we all live dangerous lives here.'

※

In May 2012, the United States Defense Intelligence Agency (DIA) found out that the ISI was plotting to 'eliminate' Asma Jahangir in order to 'quiet public criticism of the military'. A report noted that signals intelligence indicated that Pakistani spies had discussed the plan, which involved 'either tasking militants to kill her in India or tasking militants or criminals to kill her in Pakistan'. The American agency did not know whether the ISI leadership had given the green light for the operation to proceed, but if it did, it would likely result in an 'international and domestic backlash'.

Informed of the threat, weeks later, Jahangir went on the offensive. Disregarding advice from friends to flee Pakistan, she went on television to talk about the apparent plot, calculating that publicity was the best insurance policy. The military vehemently dismissed her accusations. But a year later, they were publicly confirmed when the CIA whistle-blower, Edward Snowden, leaked a copy of the DIA report to the *Washington Post*.

When I went to see Jahangir, she told me that the assassination plot was probably prompted by her criticism of the army's gross abuses in the turbulent western province of Balochistan. 'At least, that's my guess,' she said, 'but you can never know.' The head of the ISI in Punjab had been to visit, she continued – a polite, courteous man who 'basically wanted to know the source of my information'. He assured her that the ISI no longer carried out hit jobs: 'It's just a myth.'

Jahangir scoffed. 'That's like telling me lawyers don't lie,' she said.

The ISI man promised to investigate the matter. Jahangir invested in a bulletproof four-wheel-drive.

✸

By then, it was evident there would be few clear answers about Benazir's death. Khalid Shahenshah, the bodyguard seen behaving strangely before Bhutto's death, was shot dead outside his home in Karachi. Her teenage assassin was identified by forensic experts who painstakingly reconstructed his face, but then his handlers were gunned down by police officers at a remote checkpoint in Waziristan. Baitullah Mehsud, the Taliban leader, died in an American drone strike, reportedly on the basis of information supplied by Pakistan's military. A dynamic Pakistani prosecutor was shot dead in his car as he drove to a hearing in the case. And a team of United Nations investigators, who arrived in Pakistan to probe Bhutto's death, failed to reach a conclusion after complaining of unrelenting obstruction from the security forces.

Someone, it seemed, didn't want the truth to come out. Musharraf, now in retirement and facing court charges of criminal negligence over Bhutto's death, angrily rebuffed accusations that he was responsible. Bhutto's death had ultimately cost him his job, he insisted, which was true, even if it didn't preclude a role. Another theory held that Bhutto's death had been orchestrated by other military forces – reactionaries in the 'deep state' who nursed a pathological hatred of this charismatic woman, and who feared her immense political clout. In Washington before her ill-fated return to Pakistan, Bhutto delivered a speech in which she proposed that international weapons inspectors should have access to Abdul Qadeer Khan, the father of Pakistan's nuclear program – an alarming prospect for the country's national security hawks.

Whatever the truth about Bhutto's death, it was apparently too unpalatable for the military which made it clear that the episode would be consigned to Pakistan's long list of unsolved political murder mysteries. A real investigation might reveal that the generals knew too much, or not enough – complicity, incompetence, or somehow both, much like the enigma of how bin Laden had sheltered in Abbottabad for so many years.

Asma Jahangir died in February 2018, at the age of sixty-six, from a heart attack. Thousands of mourners gathered at Lahore's Qaddafi Stadium for an emotional funeral, a mixture of comrades and clients. Sobbing, black-clad lawyers clutched each other for comfort. There were also Christians, Ahmadis and others whom Jahangir had represented over the years, often for free, including a woman who wore a burka to hide the acid burns on her face. Funerals are traditionally segregated by gender in Pakistan, with women shunted into a separate enclosure or pushed to the back. Now they moved to the front. Alongside Jahangir's daughters, Munizae and Sulema, stood dozens of other women, shoulder to shoulder with the men for the first time that anyone could remember.

Salmaan Taseer

6

The Good Muslim

A Millionaire's Crusade

The killer finally got his courage up. It was January 2011, one of those cold, blindingly bright winter days in Islamabad when a powder-blue sky frames the city, casting its low-slung lines in sharp relief. Salmaan Taseer was finishing lunch with an old friend on the terrace at Table Talk, an upscale restaurant in a small market at the foot of the Margalla Hills. Taseer was the governor of Punjab, a tycoon-turned-politician who, at sixty-six, had lost little of the swagger that had propelled him through life. By turns witty, charming and crude, he was a particular kind of Pakistani power broker: a self-made millionaire, a Twitter loudmouth, and now, thanks to his lifelong service to Benazir Bhutto's Pakistan Peoples Party, the governor of the country's most populous province. In a nod to his vanity and his advancing years, Taseer usually wore a pair of expensive Italian sunglasses in public, as he did now, after lunch, strolling across the parking lot. A five-man protection detail trailed behind. One of the guards, a police constable named Malik Mumtaz Qadri, quietly released the safety catch on his service AK-47 assault rifle.

Qadri, who was twenty-six, had grown up on a scruffy street in nearby Rawalpindi, in a poor family of twelve. He had a fleshy face and gleaming eyes that were framed by a neat beard, thick eyebrows, and a 'prayer bump': a brown bruise, from his five-times-daily prostrations, that adorned his forehead like an exclamation mark. Already that day, Qadri had considered shooting his boss several times, always holding back at the last minute. Now he sprang into action. Lowering his gun, Qadri squeezed the trigger, and held it.

The long rattle of gunfire caused startled café patrons to jump in their seats. Taseer crumpled to the ground, his blood seeping into the tarmac. He had been shot twenty-eight times.

Job done, Qadri laid down his weapon, raised his hands and surrendered to his stunned fellow police officers. When the first TV crews arrived, moments later, they found the assassin seated in the back of a police van, wearing a beatific smile. He announced that he had killed Taseer for disrespecting the Prophet Muhammad – the crime of blasphemy. 'I am proud of what I have done,' he said. 'I am a slave to my prophet.'

News of the assassination whipped across Pakistan like a hurricane. It was the most high-profile hit job since the death of Benazir Bhutto three years earlier. What shocked outsiders, though, was not the killing itself. A relentless wave of Taliban attacks over the previous year had rocked the country; few Pakistanis doubted that their country was generously stocked with homicidal fanatics. What shocked was the public reaction. In any other country, Qadri might have been instantly vilified, shunned by decent folk as a delusional madman, castigated as an aberration of society. In Pakistan, he was celebrated as a hero.

Clerics fanned out in the streets to distribute *mithai*, sticky sweets used to celebrate good fortune, and exchanged celebratory text messages on their phones. Facebook pages sprang up, lionising Qadri as a warrior for Islam or calling for his release, that drew thousands of 'likes' – not just from the usual angry types who torched American flags at street protests but also from educated young Pakistanis who, to judge from their profiles, were otherwise impassioned by British soccer clubs and American pop stars. Elsewhere a queasy calm reigned. On the television chat shows, normally garrulous pundits carefully weighed their words, and some implied that Taseer was responsible for his own death. Most people said nothing.

The following morning, as Qadri arrived at Islamabad's main courthouse to face murder charges, hundreds of black-suited lawyers thronged around him, chanting slogans and showering him with rose petals. The same pugnacious lawyers who had helped to topple Musharraf now acclaimed a killer. Several offered to defend him for free. Qadri stumbled through the floral blizzard, covered in a black hood. After the hearing the police allowed him to climb onto the back of a police van, where he addressed his newfound supporters. Eyes cast to the sky, he unleashed a messianic cry.

'*Allahu Akbar!*'

In that moment of crowning vainglory, Qadri also looked physically exposed. It struck me that, in other circumstances, a man responsible for such an egregious act might have feared retribution from an outraged member of the public. But Pakistan had no Jack Ruby.

'*Allahu Akbar!*' the lawyers shouted.

Salmaan Taseer was buried in Lahore. Mourners milled about nervously on the silky lawns of Governor's House, a grand colonial-era mansion. Rumours circulated that other fanatics lay in wait outside. Thousands of party supporters had turned up but the country's army chief and president were a notable absence. The political class shivered: what good were their blast barriers and armoured vehicles if they couldn't trust their own bodyguards? Taseer's body was carried out. Hurried prayers were offered. A military helicopter landed and ferried the coffin to the cemetery, a two-mile journey now deemed too dangerous to make by road. Three of Taseer's sons huddled at the graveside, wrapped in winter coats and surrounded by soldiers in fantailed turbans. Since a group of Muslim scholars had declared it *haram*, or forbidden, to console the Taseer family, they had struggled to find a cleric to lead the prayers. (The brave man who stepped forward would later be forced to flee the country.)

A bugle sounded, the soldiers snapped to attention, and the governor's flag-draped coffin was lowered into an early grave. Across Pakistan, beleaguered progressives watched on television in horror. Some lamented the passing of 'Jinnah's Pakistan' – the tolerant and pluralist country that was envisaged by their founding father. Others, perhaps more honestly, tried to remember whether such a place had ever existed.

❋

I first met Taseer three months earlier, for lunch. The car sped up the curling drive and crunched to a halt before the colonnades of Governor's House, where liveried servants waited by the door. They led the way to the governor's office – a grand, richly appointed room where Taseer perched behind a cluttered desk, holding court in the manner of a foul-mouthed *maharaja*. 'What's wrong?' he growled at his press secretary, a polite young Scottish woman of Pakistani origin who sat at the end of the table, pecking at her food. 'Are you on some sort of fucking diet?' The woman blushed. Taseer smirked, then pivoted back to his curry, which he ate with gusto while keeping one eye on the television in the corner, which blared the news. He offered a rapid-fire stream of political tattle and trenchant opinions, interrupted only by a trio of political lieutenants that trooped in, bringing news from a by-election that the Pakistan Peoples Party, which Taseer belonged to, was contesting. 'Are we giving them a good thrashing?' Taseer asked in guttural Punjabi. 'It's going very well, boss,' the flunkeys replied, Greek-chorus style. In fact, as became clear hours later, Taseer's candidate had been trounced. No matter – after years in the political wilderness,

Taseer had transformed the stately governor's mansion into a raucous political hub, and he was having a ball.

Taseer was one of the flashiest entrepreneurs in Pakistan, with a fortune invested in telecommunications, real estate, the stock market and the media. He relished the good life – Cuban cigars, expensive cars, whisky-*paani* (Scotch and soda) – and he wasn't afraid to flaunt it. The governor was a regular fixture in Lahore's society magazines (one of which he owned), pictured at weddings and parties with his glamorous wife, Aamna, who was eighteen years his junior, and their Western-educated children. Famously handsome as a young man, Taseer had cultivated what his children jokingly called his 'Jack Nicholson look': Chelsea boots, a dark T-shirt under a blazer, sunglasses. Works by the great Pakistani artists – Sadequain, Gulgee, Shakir Ali – lined the walls of his various homes; the main one, in Lahore's Cavalry Ground, was a gorgeous villa set among drooping trees not far from the municipal polo club. When his son Shahbaz was married a year earlier, the party was a glittering, week-long affair that drew high rollers from across Pakistan.

At first glance, Taseer appeared to be a quintessential product of the Lahore elite, a group steeped in the city's rich heritage of power, art and wealth. In the Mughal era, bejewelled emperors riding warrior elephants sashayed through the imposing arches of Lahore Fort and patronised exquisite art forms like the miniature paintings for which Lahore is still famed. After partition, the city housed the mansions of feudal landlords and their families. Today, its old city is a Dickensian warren of pungent lanes, open-air butcheries and brothels, bounded by crumbling gates and a fume-choked highway. Its small traders – fiercely conservative, on the whole – are the city's deciding political force. Among the wealthy, Lahore is a city of old money where a certain unhurried elegance still rules, where breakfast might not start till lunchtime, and the *jeunesse dorée* emerge at night from their air-conditioned cocoons – silky-haired women in shimmering dresses, young men in button-down shirts – to hit the town.

While Taseer embraced the city's upper-class privileges, he also delighted in subverting them. He had risen in business thanks to a ruthless streak that cost him friendships. In politics he was an arch-pugilist, endlessly scheming against rivals or skewering them on Twitter, a platform he used to great effect. In private he swore like a sailor, even in the presence of his wife and teenage children. 'In that house it was always "Fuck this, bitch that," one disapproving neighbour told me. Where some saw a refreshing maverick, others perceived an arrogant boor, and behind the glinting smile lay a blunt man who could be cutthroat with his loyalties. His propensity for affairs with younger women was the stuff of local legend; word had it that the governor had fallen out with one of his older sons after he slept with the son's girlfriend.

Such behaviour drew appalled whispers in the more genteel drawing rooms of Lahore. But as far as Taseer was concerned, the snobs could go and stick it. In a city of old money, he had made his own.

Taseer's father, Muhammad Din Taseer, was a noted Kashmiri academic, poet and part of a circle of Muslim intellectuals who led the drive for Pakistan in the 1930s and 1940s. He married Christobel George, a spirited English suffragette he met at Cambridge; their marriage was solemnised by Allama Muhammad Iqbal, the eminent philosopher who influenced Muhammad Ali Jinnah. Taseer senior died when Salmaan was three, leaving his English wife to raise their young family in modest circumstances. Christobel couldn't afford the fees at Aitchison College, Lahore's most prestigious boys' school, so she sent Salmaan to St Anthony's High School, which was run by Irish Catholic priests. There, Taseer befriended another upper-class upstart named Tariq Ali, who shared his love of chasing girls and anti-imperial agitation. The pair went to dances dressed like Elvis Presley and got into trouble for scrawling YANKEE GO HOME in red paint on a bridge in Lahore. Arrested by the police, they got off with a reprimand thanks to family connections – a third conspirator, and classmate, was the son of a Supreme Court judge. But Ali later learned that Taseer, under pressure from the police, had implicated his friends in the affair. The betrayal stung, causing lasting damage to their friendship.

At seventeen, Taseer took the boat to London, where he worked at odd jobs and studied at night to be a chartered accountant. For a time, he worked as a croupier at the Playboy Club in Mayfair, where, he liked to tell, he bedded one of the Playmates; family legend has it that he worked for an escort agency called Eros. More significantly, London shaped Taseer's political thinking. One visitor to the Playboy Club was his uncle, Faiz Ahmed Faiz, a celebrated poet who fled Pakistan in 1960 after the military accused him of participating in a communist plot to seize the country. Taseer worshipped Faiz, whose jaw dropped when he saw his Pakistani nephew dealing cards in a white tuxedo. Later, Faiz introduced Taseer to other exiled third-world *salonniers*, such as Pablo Neruda, an experience that shaped the young Pakistani's political views and idealism.

His other great influence was Zulfikar Ali Bhutto. Like many young Pakistanis, Taseer was enthralled by Bhutto's progressive ideas and his strutting style. They first met in the bar of the Dorchester Hotel, where Taseer marched up to Bhutto and held out his hand. The student's gumption so impressed Bhutto that he bought him a beer. The drink was generously repaid following Bhutto's execution in 1979, when Taseer wrote a creditable biography of the dead leader and threw himself into the underground opposition to military rule led by Bhutto's daughter, Benazir.

Taseer's first marriage, to a childhood sweetheart, collapsed under the weight of serial affairs. 'Classic lipstick on the collar stories,' their son, Shaan, told me. General Zia's men arrested him numerous times, mostly notably in 1983 when Taseer was cast into the bowels of Lahore Fort, where he endured beatings, illness and sleep deprivation. Taseer counted the days with notches on his grimy cell walls and smuggled out letters via a cleaning person to his new second wife, Aamna. She told him she feared for his life. 'Don't worry,' he replied. 'I am not made of wood that burns easily.'

After Zia's mysterious death in 1988, Taseer stood for election several times, with mixed results, so he turned to making money, where he proved a roaring success. He had got his start in the United Arab Emirates, in the 1970s, charming oil sheikhs for lucrative accountancy contracts. He built a business empire on stocks, real estate and a cable TV company that catered to Pakistanis' endless appetite for melodramatic Indian movies. Taseer sent his sons to Aitchison College and later chaired the school's board of governors – sweet revenge for someone whose family couldn't afford the fees for him.

In 2008, Taseer had a second shot at politics when Benazir Bhutto's widower, President Asif Ali Zardari, appointed him governor of Punjab. Taseer treated the sinecure with his usual cheery cynicism. 'You know how it is in this country,' he told his school chum Tariq Ali, now a prominent left-wing writer. 'I thought that if I was in politics, and made a lot of money, at least I wouldn't have to bribe myself.' In fact, he used the largely cere-monial position as a political cudgel to attack his arch-nemesis, Nawaz Sharif, and his brother Shahbaz, with whom he had a rivalry stretching back to the 1980s, when the Sharifs were polit-ical protégés of General Zia. Taseer detested their pious politics and blamed them for a vicious beating he received at the hands of the Punjab police in 1993. The governor took his revenge on social media, mocking everything from Nawaz's lumbering speaking style to his gauche taste in home furnishings: the Sharif mansion was stuffed with gilded, Louis XIV-style furniture, and peacocks strutted in the garden, not to mention the caged tiger in the backyard.

Hillary Clinton received gentler treatment on a visit to Lahore in 2009, when Taseer treated the United States secretary of state to a lavish banquet. Even then, he could not resist his urge for playful provocation. Over dinner, Taseer boasted to Clinton that he had hurled rocks at the American Embassy in London during the student protests of the 1960s. 'Don't worry,' Clinton shot back, 'so did I.'

In political terms, though, Taseer's stint as governor was marred by a huge miscalculation. In the spring of 2009, the Sharif brothers rallied their supporters for a march on Islamabad to call for the resignation of President Zardari. In an attempt to stop them, Zardari and Taseer activated 'governor's rule', an emergency power that Taseer used to suspend the provincial government, then led by Shahbaz Sharif. A risky gambit, it backfired badly. The army stepped in to back the Sharifs, who continued on to Islamabad; Zardari was nearly ousted in a military coup; and weeks later Taseer was forced to rescind governor's rule. He appeared badly out of his depth.

Even so, Taseer stood out as a politician of unusual conviction. Since the Red Mosque siege three years earlier, Pakistan had been reeling under a storm of militant violence. The Pakistani Taliban were striking all the time in the big cities – Islamabad, Lahore, Karachi – and the security forces seemed helpless to stop them. Teenage suicide bombers, trained in Waziristan, rushed into teeming markets, five-star hotels, Sufi shrines, army checkposts and even buses carrying Pakistani intelligence officers. In 2009 alone, over 3,000 Pakistanis were killed in a wave of militant chaos that came almost to my door.

Within a few streets of my home in Islamabad, bombers hit a courthouse, a United Nations office and an army checkpost.

Yet few Pakistani politicians dared take a firm stand against these extremists. Some took refuge in conspiratorial talk of 'the foreign hand' – code for India's Research and Analysis Wing intelligence service, or Israel's Mossad, or the CIA. In Punjab, Chief Minister Shahbaz Sharif pleaded with the Taliban to spare the province because his party shared their antipathy to the West. Imran Khan, the cricketer-turned-politician, lambasted the army for its operations against the Taliban at their lair in the tribal belt, defended the harsh blasphemy laws, and derided fellow members of the Anglicised Lahore elite for what he termed their 'Westoxified' ways.

'They suck up to foreigners, playing on their fears of a Taliban takeover,' Khan told me one evening at his sprawling villa on a ridge overlooking Islamabad. Salmaan Taseer was evidently included in that category. 'He lacks a moral anchor,' Khan told one of Taseer's sons. 'He just sits there drinking his whiskeys, laughing at everything, putting everything down.'

Taseer viewed such talk as craven appeasement. During our lunch at Governor's House, he spoke of his fears that Punjab had become a petri dish for an especially virulent strain of Sunni extremism. Over the previous year, a mob had torched Christian homes in a small Punjab town, killing ten people; extremists sprayed gunfire on minority Ahmadis as they prayed, killing eighty; and a bomb ripped through Data Darbar, Lahore's revered Sufi shrine, killing forty-two pilgrims. Basant, the glorious kite-flying festival, had been banned ostensibly on security grounds, although many saw the ban as a sop to conservatives who viewed the fun as an abomination. Taseer worried particularly about the hundreds of hard-line *madrassas* in the south of the province, nourished on Saudi funding, that were churning out indoctrinated young men.

'We must show these people zero tolerance,' he said. 'One wrong move, and you gun them down.'

For Taseer, this was the struggle for 'Jinnah's Pakistan', A keen student of history, he had never been impassioned by Muhammad Ali Jinnah, a staid figure beside the freedom fighters he idolised: Mandela, Nehru, even Chairman Mao. But Taseer identified strongly with Jinnah's vision of a free and tolerant society – a noble cause he had spent his life fighting for, and would soon be called to die for.

※

The conundrum of faith and identity in Pakistan was apparent from the very start. In March 1949, six months after the death of Jinnah, the fledgling Parliament passed a law declaring Pakistan the world's first 'Islamic Republic'. What that meant in practice, though, was perilously unclear. For a start, the Muslims of Pakistan followed a wide variety of Islamic sects, legal systems and schools of thought. Which one should prevail in framing the laws of this brave new republic? Second, there was the matter of the non-Muslim minorities. At the dawn of Pakistan, Jinnah had promised members of all creeds that they would be 'free to go to your temples'. Would they now, in the Islamic Republic, be relegated to the status of second-class citizens – or worse? The first test of those thorny questions came after a few short years.

In the spring of 1953, Punjab was swept by riots that targeted the Ahmadis – a small Muslim sect that was barely half a century old. Egged on by rabble-rousing clerics, mobs attacked Ahmadis in the streets, torched their homes and places of worship, and clashed with the riot police. In speeches, the clerics painted the Ahmadis as members of a secretive cabal that they claimed wanted to seize control of Pakistan – an ugly tale with disturbing echoes of the anti-Semitism in Nazi Germany, only years earlier. In truth, the Ahmadis were despised for their reverence of Mirza

Ghulam Ahmed, a preacher who emerged from the Punjab countryside in the late nineteenth century, claiming to be a prophet from God. That belief enrages orthodox Muslims for whom Muhammad, who died in AD 632, was God's last prophet on earth. The upheaval ended, that summer, when the government declared temporary martial law in Lahore – the Pakistan military's first taste of direct rule.

To understand the causes of this ugly spasm, and prevent its recurrence, the government appointed a commission of inquiry headed by a sagacious judge named Justice Muhammad Munir. For months, the leaders of Pakistan's Islamic schools traipsed into Justice Munir's chambers, where he posed to each the same, devastatingly simple question. If an Ahmadi was not a true Muslim, then who was? All offered a similar answer: only their own branch of the faith enjoyed divine approval and competing groups were *kafirs* – unbelievers. Munir was dismayed. 'If considerable confusion exists in the minds of our *ulema* on such a simple matter,' he noted dryly, 'one can easily imagine what the differences on more complicated matters will be.'

Munir had hit upon the identity crisis at the heart of Pakistan: how to forge a nation state, respectful of all citizens, on Islamic foundations? In his final report, the judge urged Pakistan's leaders to engage urgently with this conundrum because, he said, the issues raised were so fundamental that they could 'make or mar the new state of Pakistan'. The report was a masterful piece of work – clearly written, lucidly argued, even lyrical in places. It could never be written today. In the intervening decades, Pakistan's leaders, instead of resolving the role of Islam, sought to use it to their own ends. Generals urged their troops into war with the battle cry of jihad. Politicians appealed to religious sentiment to win votes. Powerful interests cynically used Islamic laws to silence critics, quash dissent or, literally, get away with murder. Under a provision known as *qisas* and *diyat* (an eye for an eye), a killer can escape justice if he pays 'blood money' to the family of his victim – a useful loophole in cases of honour killings, or even killing American spies.

In 2011, a CIA contractor named Raymond Davis was arrested in Lahore after he gunned down two Pakistanis in the street in murky circumstances. Amid an intense furore, Davis was hauled before a court where he faced a likely sentence of life imprisonment. After unsuccessfully arguing that the trigger-happy spy enjoyed immunity from prosecution – 'Our diplomat,' President Barack Obama called him – American officials hit upon what was for them a novel solution: in return for blood price of two million dollars, the dead men's relatives agreed to let the American spy walk free.

Salmaan Taseer typified the contradictions of Jinnah's Pakistan. Like all politicians, he opened speeches with the religious invocation '*Bismillah*'. He told people he had read the Qur'an during the darkest period of his incarceration at Lahore Fort in the 1980s, but claimed to have learned little from it. At stressful moments, he touched an amulet around his neck that contained *Ayat-ul-kursi* – protective verses from the holy book – while remaining unapologetic about his affluent, free-wheeling lifestyle. His family became a target of conservatives. Photographs taken from his children's Facebook pages, and circulated widely on the internet, showed them in swimming outfits or socialising with the opposite sex – proof, to critics, of their degenerate lifestyle. Even progressives could be put off by the family's showy displays of opulence. In the autumn of 2010, as Pakistan reeled from biblical floods that killed almost 2,000 people, Taseer's children threw a lavish Halloween party that later featured in the pages of *Sunday*, the family's glossy society magazine, in a show of crass exhibitionism that to critics typified the tone-deaf sensibilities of Pakistan's super-wealthy elite. 'What la la land are *these* people living in?' wrote one influential blogger.

The most stinging judgement came from Taseer's own blood. In 2005, an unexpected visitor arrived at Taseer's door: Aatish, the product of a brief affair between Taseer and an Indian journalist a quarter of a century earlier. For years, Taseer had behaved appallingly towards his Indian son – at first denying his existence, then offering grudging assistance. Now things improved only moderately. While Aamna and the children welcomed Aatish into the Cavalry Ground villa, Taseer was supremely indifferent – behaviour that was unsurprising to Taseer's Lahore friends but that wounded an estranged son. Worst of all, Aatish later wrote, Salmaan was a hypocrite, a 'cultural Muslim' who used religion as a cloak. 'In the end this was the moderate Muslim, and it was too little moderation, and in the wrong areas,' he wrote.

Taseer, though, believed that such contradictions were precisely the point. People in countries like Pakistan (and, indeed, India) did not speak a single language or share a single culture. They had layered, complex identities that often looked different in public or in private. Taseer was fighting for a Pakistan that had space for a hard-charging, money-grubbing sinner like him. 'Surely, God is to be found in your heart and not only in the mosque,' he said. The best measure of the strength of the 'Islamic Republic', he felt, was in its treatment of non-Muslims.

Soon after our meeting in Lahore, that conviction would be put to a searing test.

❈

Itanwali, thirty miles north of Lahore, is in many respects a typical Punjabi village: an island of tin-roofed houses in a sea of lush fields. Motorbikes with rackety engines zip through rutted streets webbed with black veins of sewage. Villagers live in modest farmhouses with wooden furniture and brightly coloured crockery. On the hottest summer nights, they drag their rope beds out under the stars in hopes of catching a refreshing breeze.

Asia* Bibi, a diminutive mother of five in her mid-thirties, was in most respects an unremarkable resident of Itanwali. The daughter of a goatherd, her husband was Ashiq Masih, a swarthy, moon-faced former soldier who laboured in a brick kiln on the edge of town. Ashiq had three children from a previous marriage, and two with Asia. But they did stand out for one reason: their Christian faith.

Officially, Christians are equal citizens of Pakistan, represented by the white band on the national flag; in reality, they are treated as an undeclared lower caste. The 'Christian colony', near my house in Islamabad, was a cluster of ramshackle houses perched over a foul-smelling sewer and jammed between the spacious homes of the well-to-do. Its residents cleaned houses, swept the streets and cleaned drains – work shunned by Muslims. A friend told of how his landlord, an elderly civil servant, refused to accept a glass of water from a Christian domestic worker because it was 'unclean'. In Itanwali, Asia Bibi was familiar with such attitudes. She tugged a *dupatta* over her head during the call to prayer, attended church in a town twenty miles away, and politely resisted pressure from Muslim neighbours to convert. 'When you're a Christian in Pakistan, you have to keep your head down,' she would say.

On a scorching morning in June 2009, Asia set out to work in the fields where women were harvesting *falsa*, a tart berry used to make jam. By mid-morning, she was parched, and paused to fetch water from a nearby well. But when she offered her glass to a fellow fruit-picker, it was brusquely rejected. '*Haram!*' the Muslim woman cried – forbidden. Asia fumed. She had silently endured such indignities from Muslims for years, including this

* Despite this spelling, which appears in her book, her name is pronounced 'AH-si-ah'.

troublesome woman; now she hurled them back. Jesus died on the cross for Christians, she yelled. What had Muhammad done for them? The other women in the field gathered round. One snatched Asia's bowl of berries. Another spat in her face. 'Bitch! Filthy whore!' the first woman yelled. 'You've had it now!'

Asia ran home to her husband, who comforted her and assured her it would pass. But days later a mob turned up at their door, beat Asia and dragged her before the *imam*, or Muslim prayer leader, of Itanwali. A short man in his thirties, his stock had risen in the village since the construction of a mosque. He puffed up his chest. Asia could be forgiven, he declared, if she converted to Islam. When Asia refused, the beating resumed, and she was saved only by the intervention of two policemen who bundled her off to a police station, where, to appease the mob gathered outside, they charged her with blasphemy.

Beyond Itanwali, this unpleasant village drama went largely unnoticed. Since the 1980s, when General Zia turbo-charged Pakistan's colonial-era laws, making the offence of blasphemy punishable by death, such prosecutions had become so common that they rarely made the news. Blasphemy had become a deadly weapon of the strong against the weak. The law was abused to settle personal scores, to gain an advantage in disputes over money or land, or persecute vulnerable minorities. The law had a Kafka-esque appeal. An accuser only had to accuse a foe of blasphemy to have them jailed; in court, they were not required to repeat the offending words, because to do so would itself constitute blasphemy.

Asia was thrown in jail for eighteen months. When a judge convicted her of blasphemy, the case didn't even make it to the papers. But when the sentence was handed down, in November 2010, and she was sentenced to death – the first time a woman had received that penalty for blasphemy – a furore stirred. Human rights groups issued press releases. At the Vatican, Pope

Benedict XVI mentioned her by name during mass in St Peter's Square. Then the governor of Punjab got involved.

Salmaan Taseer was driving to Murree, a verdant hill station above Islamabad, to spend the Eid ul-Adha holiday with his family. As his jeep curled up the winding road, his twenty-one-year-old daughter Shehrbano, who had just graduated from college in the United States, read aloud a news article about Asia Bibi's death sentence. 'Spineless bloody judges,' Taseer muttered. For the remainder of the journey he said little, his brow furrowed, and his fingers pressed against his temple, staring into the distance as he often did when pondering a problem.

He knew there was little chance that Asia Bibi's dire sentence would be carried out: most cases were thrown out on appeal, owing to the lack of evidence, and nobody had ever been hanged for the crime. Yet those accused still faced mortal danger. Over the previous two decades, vigilantes had killed at least thirty-two people involved in blasphemy trials. People had been gunned down in courtrooms, or poisoned by zealous prison guards. By the time Asia's case wound through Pakistan's sclerotic legal system, she could be dead.

Four days later, Asia Bibi was summoned to the office of the superintendent of Sheikhupura Jail, where she was being held. The Christian woman was filled with dread, taking the summons as a sign her execution was imminent. Instead she found Taseer, his wife, Amna, and their daughter, Shehrbano, waiting for her. 'I'm your friend in this,' Taseer told her. He tried to put the anxious woman at ease by regaling her with jokes about his own time in prison under General Zia. He promised Asia she would see her children for Christmas. Moments later, they walked together into an adjoining room where they held an impromptu press conference. Her face wrapped in a shawl, Asia stuttered as she recounted her ordeal. Taseer held aloft a mercy petition, bearing her fresh thumbprint, and announced he was taking it directly to President Zardari in Islamabad. 'The Pakistan we want is a progressive, liberal Pakistan, not a country of darkness and persecution and cutting off heads,' he said. 'If I, as a governor, am not going to raise my voice for people like this, then what am I here for?'

It was an extraordinary sight: the powerful governor of Pakistan's most populous province seated beside a humble Christian woman in a grimy jail. His forceful advocacy had a political advantage, contrasting favourably with the stony silence of the Sharifs. Even so, Taseer seemed driven by a genuine sense of outrage. 'Somebody has to speak up,' he said. Asia's family clung desperately to this fragile hope. 'I just want to see my mother,' her ten-year-old daughter, Esha, told a reporter, tears streaming down her cheeks. But to other Pakistanis, Taseer's principled stand amounted to a declaration of war.

Protests erupted at the gates of Governor's House, where hundreds gathered to chant slogans against Taseer and to burn him in effigy. One cleric announced a $6,000 reward for anyone who managed to kill Asia; others were incensed by Taseer's call for immediate reform of the blasphemy statute, which he termed a 'black law'. It wasn't just the Christian woman, they charged – the governor, too, had committed blasphemy. Taseer was unbowed. 'Who the hell are these illiterate maulvis to decide whether I'm a Muslim or not?' he wrote on Twitter. 'Important to face – and call their bluff.'

Blasphemy has always been one of the hardest things to understand about Pakistan. In *God is Gracious*, a satirical essay published in 1954, the writer Saadat Hasan Manto envisaged a Pakistan in which poetry, arts and music were silenced by accusations of blasphemy. His words proved prophetic. In the name of protecting the honour of Islam or its prophet, children and mentally ill people have been lynched; neighbourhoods put to the torch; and prisoners murdered by their guards. Once, I was trapped in the lobby of Islamabad's Serena Hotel as a blasphemy protest raged in the street outside. The trigger was a crude video clip, posted to the internet by an obscure group of American Christian fundamentalists, that mocked the Prophet Muhammad. Now, thousands of miles from America, young Pakistanis were battling the riot police. For what, exactly?

Yet such passions *did* have a certain logic. Sometimes, blasphemy was purposefully whipped up by powerful interests – clerics, media personalities, even intelligence agencies – to serve their interests. For some rioters, it was a thinly veiled class struggle – a frustrated howl at a horribly unequal society where the super-rich shamelessly flaunted their privilege and treated the poor with unvarnished contempt.

Five days after his visit to Asia Bibi in jail, Taseer appeared on a prime-time talk show hosted by Meher Bokhari, a twenty-seven-year-old who typified Pakistan's new generation of female journalists. Glamorous and Western-educated with long uncovered hair, Bokhari offered a sharp contrast with the whiskery old men who had long dominated newsrooms. On air, she had a pointed, high-decibel interviewing style; in her spare time, she attended weddings and parties and was photographed for the glossy society magazines. Months earlier, she had come under fire over photographs that showed her carousing with American diplomats at an embassy cocktail party.

But in her interview with Taseer, Bokhari pursued her brief with prosecutorial zeal. Why was he defending Asia Bibi? What were his religious qualifications on the matter? And who was he – the Muslim governor of Punjab – to defend a Christian woman? Bokhari flourished a sheet of paper – a *fatwa*, issued hours earlier, denouncing Taseer and his actions. Bokhari quoted from it at length. Was the governor, Bokhari wanted to know, promoting a 'western liberal agenda'?

Her aggressive line of questioning shook Taseer; after the interview, he told Shehrbano that it felt like an on-air lynching. The *fatwa*, issued by an obscure cleric, carried little religious authority, but Taseer worried that the decree could further inflame public opinion. And he was perplexed. Bokhari was the kind of young woman who might feature in the society pages of his newspaper, the *Daily Times*, or attend one of his parties. 'I know this girl, she's not like this,' he told his daughter. 'Why is she pandering to the mullahs?'

I drove down to Itanwali, Asia Bibi's village where it all started. I arrived just as Qari Muhammad Saleem, the cleric who had led Asia's persecution, was preparing for Friday prayers, plugging in a crackling loudspeaker as worshippers deposited their plastic slippers at the door. Saleem was younger than I expected, with darting eyes and a *keffiyeh* scarf around his head. He delivered a rambling sermon, railing against alcohol, gambling, kite-flying, pigeon-racing and — for some reason I didn't quite understand — insurance. 'All of these are the work of the devil,' he said. People listened intently. Afterwards, over a cup of tea, he recalled his joy at the news that Asia had been sentenced to hang. 'Everyone celebrated,' he said. 'I wept with joy.'

I went over to Asia's house on the edge of Itanwali. Nobody was home — her family had long since fled — but next door I found a young woman in a headscarf, about twenty years old, who remonstrated loudly with me. 'Why hasn't Asia been killed?' she demanded, her voice swelling into a shout. 'You journalists keep coming here, asking questions. But still this issue has not been resolved! Why has she not hanged yet?'

❈

On New Year's Eve, seven weeks after Asia Bibi was sentenced to death, a preacher named Hanif Qureshi took to a stage in Rawalpindi to deliver a fiery harangue. Salmaan Taseer was an apostate who had betrayed Islam, he yelled, gesticulating so violently that his black turban fell from his head. Good Muslims were obliged to act. 'Allah has given us the courage! We know how to trigger a gun! We know how to behead those who commit blasphemy against our beloved prophet!'

'Death, death, death,' chanted the crowd.

At the back of the gathering, the police constable Malik Mumtaz Qadri listened quietly, nursing his service rifle. Born in 1985, at the height of General Zia's Islamisation drive, Qadri had grown up in a modest, working-class family – his father was a street trader – that now occupied a thirty-two-room, multi-storey compound on Al-Muslim Street, not far from the army headquarters. By most measures, the Qadris were no extremists. In religion and politics, they occupied the soft middle of Pakistani society. They were devout Barelvis, followers of Pakistan's predominant school of Islam, which blends elements of Sufism with Sharia law. For years, they had voted for the Pakistan Peoples Party. Their preacher, Qureshi, had clashed openly with followers of more ascetic schools of Islam such as Deobandism, which the Taliban adhered to.

But Barelvis do have an especially strong veneration for the Prophet Muhammad – their clerics whipped up the anti-Ahmadi riots that swept Punjab in 1953 – and Qadri, an impressionable young man, was famed in the local community for his *naats*, undulating poetic chants that praised the Prophet Muhammad. At prayer meetings, he could be seen on stage, microphone in hand, to perform a *naat*, often in his police uniform.

After Qureshi's inflammatory sermon on New Year's Eve, Qadri returned to the house on Al-Muslim Street, where he shared a few rooms with his wife and three-month-old son, and resolved to take action.

The tide was turning against Taseer. His effort to secure a presidential pardon had been blocked by conservative judges at the Lahore High Court. His call for reform of the 'black law' scared the wits out of his colleagues in the Pakistan Peoples Party, who with a few exceptions openly deserted him. The ISI warned Taseer there was a twenty-million-rupee ($250,000) bounty on his head.

Undaunted, Taseer continued with life as normal. On Twitter, he mocked the Sharifs and other critics as 'obsessional retards'; he gave a talk to students at university; he inaugurated a polo match. On 3 January, he drove to Islamabad.

The following morning, Taseer took breakfast with his youngest son, Shehryar, who was celebrating his twenty-fifth birthday. He logged onto Twitter, where he posted a verse by an Urdu-language poet named Shakeel Badayuni: 'My resolve is so strong that I do not fear the flames from without. I fear only the radiance of the flowers, that it might burn my garden down.'

Then he left for lunch at Table Talk in Kohsar Market, where he ordered his favourite dish, prawn laksa. After lunch, he stepped into a bookshop to buy a copy of *Newsweek* magazine. Then he strolled towards his security detail: five men gathered around two vehicles, including Mumtaz Qadri, who had requested to be assigned to Taseer's detail that day.

❈

The assassination of Salmaan Taseer had a ringing precedent. A quarter-century earlier, in 1984, India's prime minister, Indira Gandhi, had been shot dead by her Sikh bodyguards as she strolled across the garden of her official residence in New Delhi. The guards sought to avenge the deaths of fellow Sikhs killed by Indian commandos, months earlier, during an operation to end a protracted siege of the sacred Golden Temple in Amritsar. Like Taseer, Gandhi was shot multiple times. As with Taseer, the assassins surrendered immediately.

If the parallels suggested that such inflamed killings were a speciality of the subcontinent, Taseer's death raised a specific question that went to the heart of Pakistan's age-old ideological war. Who was the good Muslim: Taseer the reformer or Qadri the killer?

Qadri's trial lasted for five years, at times resembling that of a mafia don. Witnesses recused themselves without explanation. Prosecutors struggled to assemble a legal team. The Taliban joined a chorus of Qadri supporters. 'We would love to kiss his holy hands and gun trigger finger,' declared one commander in Waziristan. Qadri's defence was led by a pair of retired High Court judges who, as the trial progressed, acquired their own notoriety. One praised a terrorist attack on the offices of the French satirical newspaper *Charlie Hebdo*; the other said it was *haram* to express a dislike for pumpkin because the prophet Muhammad had been partial to the vegetable. In court, they sought to portray Taseer as a fallen Muslim by citing at length from his estranged son Aatish's memoir, including a passage that described the sweary, boozy atmosphere in his father's house. 'My father who drank Scotch every evening, never fasted or prayed, even ate pork,' it read.

A pernicious cult of celebrity sprang up around Qadri. At the maximum-security Adiala Jail in Rawalpindi, admiring wardens posed for photos with the inmate and excused him from regular prison duties. In Islamabad, bootleg recordings of his *naats* went on sale, and a mosque that renamed itself after Qadri doubled the size of its congregation. At Qadri's Rawalpindi home, four rooms were filled with flowers. His brothers welcomed a stream of well-wishers; extremist groups donated money to the family. A billboard depicted Qadri as a warrior astride a white horse, riding between Islam's two holiest sites in Mecca and Medina. 'The Prophet's Policeman' read one banner.

Taseer's children downplayed the cult of Qadri, describing the policeman as a symptom of a much wider malaise. 'He's just the bullet, the tool for execution,' Shehryar said. Still, a shocking example had been set. Two months later, in March 2011, extremists shot dead Shahbaz Bhatti, the federal minister for minorities and the only Christian in the cabinet. When I reached his Islamabad home, I found policemen staring into Bhatti's blood-splattered saloon. In Karachi, as thousands of Qadri supporters filled the streets to demand his release, I met with Sherry Rehman, one of the few politicians brave enough to stand publicly with Taseer, confined inside her luxurious home with an extra armed guard at the gate. 'This is dark,' she said.

Qadri's noxious influence spread far. In 2016, a British man of Pakistani descent drove 200 miles, from Bradford to Glasgow, in order to kill an Ahmadi shopkeeper. The killer was enraged by videos that the Ahmadi had posted to YouTube, which he found blasphemous. After stabbing the shopkeeper to death, the killer sat in a bus shelter and waited to be arrested. It turned out that he had been corresponding with Qadri in jail.

The Taseer family's ordeal was not over. In August 2011, armed men snatched Taseer's youngest son, Shahbaz, from his Mercedes as he sped through Gulberg in Lahore. They injected him with a sedative and spirited him to Waziristan, where he was held by Uzbek militants affiliated with the Taliban. The militants lashed Taseer's son with a whip, pulled out his toenails and forced him to record a videotape ransom demand that was sent to his family in Lahore. In exchange for his release, the kidnappers demanded several million dollars and, by some accounts, that Mumtaz Qadri should be forgiven.

⁂

When Qadri finally testified in court, he argued that Pakistan's Islamic law justified his shooting of the governor. 'Nature had to take its course, and justice was done,' he said. 'It is a lesson for all apostates.'

Qadri was executed on 29 February 2016, hanged before dawn at Adiala Jail. The newspapers estimated that 100,000 people attended his funeral, many of them wailing and kissing photos of their hero. Qadri, wearing a green turban decorated with sparkling brooches, was laid to rest in a coffin strewn with rose petals, in a mausoleum with tall white minarets. Mourners wore T-shirts that read I AM QADRI.

Asia Bibi, meanwhile, languished in jail. She spent most of her time in solitary confinement – for her own safety, wardens said – where she battled asthma and loneliness and cooked her own meals to reduce the danger of poisoning. At times, she was chained and forced to wear an iron collar that her guards tightened with a large nut. Campaigners in the West continued to focus attention on Asia's plight, and Canada offered to give her asylum. But in Pakistan, her case was largely forgotten. No minister, general or judge, it seemed, had the courage or strength to set the Christian woman free.

Sultan Amir Tarar, also known as 'Colonel Imam'

7

Lost in Waziristan

A Veteran Spy Miscalculates

In the summer of 2010, I received an email from the Pakistani Taliban. It came from the tribal belt, along the border with Afghanistan, and its senders announced they were holding hostages: a British journalist and two Pakistani companions. In exchange for their freedom, the kidnappers demanded $10 million. Failure to comply, they warned, would condemn the three hostages to the fate of the fourth – a man who had been tortured, forced to record a video saying he worked for the CIA, and then shot in the head. His body was discovered alongside a stream in North Waziristan, the most fraught corner of the tribal belt, with a handmade sign that read: AMERICAN SPY. In a macabre touch, the hostage-takers were emailing me from the dead man's account.

I wondered why they contacted me. Kidnapping was a centuries-old racket in parts of the tribal belt, but its practitioners rarely got Western reporters involved. Perhaps the hostage-takers imagined I could ratchet up pressure on the British government for the journalist, who had been on assignment for Channel Four when he was taken. (At the time, I worked for the *Guardian*.) I phoned a few friends for advice, then set the matter aside. Hostage negotiations are a delicate business. But the underlying circumstances were a reminder of the dire situation in the tribal belt, the constellation of seven tribal districts in the northwest, now a hive of jihadist ferment. Since Anwar Kamal's showdown with the Taliban a few years earlier, Waziristan had completely spun out of control. Jihadist wannabes were streaming in from across the globe – citizens of Chechnya, China, Germany, Britain and the United States – sheltering in high-walled compounds nestled amid thick forests and forbidding mountains, watching out for the CIA Predator and Reaper drones that circled overhead. Some ran suicide-bomber schools that churned out brainwashed teenagers for attacks inside Pakistan; others plotted mayhem in Europe and beyond. Anyone accused of helping the Americans, like the fourth hostage, was tortured and executed. It was impossible for reporters to go there safely.

Weeks later came a second Taliban email, this time with a video clip. It showed one of the Pakistani captives, an elderly man with a scraggly beard, sitting cross-legged against a plain backdrop that had been improvised from a white sheet. He wore the taut stare of a man fearing the worst. Holding aloft a copy of that day's newspaper, to show the date, he spoke to the camera in a slow, deliberate voice. 'My name is Sultan Amir,' he said. 'I am better known by the name Colonel Imam.'

I read the name with a jolt. I knew this man well. Imam was one of Pakistan's most storied spies – a retired ISI official who, in a career spanning four decades, had cultivated a reputation as a grizzled veteran of Pakistan's most notorious shadow wars. In the 1980s, Imam trained tens of thousands of Afghan *mujahideen* guerrillas in their fight against the Soviet Union. In the 1990s, he befriended the Afghan Taliban as they swept to power. Through it all, he demonstrated a knack for playing both sides of the equation, cultivating close ties with forces as diverse as Osama bin Laden and the CIA. Imam was also unusually open, which made him a figure of interest to scholars and journalists who sought to unpick the ISI's tangled history. I had spent hours in his company, over tea or lemonade, downloading his stories and his views, and puzzling over the details of his career. It was disturbing to see an acquaintance, even a professional one, being held hostage by the Taliban. And frankly, he was the last person I expected to see in such a predicament.

Spymaster, guerrilla trainer, provocateur – the legend of Imam stemmed from his ability to operate seamlessly in the most dangerous places with the most dangerous men. Like the best spies, he liked to keep people guessing. His real name was not Imam. His rank was brigadier, not colonel. And he had spent much of that storied career in the tribal belt, where he fraternised easily with warlords and ideologues, supplying them with weapons, money or just words of comfort.

Which was why it was so puzzling to see Colonel Imam being held hostage by the Taliban. After all, he helped create them.

※

Pink bougainvillea spills over the walls of an unmarked compound on the southern edge of Islamabad, beside a busy highway that climbs into the lower Himalayas. An electric gate slides back to reveal a neat campus, with manicured lawns and adobe buildings, that might pass for a well-funded private university. In the lobby, a solitary guard nods silently as you pass; the lift carries you to a floor where men in dark suits move along hushed corridors. You are ushered into a small reception room with deep armchairs where a uniformed waiter serves grape juice in cut-glass tumblers. Only when you lift your glass do you find a napkin with a logo that confirms you have arrived at the headquarters of Inter-Services Intelligence.

The ISI was founded, in 1948, by an Australian – General William Cawthorn, a British army officer, who stayed on after partition to help Pakistan establish its military. (He would later head the Australian Secret Intelligence Service.)

Its early decades were inglorious. The ISI badly misjudged Pakistan's calamitous 1965 war against India and, three years later, failed to anticipate an assassination plot targeting the country's military ruler, Field Marshal Ayub Khan. 'I.S.I. were fast asleep,' Khan grumbled to his diary. 'We are babes in intelligence work.'

The spy agency's fortunes were transformed, in the 1980s, by the Afghan *jihad*. Alongside the CIA, it ran the vast covert war machine that supplied money, men and missiles to the guerrillas fighting the Soviet occupation. Over the course of a decade, the ISI smuggled one million Kalashnikovs to the *mujahideen* – not to mention crates of American-supplied Stinger missiles that knocked the Red Army's helicopter gunships from the sky. By the time the last Soviets stumbled from Afghanistan in 1989, bloodied and humiliated, the ISI had become a powerful, well-resourced organisation and a centre of power in its own right. Its generals were important allies of the CIA and Saudi intelligence, and some had become rich. When the longtime spy chief, General Akhtar Abdur Rahman, died in the same mysterious plane crash as General Zia in 1988, he left behind a considerable fortune. (Today, his son is among Pakistan's most successful businessmen.)

But the most profound effect of that era was on the Pakistan military's thinking. Intoxicated by victory, the ISI sought to replicate its success in Afghanistan by employing the same tactics elsewhere. Through the 1990s, it established its own jihadi groups and deployed them to attack Indian soldiers in Kashmir, and it funnelled cash to foreign Islamist guerrillas as far afield as the Philippines. At home, the emboldened spy agency meddled aggressively in politics, mostly in an effort to oust Benazir Bhutto. ISI officers rigged elections, bought politicians and strong-armed troublesome judges. Critics began to speak of a 'state within a state'.

My own relationship with the ISI was mostly respectful. My phone beeped and echoed occasionally; sure signs the line was being monitored. On reporting trips to sensitive corners of Pakistan – towns where militants roamed freely, or with secretive nuclear facilities – stiff-looking men lingered in the lobby of hotels where I stayed, watching me come and go. At home in Islamabad, strangers would come to the gate, asking the cook or the guard – but never me – for details about whom I was meeting and where I was going. Sometimes it was my guests who were being shadowed. On the evening I celebrated my thirty-sixth birthday, I counted three sets of intelligence operatives loitering outside the gate: one for an Indian reporter (members of the Indian media were tailed as a matter of course), another for a Pashtun guest (I later learned the Pakistanis suspected him of spying for the CIA), and the third set for a Pakistani journalist who worked with me.

The ISI even had a semi-official spokesman, an affable and well-read naval officer with a ponytail, a wry sense of humour and an easy smile. Let's call him 'Commodore Z'. Over endless coffees in the lobby of the Serena Hotel, Z had the thankless job of putting a positive spin on the agency's work, offering wounded denials that the ISI was up to its old dirty tricks. He also had a passion for golf – call him with a query about a drone strike, and you might hear a thudding five-iron in the background – and a taste for darkly portentous messages. After Benazir Bhutto's assassination in 2007, when suspicions of an ISI hand in her killing led to violent upheaval in parts of the country, Commodore Z sent me a text message. 'Read *Julius Caesar* again,' it read. 'His will was used by Antony to incite statements and his wounds were shown to citizens to trigger rebellion. Rome paid dearly.'

Of course, I was a foreign correspondent; different rules applied to Pakistanis. One reporter who worked with me was abducted by masked men and taken to a safe house, where he was interrogated, punched and had cigarettes stubbed out on his chest. When his assailants dumped him on a roadside the following morning, they warned that if he went public about his experience, they would rape his wife and post a video of the assault on YouTube. The reporter and his family now live in Switzerland.

The ISI does little to dispute its reputation as an omnipotent force. Fear is a powerful weapon. But talk of a 'rogue agency' is misplaced, and its abilities are frequently overestimated. While it is effective on street level, and seen by Western spy agencies as superior to its Indian rival, the Research and Analysis Wing (RAW), the ISI is not a professional service in the mould of the CIA or Britain's MI6. The army officers who run the agency rotate out, every few years, to other branches of the military. The organisation is afflicted by the same bungling and corruption as the rest of the Pakistani state. It has frequently lost control of its most dangerous assets – 'Puppetmasters who can't control their puppets,' as Robert Grenier, a former CIA station chief in Islamabad, put it. And when it comes to analysis, the ISI has a poor record. 'They saw everything through pre-determined ideological prisms, rather like the KGB during the Cold War,' a senior British official who worked with the ISI for decades told me. 'Frankly,' he added. 'None of their analysis was worth the paper it was written on.'

In recent decades, the ISI leadership has made a series of major miscalculations that have had grave consequences – not only for Pakistan, but for the spy agency itself.

Colonel Imam lived in a corner of Rawalpindi called Askari Seven, a military housing estate of modest, closely spaced villas. Its residents were, for the most part, mid-ranking army officers – men with neat moustaches who played golf and drove sensible cars, were unthinking in their nationalism and unaccustomed to the West, and therefore almost nothing like Imam.

Imam filled the front door when he opened it, still broad and tall despite his sixty-odd years. He had a wispy grey beard and a crooked smile, and he spoke with a slur that suggested someone who had once been punched very hard in the jaw and suffered a lasting injury. He dressed in an unusual fashion, with a small white turban folded in the manner of certain Arab preachers, and a collarless *shalwar kameez* finely embroidered in the style of Pashtun tribesmen from the Kandahar region of southern Afghanistan. His sandals were oddly heavy (three kilos, he liked to boast), and he wore a faded, olive-green paratrooper jacket that was issued by the British army in 1942. Imam had replaced its Union Jack with an Islamic insignia.

Imam steered me into a small drawing room that, judging from the dust-smeared coffee table, didn't see visitors very often. He disappeared in search of refreshments. War mementos covered the walls: a set of daggers gifted by an Afghan warlord; a Kalashnikov that had been pried from the hands of a dying Russian general; and a large missile casing, intricately decorated with verses of poetry. On a cabinet, a faded photo showed a burly man with dark hair and blazing eyes leading a line of fighters down a snowy mountain path: Colonel Imam and the *mujahideen*. But the most intriguing item was a chunk of spray-painted concrete, mounted in a small case: a piece of the Berlin Wall, presented to Imam by the Islamabad CIA station at the end of the Cold War. 'With deepest respect to one who helped deliver the first blow,' read the inscription.

Imam returned, carrying a silver tray laden with glasses of pineapple juice. Noticing my interest in the memento, he gave it an odd look, somewhere between pride and disdain.

'So,' he said, 'what was it you wanted to talk about?'

Everything. The legend of Imam started with the *jihad* of the 1980s, when he ran a network of covert guerrilla training camps, along the border with Afghanistan, that supplied fighters to the *mujahideen*. He scuttled down remote border roads in his hulking Toyota, scouring refugee camps and *madrassas* for recruits, who were then armed, fired up with talk of Islamic glory and dispatched across the border to kill the godless communists. But Imam was more than a sergeant major. While other ISI officers looked down on the Afghans as expendable battle fodder, Imam dressed like them, led them in prayer and charged into battle at their side. 'It wasn't just that Imam dressed like an Afghan – he thought like one, too,' said Michael Scheuer, a CIA analyst who later headed the unit dedicated to hunting Osama bin Laden. Those missions took Imam deep into Afghanistan, as far north as the Panjshir Valley, where he ambushed *Spetsnaz* commandos, shot down helicopter gunships and interrogated Soviet prisoners. The Afghans repaid him with a *nom de guerre*: Imam, meaning 'prayer leader'. 'Soon, even my own family forgot my real name,' Imam told me.

The experience left Imam with a veneration for Pashtun culture – specifically, its narrowly warlike aspects – that bordered on the extreme. 'They are my superior people, my superior culture,' he told me. 'They are scrupulously freedom loving, always have been, right since Alexander the Great. They cannot tolerate any foreigner coming onto their lands, dictating to them.' He liked to say that the Soviet troops were so terrified of the *mujahideen* that they preferred to urinate into their helmets than leave their tanks and risk a fight – a claim that sounded like bombast, but which Mikhail Evstafiev, a Russian writer who served in the war, suggested was accurate. 'A man felt safe and secure only inside the garrison, surrounded by barbed wire, tanks and machine guns,' Evstafiev wrote, in testimony that would be echoed by American soldiers two decades later. 'Fate had strewn

Soviet military divisions all over Afghanistan, they were islands in an ocean, lonely, far from the mainland.'

Some accounts of Imam's life, generally in histories of that war, described him as an ethnic Pashtun, but that was wrong. He was born Sultan Amir Tarar in Chakwal District, in the rich, canal-fed farmland of northern Punjab. His father fought in World War II with the British Indian army, and was wounded in the Italian campaign. Imam graduated from the Pakistan Military Academy, Pakistan's version of West Point, in 1971, then spent time at a Special Forces training course in Fort Bragg, North Carolina – part of a long-running American effort to ally with foreign militaries by offering specialised training to their most promising officers. Three years later, back in Pakistan, he reported for duty at Bala Hissar, an imposing Mughal-era fort in Peshawar, for his first covert mission: to train up a group of young Afghan revolutionaries who sought to overthrow their government.

The rebels were student Islamists from Kabul University who resented the growing communist influence in their country, where King Zahir Shah had been ousted a year earlier. Pakistani intelligence backed them as part of the decades-old grudge match between the two countries. The effort was a flop: Imam singed his moustache during an explosives lesson, and the scrappy uprising never took off. But it cast the die for the bigger fight, in 1979, when the Red Army invaded Afghanistan. Some of those revolutionaries, such as Ahmed Shah Masood, would become fabled commanders in the anti-Soviet resistance, and Imam, their Pakistani mentor, would become a central figure in Pakistani efforts to arm and train them.

During the decade-long war, Imam's job involved giving guided tours to high-level visitors from Washington such as Charlie Wilson, the playboy congressman from Texas who championed the covert war in the US Congress. But some CIA officers found him terse and guarded, and suspected that he was cooperating out of obligation rather than any shared values. 'He made it clear he didn't like us,' said Michael Scheuer. Imam preferred the company of radical Afghan commanders and foreign ideologues like Osama bin Laden, the skinny twenty-three-year-old son of a Saudi billionaire.

In fact, Colonel Imam himself had become radicalised – one of several ISI officers who had drunk the jihadist Kool-Aid, imbibing the ideology they used to motivate the Afghan guerrillas. Now he, too, was a true believer.

Imam was deployed back to Afghanistan in 1994, under diplomatic cover, as Pakistan's consul general in the western city of Herat. Following the Soviet retreat, Afghanistan had sunk into a vicious civil war, and a new fundamentalist group called the Taliban began to assert itself. Pakistan's spy agency, in search of a new Afghan client, offered help. Imam drew close to the Taliban's reclusive one-eyed leader, Mullah Muhammad Omar, who, it turned out, had graduated from one of Imam's *mujahideen* training camps in the 1980s. The Pakistani spy became known as Mullah Omar's *consigliere*, a reputation that reached the floor of the United Nations, where, in 1995, a diplomat with the beleaguered Afghan delegation denounced 'a Pakistani by the name of Colonel Imam' who was 'acting as de facto governor' in Taliban-held territories. Three years later, as the Islamists crushed a major pocket of resistance in northern Afghanistan, Western intelligence intercepted Imam's voice on a battlefield radio. 'My boys and I are riding into Mazar-i-Sharif!' he cried.

Imam remembered those days quite differently. As he related it, the Taliban were a bunch of pious naïfs who stumbled to power, guided by God and a grateful public. Certainly, he conceded, they made mistakes. But he downplayed their most barbaric acts – the stoning of men and women accused of adultery, or the demolition of the sublime Buddha statues at Bamiyan – as the product of youthful excess. 'Of course, sometimes they could be naughty,' he said with a mischievous smile.

For the most part, Imam was polite and disarmingly earnest. He engaged easily in debate and, in a mark of the bloodless morality of intelligence men the world over, rarely took offence at even the most provocative remarks. He loved to revel in his former glory, punctuating his stories with a fruity chuckle. But when it came to the Taliban, his manner could be hectoring and insistent, and the eyes that had shone with warmth now flashed with icy steel. 'Look here,' he challenged me once. 'Where do you educated people get all this propaganda? The Taliban are lovely people, friends of Pakistan and the world. It is pure disinformation that they are terrorists.'

Woe betide any foreign force, such as the United States, that thought it could vanquish them, he warned. 'They are not warlords. They have an ancient culture, ten centuries old. It cannot be defeated by technology.'

I heard versions of that speech from other Pakistani officers, who, it seemed, purposefully distorted Pashtun culture for their own purposes. Imam, for his part, didn't even speak Pashto properly, and the way he talked was reminiscent of the old colonial writers, like Olaf Caroe, with their romanticised versions of the 'noble savage'. But there was also no doubt that he considered jihad to be a sacred calling – as a soldier, a Pakistani and a Muslim. I think he viewed himself as a kind of Pakistani T. E. Lawrence: the army officer who turned unruly tribesmen into disciplined warriors, and now, through the toil of battle, had joined their ranks.

But orientalism, even of an Islamist variety, can cloud one's vision, and the world that Imam helped create was shifting rapidly beneath his feet. Around the time of our first meeting, in the mid-2000s, the powerful forces unleashed by the Afghan jihad of the 1980s were mutating in wild and unpredictable ways inside Pakistan. Nowhere were those changes more starkly evident than in the tribal belt, where it had all started.

❦

My first glimpse of Waziristan came through the porthole-shaped window of a clattering Pakistan army helicopter. Below, a breathtaking vista stretched in every direction. Castellated houses clung to vertiginous slopes. A jeep scrambled, insectlike, across a desiccated riverbed. Giant shafts of sunlight pierced the clouds.

It was 2005, and the military had agreed to take me to Waziristan to show that it was in charge. But the area has long been a tricky proposition for those who presume to rule it. In 1920, the British viceroy, Frederic Thesiger, noted wearily that his troops had quelled an uprising in Waziristan on average once every four years, for the previous seventy years. 'A forbidden land,' one British officer wrote in his diary. 'It was impossible to go; and if you did your bones would be left there.'

At the district headquarters in Miram, Tariq Khan, the political agent, posed behind an antique desk with the satisfied air of a well-fed cat. 'I am the law around here,' he declared, reclining into his armchair. 'I double up as the judge, the chief of police and the head of development. I can grant relief to a man or I can come down on him like a ton of bricks.' He paused for effect. 'You could call me a benevolent despot.'

Khan seemed to relish his role as provocateur, but he was only mildly exaggerating. At that time, the tribal belt was still governed by the Frontier Crimes Regulations, a colonial-era law that endowed him with astonishing powers. Khan could imprison any tribesman at will, fine his relatives or order his village razed to the ground; a wooden board behind him listed political agents back to the 1890s. The archaic legal framework was symptomatic of wider dysfunction. For decades, Pakistanis had treated the tribal belt as a kind of lawless colony, famed for smuggling, hostage-taking and hashish production. The government exerted its authority through political agents like Khan and the *maliks* – handpicked elders whose loyalty was purchased with cash payments and sinecures. In the movies, villains escaped the law by fleeing into the tribal areas, where they vanished into a world of high-walled compounds and biddable tribesmen.

The sense of a land frozen in time deepened when the military took me to its base in Jandola. A plaque outside the mess hall recalled the 1930s, when hard-drinking, cigar-smoking British officers played billiards and a portrait of 'a luscious brunette' adorned the fireplace. In 1930, the plaque noted, the airman Lieutenant Colonel T. E. Lawrence – Lawrence of Arabia – spent a night here, travelling under a pseudonym. He left behind a copy of his 1927 book *Revolt in the Desert* (the abridged version of his vaunted *Seven Pillars of Wisdom*).

At the entrance to South Waziristan tribal agency, a line of rock slabs jutted from a desiccated riverbed at an acute angle, like an ancient palisade. Our military convoy descended into the capital, Wana, a shabby town squatting on an orchard-studded plain, where a woman in a bright blue burka squatted wordlessly outside a dilapidated petrol station, and old men glared as we passed. Nobody waved, not even the uniformed boys jaunting to school.

We plunged into the mountains. The road melted away as we jolted along a dirt track at a grinding pace, splashing through chocolate streams and passing stacks of freshly cut lumber. I spotted flashes of movement in the walled compounds that clung to the steep slopes. We were being watched. Globs of rain splattered the windshield as we slithered up a greasy slope, wheels spinning, then skidded to a halt at a checkpoint: a rope pulled across the road. A pair of skinny levies, or tribal policemen, emerged and, after a minimum of formality, waved us through. We turned the corner to be confronted with a spectacular vista: the pine forests and snow-capped peaks of the Shawal Valley, the world's premier al Qaeda sanctuary.

A band of al Qaeda fugitives arrived here in late 2001, after fleeing American bombardment in the caves of Tora Bora in southern Afghanistan. (By one account, bin Laden's Egyptian deputy, the surgeon Ayman al-Zawahiri, crossed the border on horseback in March 2002, wearing a white turban and 'a beautiful coat'.) I could see why it was their preferred destination. Thickly forested mountains soared up to 10,000 feet. In winter, the valleys were snowbound for six months at a time. Every twist in the road presented a textbook opportunity for an ambush.

The Pakistanis claimed to have the situation in hand. Before leaving for Waziristan, the regional commander, General Safdar Hussain, boasted to me how easy it was to buy the loyalty of troublesome tribesmen. He named Baitullah Mehsud, then an obscure militant commander, who, according to Pakistan press reports, had received $840,000. Hussain flicked through graphic photographs of slain al Qaeda fighters, pausing to mock their weak religious conviction. 'Some weren't even circumcised,' he sneered. Our interview ended when Hussain left to play golf.

In truth, the Pakistanis were recycling the tactics employed by the British in their efforts to subdue Waziristan – cash, coercion, blunt force. They would enjoy a similar level of success.

Within a few years of my 2005 trip, Waziristan had spun completely out of control. Aspiring jihadis flooded in from across the globe to sign up with al Qaeda. In Miram Shah, where I had taken tea with Tariq Khan, the restaurants and internet cafés burbled with foreign accents. 'This bazaar is bustling with Chechens, Uzbeks, Tajiks, Russians, Bosnians, some from EU countries and of course our Arab brothers,' David Coleman Headley, an American-born jihadi, marvelled in an email in 2009. 'Any Waziri or Mehsud I spoke to seemed grateful to God for the privilege of being able to host the "Foreign Mujahideen".' Headley had participated in the terrorist assault on Mumbai a year earlier, in which 163 people were killed, and was plotting an attack on a Danish newspaper, *Jyllands-Posten*. Other foreigners planned mayhem in Madrid, London, Amsterdam and New York. Waziristan had become the cockpit of global jihad. 'It's like an Elvis fan coming to Graceland,' a British diplomat in Islamabad told me of the influx. 'It confirms you.'

The Americans, alarmed at Pakistan's loss of control, took matters into their own hands. The CIA dramatically ramped up its campaign of drone strikes in the tribal belt, hitting at least fifty-four targets in 2009, and then 118 in 2010. For President Barack Obama and Washington lawmakers, the drone strikes had an antiseptic appeal, decimating the top al Qaeda ranks while posing little danger to American life. But they also killed hundreds of innocent civilians – the exact numbers were hard to know – and fed into a groundswell of anti-American sentiment across Pakistan.

The chaos in Waziristan, and all along the Durand Line, posed a dilemma for Pakistan's military leaders, who were torn between their alliance with the United States, which was worth more than $1 billion in military aid every year, and their desire for continued influence in Afghanistan. Strategists worried that when American efforts to build democracy in Afghanistan foundered, as they inevitably would, Washington would pull out its troops and go home – offering India an chance to establish a toehold on Pakistan's northern border. At that moment, the thinking went, Pakistan would need the Taliban.

The military's solution to this conundrum was to play a complex double game. In places like Balochistan, at the western end of the Durand Line, the ISI covertly assisted fighters who directed their fire on Afghanistan – the 'good Taliban'. But in

Waziristan, the agency was at war with militants who threatened the Pakistani state – the 'bad Taliban'.

For this delicate policy to succeed, the ISI needed help from its most seasoned operators – men like Colonel Imam, who knew the Taliban better than anyone else.

※

Soon after my 2005 trip to Waziristan, Colonel Imam invited me to meet him at an orphanage halfway between Islamabad and Rawalpindi. It was a large complex, run by a Saudi government charity, that was home to hundreds of young boys. A puppet show was under way, and the audience of blue-uniformed orphans laughed riotously as they dipped their spoons into small tubs of ice cream. After the performance, a Saudi diplomat, resplendent in headdress and flowing robes, posed on stage for photos. I found Imam in the back row, fingering his prayer beads, occasionally smiling.

Imam's glory days were apparently over. He had been called home from Afghanistan in late 2001, after the attacks on America, when Pakistan publicly ditched its support for the Afghan Taliban and the Americans prepared to invade. Robert L. Grenier, the CIA station chief in Islamabad, bumped into Imam at Quetta Airport, as he travelled home. On a flight to Rawalpindi, the American spy peppered Imam with questions about the jihad and found him to be fine company; once the plane landed, Imam rushed off 'like a scalded cat' to join a group of airport workers, spread out in a field beside the runway, who were offering the evening prayer.

The orphanage was his retirement plan. The first of the boys to be admitted were terribly undernourished and suffering from hepatitis and scabies, he told me. 'Now look at them,' he told me, pointing to the smart young fellows licking ice cream. But questions were being asked about whether Imam had truly hung up his boots. In Afghanistan, the sudden resurgence of the Taliban stoked suspicions that the ISI was re-arming and training its old allies. There came reports that the agency was using retired officers to liaise with the militants. Invariably, Imam's name entered the picture.

The evidence was fragmentary. In Afghanistan's Uruzgan Province, unnamed Australian soldiers told a *Time* magazine reporter that Imam had supplied the Taliban with motorbikes and cash. Others said he was circulating in the tribal belt again, reviving his contacts. Grenier, who had just retired from the CIA, learned that Imam had been called back to duty at the ISI. 'As soon as I heard that, I knew what it meant,' he said.

Imam laughed heartily when I asked him about this. 'If anyone was helping the Taliban, it would be me,' he said. 'But I am not. Why should I? They don't need it. They are lovely people, friends of Pakistan and the world. If I'm doing anything for them, it's just praying.' At the same time, he made little secret of his sympathies. When he learned that I was just back from an embed with British troops in Afghanistan's Helmand Province, at one point coming under fire from Taliban insurgents, he launched into a lengthy reminiscence. 'A wonderful area!' he said. 'I used to spend a lot of time over there. Rough people – the naughtiest in Afghanistan! But good fighters.'

A similar enigma surrounded Imam's old boss at the ISI, Hamid Gul. A fellow true believer in jihad, Gul regularly went on Pakistani television to express his admiration for the Taliban and Osama bin Laden. Among Afghans and some Westerners, Gul became the embodiment of the Pakistani 'hidden hand'. American military reports from Afghanistan published by WikiLeaks in 2010 portrayed the septuagenarian retiree as the Scarlet Pimpernel of the frontier, travelling here and there in support of the Taliban, often in pursuit of fantastical plots – poisoning American soldiers in their canteens, and suchlike. But much of that information came from paid Afghan informants, who had a history of telling their interlocutors what they wanted to hear, and many Western officials doubted that Gul ever got much further than a TV studio.

Whatever the truth, Imam and Gul belonged to a generation of Pakistani military officers who nursed a great bitterness towards the United States over a perceived betrayal. In 1990, a year after the Soviets were routed from Afghanistan, Washington imposed heavy sanctions on Islamabad over its nuclear programme and cut off military ties. The about-turn deeply stung old jihadi warriors, like Imam and Gul, who had worked closely with the Americans, as Milt Bearden, an American spy who ran the CIA station in Islamabad in the late 1980s, told me. 'Every senior Pakistani officer I knew had a love–hate thing going with us,' he said. 'They wished they could love us. But they also knew it would not be long before we would screw them again.

Even inside the ISI, not everyone shared Imam's passion for jihad. 'He's a big bloody show-off,' Javed Ashraf Qazi, a former ISI director general and Imam's boss during the early 1990s. Qazi hailed from the pseudo-British wing that once dominated the Pakistani military – whisky-swilling types with twirled mustaches and a respectable golf handicap. He lived in a tastefully appointed hilltop villa that overlooked the Soan River, and had little time for the army's self-appointed jihadi cheerleaders. Just the mention of General Zia was enough to trigger an impassioned outburst.

'Muslim *ummah*, Muslim *ummah* – there is no fucking such thing as a Muslim *ummah*,' he said, using the term for the global community of Islam. 'They hate each other. They are at each other's throats. What Muslim ummah? Zia should be taken out of his grave, whatever is left of him, and hanged. He has ruined the psyche of this country.'

Even so, the old spymaster was no stranger to the benefits of jihadi warfare. Qazi's tenure at the ISI, between 1993 and 1995, coincided with the start of the agency's support to the Afghan Taliban, and the deployment of Islamist guerrillas to Kashmir. As I left his home, I noticed a rifle hanging in his hall. An Indian weapon, Qazi said – a war trophy from Kashmir, presented by an ISI-sponsored jihadist.

❧

Was Colonel Imam really back in action, running Pakistan's latest secret war? Or was he just a washed-up blowhard, running his mouth and reliving his glory days? It was hard to know. Whatever the truth, the situation was rapidly evolving. In January 2010, I drove out to Rawalpindi to pay him a visit, my last before his appearance in the video clip sent to me by the Taliban.

The city was tense. On the road to Imam's house, soldiers with hard faces manned newly erected checkposts. A week earlier, the Pakistani Taliban had attacked the Parade Lane mosque, near the General Headquarters, during Friday prayers. Forty people died in a hail of bullets and bombs, including several army generals, their sons and their grandsons. As Imam walked me to his gate, I noticed a sniper perched on the roof of his local mosque. Some neighbours had remonstrated with Imam, blaming him for the Parade Lane atrocity, he told me. 'They said "You trained these people, now look at what you have brought on us".'

At his home, we discussed the situation in Afghanistan, where President Obama had deployed thirty thousand troops in a surge that aimed to halt the Taliban insurgency. Imam felt vindicated. The foreigners would soon have to sue for peace with his old comrade, Mullah Omar. 'He doesn't want any more adventure,' Imam said. 'He has had enough of that.'

I asked about the Parade Lane mosque bombing. 'They are not true Taliban,' he replied, speaking slowly. 'Still, they have their tribal ways, as Pashtuns. They believe in revenge, and that is a most fierce thing.' He paused, much as an indulgent uncle might do when speaking of a mischievous child. 'Still, I like them.'

It was Friday, and the call to prayer rang out. Imam's eldest son, a burly facsimile of his father, bustled into the room clutching a Kalashnikov and handed a shotgun to his father. They prepared the weapons, clicking the chambers and slotting ammunition into place, to take them to prayers. 'I don't trust those army people to defend me; they are not that dedicated,' Imam said of the regular army. 'But when I am around, *Insha'Allah* we will be safe. I may be consumed. But I will not allow anyone to reach the mosque.'

It was an extraordinary sight – a legend of the ISI, and a true believer in jihad, arming for battle in a mosque in Rawalpindi. Maybe the neighbours were right, I ventured: maybe this *was* Imam's fault. 'No, it's not!' he retorted. 'It was the Americans. They told me to do it. They provided the money. And they gave me this.' He was pointing at the case containing the Berlin Wall fragment.

Imam stood up, walked to the mantelpiece and picked up an artefact I hadn't noticed previously. It was a smoker's pipe, presented to his father by an elderly Italian woman as he lay wounded in hospital at the end of World War II, in gratitude for his service against the Nazis. Imam gave the pipe a wistful look and, for an instant, his bravado seemed to melt away.

'You see,' he said in a low voice, 'in a way, we are all mercenaries.'

Two months later, a British filmmaker named Asad Qureshi and his team set out from Islamabad on the road to Waziristan. To anyone who asked, Qureshi said he was making a documentary about American drone strikes in the tribal belt. In fact, he was chasing a scoop – an interview with Pakistan's most wanted, the Taliban leader Hakimullah Mehsud.

Charismatic, flamboyant and ruthless in equal measure, Hakimullah rose to the top following the drone strike that killed his cousin, Baitullah Mehsud, in 2008. As a young commander, he hijacked a consignment of American Humvees as they were being transported through the Khyber Pass, then released a video that showed a laughing Hakimullah joyriding the vehicles around the tribal areas. Months earlier, he had pulled off his most audacious operation yet. Hakimullah helped an al Qaeda triple agent slip into a CIA base in Khost, southern Afghanistan, where the man blew himself up and killed seven American intelligence operatives – the CIA's greatest loss of life in a quarter of a century.

Qureshi, on assignment for Britain's Channel Four, knew his ambitious trip was fraught with danger. David Rohde, a *New York Times* reporter, had been kidnapped trying to interview a Taliban commander and spent seven harrowing months in captivity before making a miraculous escape. The Obama administration, incensed by the CIA deaths, had redoubled its efforts to take out Mehsud in a drone strike. 'The shackles were unleashed,' one American official said. Qureshi mitigated the risk by hiring a pair of retired Pakistani intelligence officials to escort him into the lion's den. Khalid Khawaja was an advocate for jihadist causes who campaigned for the release of Islamists held in military custody. He claimed to have met Hakimullah Mehsud on an earlier trip to Waziristan. The other person in the car was Khawaja's friend, Colonel Imam. Qureshi relaxed. Who better to ensure his safety in Waziristan than two retired

ISI officers of impeccable jihadist pedigree? 'The adventure of a lifetime,' he thought.

The group advanced slowly towards Waziristan, spending two nights at *madrassas* on the frontier, as they prepared the way ahead. But Qureshi soon grew nervous as it became apparent that Khawaja and Imam had their own agendas, hoping to use the meeting with Hakimullah to establish a back channel for peace talks between the Taliban and the Pakistani government. His apprehensions sharpened when a guide organised by Khawaja to take the group into Waziristan, failed to show up. Khawaja's son sent an ominous text message: 'They know you are coming. Permission for journalist not granted. Please return home.'

Colonel Imam concurred with that advice. Khawaja insisted that they press on.

The following morning, the journalist and his team entered Waziristan. As their hired Toyota Corolla bumped along a dirt road, a crack of gunfire rang out. Armed men wearing balaclavas halted the car, yanked out Khawaja and beat him. A local taxi driver, hired by the group hours earlier, tried to make a run for it, and was shot dead. Imam tried to reason with the gunmen 'I am your friend. Why are you doing this?' he asked. They struck him in the face with the butt of a rifle, bundled him into the boot of the car and drove off with four hostages: Khawaja, Qureshi, Qureshi's regular driver, who had left his car behind, and Imam, who could be heard saying his prayers in the boot.

The 'Asian Tigers', as the kidnappers styled themselves, were a hybrid of Taliban from Waziristan and sectarian thugs from Punjab. They softened up their hostages with cruelty, lashing Imam with a studded whip that scored his flesh, and subjecting him to a mock execution. Khawaja was in greater peril. Shortly after his previous trip to Waziristan, a CIA drone strike had narrowly missed Hakimullah Mehsud. Now the militants accused

Khawaja of planting a homing device on their leader's vehicle that led the Americans to him. They tortured Khawaja, forced him to record a video-taped confession, then shot him in the forehead. A note pinned to his bloodied corpse charged him with treachery. 'If someone tries to spy for America, this will be his fate,' it read.

Soon after that, I received via email the video that showed a bedraggled Imam pleading for help.

'Khalid Khawaja is no more,' the militants wrote. 'This is the last warning to set your minds. What would be the next?'

Their opening demand was $10 million in exchange for Qureshi, and 150 Taliban prisoners for Imam. The British and Pakistani governments refused to negotiate, so the desperate families sought out intermediaries to plead with the kidnappers. The leader of the Afghan Taliban, Mullah Omar, meanwhile, was rumoured to have sent a delegation to Waziristan to press for the release of his former mentor, Imam.

The hostages were transferred to a compound on the edge of Miram Shah, where I had met the political agent Tariq Hayat Khan. Their guards were psychopathic teenagers who alternated between cruelty and chumminess – one day thrashing them with rubber whips, the next fantasising about Indian actresses or inviting the captives to play Ludo. The teenagers boasted of disembowelling their slain enemies, and insisted that the graves of Taliban fighters smelled of perfume. One claimed to be a former detainee at Guantánamo Bay.

The summer dragged on, bringing the holy month of Ramadan, whose daily fasts were punishingly hard in temperatures that touched 40 degrees Celsius. The hostages were moved to a scorpion-infested hut with sealed windows that turned their cell into a baking oven. Qureshi and his driver suffered bouts of food poisoning and grew thin. Imam retreated into himself, sitting quietly in a corner, where he read the Qur'an and books in Arabic through a pair of old red glasses with scratched lenses. (Among the permitted books was a sectarian text that castigated Shias as heretics.)

The captives irritated each other. Qureshi, a germophobe who panicked at the sight of a mouse, berated his fellow captives if they failed to wash their hands. He yelled at Imam for snoring and for his habit of loudly swilling water in his mouth before swallowing. But there were also moments of solidarity. On good days, Imam regaled his fellow hostages with tales of his exploits on the frontier during the 1980s. He taught them a prayer for deliverance, attributed to the prophet Jonah while trapped in the belly of a whale.

There is no god, but You.
Limitless are You in Your glory!
Verily, I have done wrong.

The outside world soon forgot about the hostages. That summer, Faisal Shahzad, a Pakistan-born American citizen, tried and failed to detonate a car bomb in New York's Times Square. He had been trained by Hakimullah Mehsud in Waziristan. Later, biblical floods washed across Pakistan, inundating 40 per cent of arable land and displacing millions. A passenger jet slammed into the Margalla Hills, just behind my house, killing all 152 people on board. And in the sleepy town of Abbottabad, in the foothills of the Himalayas, the CIA sent operatives to investigate a secretive high-walled compound where tentative intelligence reports indicated that Osama bin Laden might be hiding.

Deliverance arrived for Qureshi and his driver in August. For weeks, tensions had been building between the Pashtun and Punjabi commanders of the 'Asian Tigers' over who would pocket any ransom they would receive. One evening during Ramadan, the Pashtun, convinced he was being double-crossed, invited the Punjabi to break their fast together. Once they were seated, the Pashtun drew his weapon and killed the Punjabi and his four bodyguards. Soon after that, Qureshi and his driver were released. They spent their last night at a compound in Miram Shah run by other militants – al Qaeda followers, they told him – before continuing to Islamabad the following morning. After six months of hellish captivity, Qureshi was free. But as he drove to Islamabad, a CIA drone fired missiles into the compound where he had slept, obliterating the men who had hosted him. It was unclear whether the two events were connected, but the strike offered a final reminder of the perilous world he had narrowly escaped.

Several years later, I met Qureshi on a bright spring afternoon at BAFTA (British Academy of Film and Television Arts) in London's Piccadilly. Sunlight flooded through the tall windows of a handsome room where film-industry types sipped lattes. The filmmaker slipped back to a darker place. He declined to say if a ransom had been paid. Despite the time that had elapsed, the scars of his trauma seemed fresh, and he brimmed with anger as he recalled his captors and their senseless brutality.

There was no cavalry, however, for Colonel Imam. The Taliban had raised the price of his release to an impossible level: freedom for 159 imprisoned militants, including men who had committed heinous crimes. Whatever the ISI was doing to free him, it wasn't working. Did the spy agency lack the funds or political will to spring him free? Did it see him as an anachronism – a redundant asset of an old espionage operation like his clunky Land Cruiser, not worth saving? Or maybe the truth was more prosaic: that the ISI was powerless to help him. Trapped in the impenetrable wilds of Waziristan, his legend had amounted to nothing.

Winter drew in. Snow fell gently on the thick forests and mud-walled farmhouses of the tribal region. Twisting highland roads glistened with ice. In the markets, burly men wrapped themselves in wool shawls. Imam was sixty-six. His story went dark for a brief period – we have no accounts – but going by the experience of other captives, he was likely held in a squalid corner of some remote farmhouse. His family scrambled to pool money to pay the ransom; hopes for a deal rose. Then, suddenly, Imam moved back into view.

One day in January, the Taliban drove Imam to a quiet spot on a road that curled through a tree-studded valley. Snow was heaped high on the ground. A dozen fighters stood over him. Unusually, they were led by their supreme leader, Hakimullah Mehsud, who by now preferred to avoid public appearances, fearing the deadly gaze of the CIA drones. Someone produced a camera and started to record.

Imam sat dejectedly on the ground, eyes downcast. Hakimullah turned to the camera, and delivered a speech in the firm, undulating manner of a court prosecutor. Imam and other men like him in the Pakistani military had betrayed the *mujahideen*, he charged. They took money from Osama bin Laden in the 1980s but reneged on their promise to turn Pakistan into a true Islamic state. After 2001, they committed the greatest sin of all: selling out to the Americans. Hakimullah's voice rose, swelling with righteous indigation. He jerked a thumb at Imam. 'He cheated the people,' he said. 'He cheated the people who gave him honour, respect and blood. He is a traitor.'

It was an unsophisticated speech that offered a searing repudiation of Pakistani policy. Once, men like Colonel Imam had been welcomed to the tribal belt by fighters sought to repel unwanted foreigners. But the new generation, indoctrinated and tutored by al Qaeda, had bigger goals. They dreamed of overthrowing the Pakistani state and establishing a global caliphate. Others were just brigands. Either way, they had turned on the men who created them.

Imam sat wordlessly: Frankenstein confronted by his monster. The Taliban fighters cocked their guns and dragged him to his feet. A masked man pointed a pistol at Imam's head and pulled the trigger. He crumpled to the ground, his wool cap tumbling from his head. The gunman fired another four rounds.

The proud man I had known, now lying prone, looked tragically diminished. The years of playing different sides off against each other had finally come to haunt him, his blustery confidence and professed love for jihad now draining into the cold mountain soil.

'*Allahu Akbar!*' shouted the fighters, raising their weapons in celebration.

Hakimullah, though, did not budge. The young Taliban leader stood there, wordless, staring intently at the bloodied body at his feet.

Chaudhry Aslam Khan

8

Minimum City

Faith in God and Glock

It was after midnight and Chaudhry Aslam was getting down to work. Markets had emptied, the last rickshaws skittered home along streets bathed in flickering amber light, and a dark, heavy heat smothered everything. The homogeneity of the tribal belt felt distant here in this brooding megalopolis that was home to migrants from every corner of Pakistan.

Aslam's office had the gleam of a mortuary and the furtive bustle of a mobster's den. Naked light bulbs hovered over a low room with white tiles and a thrumming air conditioner. The musty tang of cheap cigarettes hung in the air. Men streamed in and out, lean types who spoke in curt mumbles. Aslam slouched behind a long desk, pistol bulging under his shirt, firing off orders. 'Bring him now,' he would say, sparking up a Gold Leaf, the cigarette of the streets. 'Do it later.' Or: 'Let's wait and see.' Out in the yard, guards slinging Kalashnikovs loitered under a wall topped with sandbags and razor wire. Beyond that, a yard strewn with abandoned vehicles. And beyond that, Karachi: a slumbering expanse of shacks and mansions, ribboned with highways and bounded by the Arabian Sea, now twinkling in the night.

Aslam was Karachi's most famous cop, a legend in the notoriously messy business of imposing order in Pakistan's largest city, home to perhaps twenty million people, perched on the rim of the Arabian Sea. At first glance, he might have been a trader at Bohri Bazaar, the city's century-old warren of stalls: a bear of a man with a peppery beard and yellowed fingers, in a pressed white *shalwar kameez* that draped easily over his generous belly. A Rolex gleamed on his wrist. The rest bespoke a creature of the night: the pallid skin, puffy eyes and tobacco-stained growl that sounded like a chainsaw when he laughed. At rest, Aslam's demeanour was sleepy and watchful, but it took only the smallest spur – a nudge, a joke, a fresh nugget of information – to make him spring to attention, eyes gleaming.

My questions bored Aslam. His gaze drifted as he proffered pat answers about the tribulations of policing a city like Karachi, the ingenuity of its criminals, or that ultimately, success or failure in the hands of God. (A meandering rumination on the inescapability of divine will, I realised, was a favoured diversionary tactic of Pakistani officials.) During our interview he would break off, mid-sentence, to field a call or crack a gag with a subordinate. But when I asked how many crime lords he had collared, Aslam sat up straight.

'Dozens,' he said, reaching into a drawer.

He produced a folder filled with photocopies of checks issued in his name: government rewards, totalling several hundred thousand dollars, for the criminals he had captured or killed over his twenty-five-year career on the city police force. The list of names read like a Who's Who of Karachi's criminal royalty – swaggering gangster dons, jihadi masterminds, hit men who were household names. There was Shoaib 'Rummy Wala' Khan, the gambling kingpin who ran a network of backstreet *satta* gambling dens; Rehman 'Dakait', or dacoit, a Robin Hood-style slum bandit in Lyari, one of the city's oldest neighbourhoods; and Rafi 'Bubbly', a notorious cop killer. A few languished in the city's grotty prisons, but most were dead, having been dispatched by Aslam's Glock pistol.

In the local parlance, Aslam was an 'encounter specialist', a cop who shoots first and asks questions later – or, just as often, asks questions first and then shoots the suspect anyway. Hundreds of people died like that in Karachi every year, gunned down by the police in empty alleys or on the city's lonely fringes, where the shanty towns and belching factories bleed into the desert. Human rights groups called them extrajudicial killings, the mark of a rogue police force that had become a law unto itself. Cops like Aslam shrugged. They did what was necessary, they said. What other choice was there in Karachi, where the judges ran scared, the politicians were indistinguishable from the criminals, and the law, like everything else, was a commodity to be bought and sold?

Aslam stubbed out his cigarette and stood up. 'Let's go.'

We climbed into his jeep, a hulking four-wheel-drive with tinted windows and armoured doors that closed with a heavy thunk. It wheeled out onto a wide boulevard, trailed by a pick-up carrying half-shaven detectives in civilian clothes. Downtown Karachi blurred past: Frere Hall, an elegant colonial relic that peeked over a line of trees; the United States Consulate, huddled behind blast barriers (soon to be moved to a safer, more distant location); and the Pearl Continental, the swanky hotel where the city's most stylish burghers held their fashion shows and five-star weddings. Karachi's beating heart, though, lay in the distance, under a tangle of cranes at the city port. Day and night, trucks trundled from its gates, great steampunk beasts adorned with spiked hubcaps, skirts of jangling metal chains and rainbow paint jobs, an aesthetic that combined Mad Max and Mardi Gras. Some carried military supplies for Western armies in Afghanistan – occasionally the exposed backside of an American Humvee poked through a flapping tarpaulin – which made them a peachy target for Karachi's restive Taliban fraternity, and a growing preoccupation for Aslam.

He headed the Anti-Extremism Cell, an elite unit of the Crime Investigation Department that combined detective work with paramilitary action. The team worked at night, drawing on tips from paid snitches, to hunt their quarry in Karachi's most dangerous corners – smashing doors, tugging criminals from their beds and squealing out at speed before the neighbours could start a gunfight. Aslam was the public face of the squad. In the newspapers, he was photographed leaping from a jeep, Glock in hand, or sparking up a Gold Leaf after another successful raid. Reporters loved him for his blunt, staccato speaking manner; Aslam invited them to impromptu press conferences at his fortified compound, to view the spoils of a raid the previous night: tables filled with Kalashnikovs and rocket launchers, and hooded, newly captured criminals. Aslam was 'box office', as one admiring colleague put it – the uncompromising tough guy willing to wade into the city's dirtiest waters, Karachi's Dirty Harry.

Others – political parties, human rights groups, judges – were less enamoured of his methods, which they said represented everything that was rotten in the force. Years earlier, Aslam had faced murder charges over the death of a man he had mistaken for the kidnapper of a rich businessman. Aslam insisted it was an honest mistake – the dead man was also a kidnapper, he said, just the wrong one. As the case proceeded, Aslam was housed in Karachi Central Jail alongside crime lords he had arrested, but after sixteen months the prosecution collapsed and he was released. Witnesses said they had been threatened.

The convoy swooped into Defence, one of Karachi's wealthiest neighbourhoods – a expanse of spacious villas and lush gardens, built on reclaimed land that had been parcelled out to senior army officers. Defence was the top rung of Karachi's social ladder, a sign you had made it; Aslam lived in Phase

Eight, one of the more recent sections, in a mini-mansion with Roman colonnades and gilded furniture. It was considered impolite to ask how a police officer on a monthly salary of at most 1,000 dollars might afford such a home, even with the reward cheques for nabbing criminals. In any case, the question had become redundant when it came to Aslam's house, because there wasn't much left of it.

The entire façade had been sheared off, exposing rooms filled with dust and rubble. In place of a gate there was a gaping crater. A charred vehicle slumped against a wall. Days earlier, a Taliban militant rammed an explosives-laden vehicle into Aslam's gate, setting off a dull boom that rang across Defence. Eight people died in the blast, including a mother and her five-year-old son walking to school. Aslam's wife and children, taking breakfast at the rear of the house, escaped unhurt. He woke to see his bedroom walls juddering and a door tumbling from its hinges. He phoned Irfan Bahadur, his loyal lieutenant of fifteen years' standing – 'My house has been attacked!' – then picked up a gun and headed outside. A television crew found him in a cold rage. 'I am going to find the people who did this,' he said, pointing at the smouldering crater. 'And I'm going to bury them in here.'

Aslam led me through the house by torchlight. We clambered over the rubble and up a broken staircase to the salon, where a chandelier had been ripped from the ceiling. As I took photographs, Aslam lingered in the shadows, his grizzled face illuminated by cigarette glow. He'd been shot five times and was said to have survived eight assassination attempts – a record he joked about with reporters, telling them that one day his white *shalwar kameez* would become his funeral shroud. Yet he refused to wear a bulletproof vest, preferring to put his faith in God and his Glock. 'I've seen too much,' he told me, standing in the half-light. 'As a Muslim, I know that I will die one day.' What bothered him, in fact, was the attitude of his neighbours. A petition urging Aslam and his family to move out of Defence had collected 500 signatures; there was talk of a court action. 'Our police are not like the English ones,' Sami Mustafa, the headmaster of a private school across the street, told me. 'When you see our police, it means trouble is coming your way.'

That attitude angered Aslam. At any time, about one-third of Karachi's 30,000 police officers were on 'VIP duty' – sitting in police pick-ups that trailed the luxury vehicles of political or business bigwigs. Every rich person had a police 'uncle' to turn to in a moment of need – a son arrested with a bottle of liquor in his car, a business dispute that required resolution, or even a family member facing manslaughter for knocking over and killing a poor man with their Porsche. Then, the rich were all polite smiles and unctuous solicitation. 'Please, uncle, we're counting on you.' But once the problem had been solved, the police were quietly escorted out, via the back door, like tradesmen who had served their purpose.

Aslam flicked his cigarette, his tired eyes following the glowing stub as it tumbled into the blackness. It wasn't just the super-rich. Muscle was a prerequisite to survival in Karachi, and everyone used the police to their own ends: the politicians, the army generals, even the criminals. A good cop knew how to play the system – when to swim with the tide of fortune and when to change course; when to take money and when to give it; when to break the law and when to enforce it. The cops were the grease of the city, the element that lubricated its cogs and kept the whole messy, corrupt, infernal machine turning.

And that, more broadly, was the way of Karachi, a city that represented the soaring potential of Pakistan yet also had become a symbol of its heart-wrenching failures.

If Pakistani cities were caricatures, most would be easy to draw. Lahore is corpulent and languid, stretched out in a *shalwar kameez*, twirling its moustache over a greasy breakfast. Islamabad cuts a more clipped figure, holding court in a gilded drawing room, proffering Scotch and political whispers. Peshawar wears a turban or a burka, scuttling among the stalls of an ancient bazaar. But Karachi is harder to sketch. It has too many faces: the shiny-shod businessman, rushing to the gym; the hardscrabble labourer who sends his wages to a distant village; the slinky young socialite, kicking off her heels as she bends over a line of cocaine.

You can feel the difference as soon as you step off the plane. A breeze slings in off the Arabian Sea, tangy with a lick of salt. There is a palpable zing, a sense of scale and motion. People dress differently, jeans rather than *shalwar kameez*. The buildings are unlovely glass and concrete, no Mughal splendour here. Unruly buses lumber through seething streets filled with opportunity and peril. A newcomer to Karachi might make a million, or have his wallet stolen at gunpoint in traffic. 'Lahore may be the heart of Pakistan,' wrote the columnist Mosharraf Zaidi. 'But Karachi is its wallet, its BlackBerry, its cologne. Karachi is its mojo.'

A century ago, Karachi was a sleepy backwater, a Raj-era port of stout bungalows, art deco cinemas and neat streets that were hosed clean every morning. The city fathers were midshipmen of empire: Hindu gold merchants, British bureaucrats, Parsi shipping magnates and a handful of Jews. In 1919, Abraham Reuben was elected to the Karachi City Council; still today a Star of David adorns the Merewether Clock Tower, named after a British officer who fought in Abyssinia. Partition changed everything. Hindus fled by train to India; Jews boarded steamships for Palestine, where Israel would be founded a year later; and Muslims flooded in from northern India – United Provinces, Bihar and New Delhi, mostly – all drawn by Jinnah's splendid promises. Language changed. Previously people spoke Sindhi, Gujarati and English, but the newly arrived migrants from India, known as *mohajirs*, spoke Urdu. In the space of a few frantic months, the population doubled to one million people.

That was just the start. In the decades that followed, successive waves of migrants crashed on Karachi's shores: refugees from China's civil war in the 1940s; Bengalis seeking economic opportunity in the 1960s; Iranians after the fall of the Shah in 1979; Afghans throughout the 1980s. Mostly, though, they hailed from small-town Pakistan, hopeful newcomers laden with cheap suitcases and modest dreams. Still today they come at a rate of 350,000 a year, propelling Karachi into the ranks of global megacities such as Lagos, Rio de Janeiro, and, 500 miles down the coast, Mumbai.

The rich tide of migrants has imbued Karachi with a mercantile, cosmopolitan ethos. While other Pakistani cities are ethnically segregated – Punjabis in Lahore or Pashtuns in Peshawar – in Karachi, they all live side by side, albeit uneasily. (An estimated one-quarter of the population is Pashtun, making Karachi a more populous Pashtun city than even Peshawar or Kabul.) Class, creed and clan matter less; wealth is the principal determinant of status. 'Here, people don't worry where you are from,' an investment banker told me as he poured a generous Scotch, seated on a sofa before a huge window overlooking a tropical garden. He was in his forties, divorced, with a thick bush of silver hair, recently returned from stints in London and Hong Kong. Jazz drifted from the speakers; an abstract painting depicted a copulating couple. 'The attitude is different,' he continued. 'People don't care about your antecedents or your family. They want to get to know you with a view to making some money – or just having fun.'

Oddly enough, the hardest person to find in the city was the man who controlled it. Altaf Hussain's face was ubiquitous, staring down from billboards in the mould-stained *katchi abadi* slums and from a gilded frame in the mayor's air-conditioned office. He was tsar of the *mohajirs*, the migrants who came from India at partition, now estimated to account for 40 per cent of the city's population; his party, the Muttahida Qaumi Movement, or MQM, was an electoral juggernaut which had swept every election in the city for two decades. Yet Hussain himself was in England, where he had been living for over twenty-five years, running his party – and, by extension, Pakistan's largest city – from an anonymous office block in a rundown corner of north London. He kept up with events in Karachi via satellite TV and communicated with the party faithful from London via 'phone rallies' – giant street meetings that he addressed by telephone or videoconference. It was not unusual to turn a corner in Karachi and see tens of thousands of people, sitting raptly before a stage that was empty save for Hussain's portrait, listening to his disembodied voice as it boomed over the loudspeakers.

Hussain's political appeal was not immediately evident. A barrel-shaped man with a caterpillar moustache, he wore unfashionable, amber-tinted glasses and spoke in a squeaky, high-pitched voice. He addressed his followers in the hectoring style of a 1930s fascist – now smirking, now scowling, or jabbing a finger in the air – and was prone to absurdist turns. Mid-speech, Hussain could suddenly launch into song, a kind of mystical caterwauling, or burst into tears, sending salty globs down his glistening cheeks. Critics speculated that he was intoxicated, or mentally disturbed. Yet among his legions of supporters, Hussain was the object of feverish adulation. Some supporters had sworn a secret oath of allegiance to him; others, apparently believing he possessed mystical powers, implored him to bless their babies with a kiss. At Nine Zero, the MQM headquarters named after the last two digits of Hussain's phone number, party officials stayed up late into the night to await his instructions, in a room where the clocks were set to Greenwich Mean Time. They handed me hagiographical books about their great leader, or collections of essays that lauded his wisdom. In 2014 Hussain published a book, *The Philosophy of Love*, that featured his beatific portrait on the cover. But it was on the streets of Karachi that Hussain's grip was most evident. At a couple of hours' notice, he could bring the entire city to a grinding halt by calling a *hartal*, or general strike. Shopkeepers would whip down their shutters and office workers would scurry to their cars and rush home with anxious haste.

Electoral politics only partly explained this formidable show of strength. The MQM was a beacon of middle-class ambition – a party filled with articulate, well-educated officials, women as well as men, who espoused progressive ideas and presented themselves as an antidote to the tired political dynasties like the Bhuttos and Sharifs, or the conservative mullahs of the religious parties. But the true source of Hussain's power was old-fashioned muscle. From his perch in London, he controlled a network of armed gangs that enforced his will across the city with ruthless acts of violence. The gangs extorted businesses, intimidated voters and carried out gun attacks on police officers, journalists and members of rival political parties, mostly ethnic Pashtuns who were themselves armed. In 2009, American diplomats estimated the MQM had 10,000 men under arms, with another 25,000 in reserve. 'A frightening military organization cohabiting within a political party,' judged the Human Rights Commission of Pakistan.

But Hussain, oddly unbothered by the British authorities, seemed untouchable. Nine Zero, which was located inside a maze of streets patrolled by armed gunmen, had the air of a neighbourhood militia base. At a nearby traffic junction, a monument depicted a giant fist smashing through a granite plinth. DISTANCE DOES NOT MATTER, read the inscription.

Karachi's volatile politics contributed to its unenviable international reputation. The American journalist Daniel Pearl died here in 2002, executed in a garden shed by the 9/11 mastermind Khalid Sheikh Muhammad; in the years that followed, the fugitive leader of the Afghan Taliban, Mullah Omar, was often reported (probably erroneously) to be hiding in its slums. India's most notorious gangster, Dawood Ibrahim, lived quietly under ISI protection in a mansion behind the popular Abdullah Shah Ghazi Sufi shrine. Western diplomats travelled in bulletproof jeeps, as they would in Kabul or Baghdad.

Yet for many Pakistanis, Karachi was a city of exciting possibilities.

One day I went for lunch with Shakir Husain, a thirty-something software entrepreneur. We met at a Korean restaurant near his office – a loud, intimate place where other young professionals, ties tugged open, slurped noodles and swigged bottles of Murree beer. At the table beside us, women were giggling and taking selfies. When the call to prayer rang out, nobody budged.

The son of a senior bureaucrat, Husain had been educated in California, worked a few years in the Persian Gulf ('Can't stand the Arabs,' he said), and then returned to Pakistan to set up a software company. 'Love of the motherland, and all that shit,' he said, dragging on another cigarette. After lunch, we went over to his office. From the outside, it didn't look like much: a broken pavement, a filthy stairwell and a modest sign. Inside was a bright, open-plan office filled with twenty-something website designers and programmers hunched over chrome monitors. The company had a global roster of clients, from American police departments to Pakistani mobile-phone companies. The 'kids', as Husain called his 150 employees, made as much as $1,000 a month – about the same as a one-star general in the Pakistani army. Some went on to work for Google or Microsoft.

'The internet is a great leveller,' he told me. 'In essence, we could be anywhere.'

That was almost correct. An old man pushing a trolley laden with steaming cups of tea – the *chai-wallah* – weaved between desks. At first, Husain tried to emulate Silicon Valley start-up culture by providing a pinball machine, free soda and other perks. But his employees took home the soda by the crate and their pinball game improved faster than their coding. So, the *chai-wallah* was hired back and Shakir offered more practical perks, such as night classes.

One beneficiary was Maryam, a petite twenty-five-year-old in a bright orange headscarf. Conservative relatives had initially disapproved of her job designing web pages. 'In my social circle, girls get married at eighteen,' she explained. 'They cook. They clean. They don't do this kind of stuff.' But her parents supported her now that she had carved out an independent life of sorts, with gym memberships and shopping on her own dime. Still, some things were unavoidable. Her parents had arranged a match with a Pakistani software engineer in England, and they were due to get married. 'Not exactly my choice,' Maryam said awkwardly, then straightened up. 'But practically speaking, it's a good future.'

Aptly, the firm was called Creative Chaos. A pair of generators in the basement kicked into action during the frequent electricity outages. Shakir funded home internet connections for his employees so they could keep working during the sudden calamities that occasionally struck the city, such as an explosion of political violence, or a torrential downpour, or a *hartal* imposed by the MQM. Shakir himself contended with extortion demands from gangsters. Foreign clients preferred to meet him in Dubai. His psychiatrist wife, who had been raised in California, worried about their safety. Yet he was immensely proud of his ability to keep his business rolling no matter what Karachi threw at it.

I heard a lot of that. Resilience was an article of faith for Karachiites, an integral part of their psychological makeup. The city was plagued by shootings, bombings, strikes and floods. But as soon they had passed, the city would snap back into shape, often in a matter of hours. Shops opened, kids returned to school, society queens continued on their way to their beauty salons and fashion shows. 'Our city takes no shit,' remarked one resident after a major Taliban attack. But was that something to be proud of? Karachiites seemed to be making a virtue of necessity, glossing over the realities of their chaotic, cruel city where it seemed that nobody was in charge, not even the police.

In a city of migrants, Chaudhry Aslam had a typical story. His parents arrived in the 1960s, from Abbottabad in the northwest, and settled in a duplex house in Civil Lines, a middle-class neighbourhood near the city train station. His father was a lawyer – not one of the showboating barristers of the Karachi High Court, with their Anglicised vowels and imperious manners, but one of the more modest types in worn, faded black suits who toiled at a nearby warren of offices. Aslam's father was also a political animal, and in 1985 he supported Hussain Haroon, the scion of an old Karachi family, helping him get elected to the Sindh Provincial Assembly. In return, Haroon arranged a job for the lawyer's wayward son.

By his own admission, the teenage Aslam was a ne'er-do-well who enjoyed street fighting more than schooling. One afternoon, he was knocking a ball about with friends when a car pulled up. Haroon, sitting inside, beckoned Aslam and handed him a piece of paper – an offer to enrol at the nearest police station.

Aslam became a cop in 1986, a year of jolting change in Karachi. One day a speeding bus driven by a Pashtun knocked over and killed a female student named Bushra Zaidi, who happened to be a *mohajir*. The accident triggered days of rioting between mohajirs and Pashtuns in which over forty people were killed. A fuse had been lit. The mohajirs, who thrived in the early decades of Pakistan, felt marginalised by the wave of incoming migrants. Now they rallied behind a charismatic young leader, a student pharmacist named Altaf Hussain, who urged them to arm themselves with newly available guns, most of which had fallen off the CIA's secret pipeline that smuggled arms to the *mujahideen* in Afghanistan. 'Sell your TVs and buy a Kalashnikov!' Hussain famously cried at one rally.

Karachi descended into anarchy. Through the 1980s and 1990s, the MQM battled for supremacy with other ethnic and political factions – at first Sindhis, then Pashtuns, and finally the government. Parts of the city became battlegrounds that were compared to war-torn Beirut. Schools were frequently forced to shut down. Atrocities were common, on all sides.

The MQM dispatched one of its leading hit-men to kill the wife of a police superintendent, with orders to avoid using a gun. 'Not an easy kill,' they said. But once he broke into the officer's home, the assassin, Arshad was confronted with a pregnant woman. 'I went in,' he recalled. 'I saw she was pregnant and stabbed her with a knife in her belly. "For the name of God don't kill me," she said. The details were so horrible. I killed her with a knife, then took off her head and put it on top of the refrigerator. I made it horrible so that when it was reported in the papers MQM's enemies would be afraid.'

'Well, it worked,' he told a researcher years later. 'Now she comes in my dreams, I can't get rid of her.'

In 1995, three years into its war of attrition with the MQM, the Islamabad government dispatched a leathery police veteran named Shoaib Suddle to get Karachi under control. Suddle arrived to find a force under siege. Officers huddled inside fortified police stations that resembled army bases, and refused to wear their uniforms for fear of being shot on the way to work. Three hundred people had died violently in the previous month. Suddle quickly concluded that he needed to dispense with the usual tools of law enforcement, such as arrest and trial, in favour of a more robust, hard-shooting approach. He began searching for officers to carry out that vision.

At the time, Chaudhry Aslam was in charge of a besieged police station in the MQM stronghold of Gulbahar. Party gunmen perched in apartment blocks overlooking the police station and occupied an empty school that served as a weapons depot and torture centre. 'They cut people's genitals, drilled their eyes and suspended them from poles,' Suddle told me. One night, Aslam, wearing civilian clothes, led a small team of officers in a commando-style raid on the MQM lair. After an all-night gunfight, they emerged victorious and seized four truckloads of weapons. A police legend was born.

By the time I met Aslam, fifteen years later, following the Taliban attack on his home, his hard-charging, law-breaking approach to law enforcement was not universally appreciated. Instead of fighting the gangs of Karachi, critics claimed, the police had become one of them. Officers who racked up 'encounters' were promoted, not punished. Corruption was rife. The cops were taking a cut from the brothels on Napier Road; from the backstreet gambling dens where gamblers played *mang patta,* a local version of craps; and even from the gun-toting thugs who snatched purses and mobile phones while officers at nearby stations did nothing.

Corruption was even endemic *inside* the police force. To get a decent posting, an officer had to bribe his superiors, often to the tune of thousands of dollars. Then he used low-level officers, known as 'beaters', to collect his money from smugglers or pimps. A percentage was reserved for officers at the top. It was classic Karachi: the poor robbed the rich, the rich robbed the government, and the cops – well, they had to get their cut, too.

Aslam acknowledged that he operated in a morally complex world where the line between criminal and cop could be hopelessly blurred. But compromise was the only way to survive.

Aslam took a cut from the bookies but not from the pimps; he offered his services as a mediator between warring businessmen; and he sold prison privileges to the better-off criminals – a nicer cell, a good meal, or a promise to water down the charges, in return for cash. One colleague who saw his ledger of receipts told me it amounted to thousands of dollars a day. Aslam argued this was not corruption, per se – it was the cost of doing his job. Although he was famed for his ability with a Glock, the secret of his success was in fact his citywide network of informants – street children, traders, prostitutes, criminals. It cost up to $10,000 to nab a major criminal. Where else would he get the money for that?

He had other outgoings. During the Eid holiday, Aslam sent bundles of cash to the wives of slain officers. He gave a slice of the profits to the police leadership. And he kept a cut for himself, which helped explain the mansion in Defence and his investments in Dubai. To Aslam, this quasi-feudal system was a matter of loyalty. 'He gives, and the men give it back tenfold,' one officer told me.

And he insisted that it was possible to fight for the law while breaking it. Somehow, he was sure, all the bloodshed and mayhem would lead to a safer city, even a better Pakistan. Besides, what choice was there? 'Who are we?' he rhetorically asked one reporter in a private conversation. 'We are killers. But who do we kill for? The State. We just do our job. On our own, we are nothing.'

Karachi's wealthier residents enjoyed little more than to wax lyrical about the glorious sixties and seventies – a halcyon era of nightclubs, racecourses and casinos, when Duke Ellington and Dizzy Gillespie played the cabarets, the Beatles were swamped by screaming schoolgirls and Che Guevara was photographed on the beach. Long-haired Western hippies passed through, on the trail between Iran and India, arriving in Volkswagen buses emblazoned with slogans about love and peace. Some paused to smoke dope with the Sufi fakirs at the Abdullah Shah Ghazi shrine. The city boasted hundreds of cinemas, including one, the Bambino, run by the family of a brash young playboy named Asif Ali Zardari. Guns were rare: the greatest trouble came from gangs of macho young men who roamed the streets armed with knuckledusters.

That era drew to a close after 1977, with the ban on alcohol and the start of General Zia's Islamising drive, which injected Karachi's middle classes with a cloying piety. Among the witnesses to this change was a twenty-year-old American college student named Barack Obama, who visited the city with a college friend in 1981. In any case, fond memories of Karachi's glamorous past are tinted in rose: even in its heyday, the good life was accessible only to a minority of Pakistanis, and it ignored the ethnic and social tensions that would explode with such destructive force decades later. Like resilience, nostalgia was a psychological crutch for Karachiites struggling with the present.

Even so, Karachi remains a cosmopolitan ideal for many Pakistanis. Professionals and women thrive here in a manner that is difficult, or impossible, in other parts of the country. Gay couples discreetly cohabit. A working woman can rent an apartment on her own without, as happens in other cities, being accused of prostitution by a suspicious landlord. At weddings, women wear belly-baring saris, a form of dress shunned in other parts of Pakistan for its associations with the culture of Hindu-dominated India.

My regular digs in Karachi were at Bhopal House, a ram-shackle, century-old mansion in Clifton, a patrician neigh-bourhood by the sea. The house was a high-class wreck, with deserted rooms and ancient plumbing and a large, weed-infested garden. I stayed in a room with an ancient air-conditioning unit that thrummed so hard that it gave the pleasant sensation of sleeping in the bowels of a rumbling ocean liner. My host was Faiza Sultan Khan, a young editor descended from subcontin-ental royalty.

The house once belonged to Faiza's grandmother, Princess Abida Sultaan, one of the most eccentric figures of post-independence Pakistan. She was born in Bhopal, a gigantic, Muslim-majority princely state in the centre of British India, said to have one of the world's largest palaces. The people of Bhopal boasted an unusual distinction: for a century they had been ruled by a succession of powerful matriarchs known as the Begums of Bhopal. Abida, who was recognised as the heiress apparent in 1928, was an iconoclast, with passions that included hunting tigers, flying aeroplanes and repairing car engines. One photo, taken in her thirties, shows her with cropped hair and riding boots, standing over an engine block.

Three years after Bhopal was forced to accede to India in 1947, Princess Abida, aged thirty-seven, abandoned her hus-band and flew to Karachi with their infant son, Shehryar – Faiza's father. She also carried a portion of the crown jewels of Bhopal. To help get Pakistan on its feet, she offered the new state her Karachi residence for its foreign ministry – Bhopal House. Later she became Pakistan's ambassador to Brazil, and Shehryar become ambassador to the United Kingdom and India.

But after the capital was shifted to Islamabad in 1960, the government refused to relinquish possession of Bhopal House, marking the start of a knotty legal dispute that was still dragging on, decades later, when I got there. The state had already staked its claim to half the property by erecting an ugly office block that served as the local headquarters of the Intelligence Bureau, a civilian intelligence agency controlled by the interior ministry. Faiza's family had clung to the rest – the crumbling mansion and its abandoned garden – and was disinclined to invest any further until the dispute had been resolved. There was little sign of that.

Faiza downplayed her royal roots, the Indian cousins who lived in palaces and her storied grandmother (who, by several accounts, could be a demanding relative). 'Darling,' she said in an accent shaped by private schooling in England, 'I find people who discuss their family history utterly odious.' Instead she wrote pieces of acerbic social observation for Pakistani and Indian publications, mulled over a novel on the sexual mores of upper-class Pakistanis and ran a short-story competition that attracted a wide range of entries, including a fascinating piece of erotic pulp fiction in Urdu that was set on a Karachi bus.

Much of the time, Faiza was in her room, smoking and reading; occasionally she floated through the baking corridors in her pyjamas. But a couple of nights a week, the old mansion sprang to life for impromptu gatherings that opened my eyes to a different aspect of Karachi. The guests were writers, architects, singers and professional dilettantes, and they would sit on her balcony for hours, drinking warm beer and sickly vodka concoctions. The crowd typically stayed late, smoking and gossiping and conducting long arguments on subjects from weighty politics to arcane pop trivia. Under orders from Faiza, nobody took mobile-phone photos of the Intelligence Bureau building over the wall. We tried not to think about the jihadi sympathisers said by human rights groups to have been tortured inside.

The balcony scene was a bubble of privilege, of course: part of a world of coffee shops with tasteful furniture and stone gardens, art galleries and expensive French restaurants where the ladies who lunched drank freely, sometimes even from an open bar. But the other city – Karachi Noir, with its Dirty Harry cops and strutting gangsters and simmering ethnic tensions – was never far away. Growing up in the 1990s, wealthy friends told me, their posh schools would close sometimes every week as gun battles rocked the city. Uncles or cousins were kidnapped for ransom by criminals and spirited off to the tribal belt. Now the enemy was dysfunction. Giant diesel-powered generators squatted in their gardens, to combat power shortages, and armed guards stood at their gates. Some showed me their extensive private gun collections. But it was impossible, even for the rich, to completely isolate oneself from Karachi, which was the tension, and occasionally the thrill, of the city.

Perhaps that explained the pervasive sense of decay and rot. Unlike stately Lahore or modern Islamabad, Karachi resembled the set of a dystopian thriller. In the city centre, the stately Raj-era buildings cowered behind tangles of power lines and garish neon signs. Rubbish was piled outside elegant mansions in upmarket Clifton. In the summer, when power cuts were frequent, slum dwellers slept on the rooftops, and clouds of flies swarmed around people as they walked to work. Every day, 400 million gallons of untreated sewage poured from the city into the Arabian Sea. Karachi's conservationists were a suicidal lot. 'Loving Karachi is like loving an unfaithful mistress who has not hesitated to discard her earlier charms and replace them with the tear-streaked makeup of an unhappy harlot,' noted one.

And yet, Karachi has a unique vibrancy and urban sensibility that many residents wanted to celebrate. One Sunday morning, I went to visit Hameed Haroon, who was in his sixties, the chief executive of *Dawn* newspaper. The Haroons were among the oldest families in Karachi, and Hameed lived in half of a rambling mansion located on a road named after his grandfather. (His brother, Hussain, the politician who boosted Chaudhry Aslam into the police and was later Pakistan's ambassador to the United Nations, lived in the other half of the building.) Hameed had transformed his abode into a temple to art, its rooms filled with sculptures, paintings and silks by Pakistan's most celebrated artists. When I arrived, the door was opened by Hameed's friend George, a chirpy Greek art dealer. After some conversation about how to make a decent *foie gras*, Haroon announced we were leaving for Gadani, a coastal village thirty miles to the north.

Known for its ship-breaking yard, Gadani had once been home to Sadequain, a towering figure of Pakistani art and an eccentric recluse. His most famous paintings adorned Haroon's house, and Haroon had published a giant book about Sadequain, a 700-page tome that weighed twelve kilos. Sadequain's work was risqué by the standards of orthodox Islam, with naked figures often disguised as calligraphy. 'You see this breast?' Hameed said, pointing to a squiggle. 'If a mullah came in, Sadequain could transform it into a "noon",' a reference to the letter N in Urdu. His themes varied: the crucifixion of Christ, the death of Martin Luther King, sex, the mysteries of Islam, often expressed through sweeping strokes. Unconcerned with money, he donated paintings to friends and admirers, and the story goes that he once painted a large mural on the wall of a travel agency in exchange for a bottle of whisky.

Hameed's summer house at Gadani, overlooking the sea, was still under construction – a grand edifice with colonnades, steam rooms and a swimming pool. Fibreglass lions, replicas of the ones in London's Trafalgar Square, stood guard on the lawn. In the distance, I could see the cranes, jibs and rusting hulks of the ship-breaking yards. Sadequain lived here, in a modest house between the desert and the sea, fascinated and inspired by cactuses and gnarled brambles, which became prominent motifs in his work. I could see why he might have liked Gadani, although it also must have been a lonely existence. By the time he died, in 1987, his painting strokes had become harder and more dramatic: one of his last works depicts an exterminating angel.

❈

Those who tried to make Karachi better often found themselves frustrated. Ardeshir Cowasjee sat in a cane chair in his study, a small Jack Russell terrier resting in his lap, as he stirred his pre-lunch vodka-and-tonic. By way of small talk, I asked how things were going. 'Down,' he said with a sad clown face, pointing a finger to the floor, 'because otherwise it would be like this.' Cowasjee slowly flipped his middle finger up until it was pointing directly at me. His face cracked into an impish grin.

Even at eighty-one, Cowasjee revelled in his role as the city's provocateur-in-chief. A small man with a snowy goatee, he had devoted his life to the art of laser-guided offence. He lived in an elegant mansion in Bath Island, near the sea; kept cats, cockatoos and Jack Russell terriers; and liked to drive through the city in his silver open-top Mercedes, resplendent in a tailored suit, silk handkerchief and hat. Accounts of his social japes were legion in Karachi high society. He once attended a board meeting of the city electricity company dressed in Bermuda shorts; at a dinner, he provoked French diplomats with lewd comments about their president's wife. The pious were favoured targets. As he led the way to the lunch table in his home, he gestured towards a cluster of nude sculptures, saying that he made a point of showing them to any Muslim cleric who came visiting. 'They do like this,' he said, half-shading his eyes with one hand, again in cheeky schoolboy mode. 'Great fun.'

The Cowasjee family once had a fortune in steamships and stevedoring. But their business, the East and West Steamship Company, was nationalised in the 1970s by Prime Minister Zulfikar Ali Bhutto, and with it the family's six ships. The loss still rankled with. 'One of ours,' he said wist-fully, gesturing to a model ship in a glass case. 'Bhutto was an evil man.'

But for all his affected curmudgeonliness and comic-book venom, Cowasjee was a man of principle and purpose, and his outsider status came as much from his bravery as from his Zoroastrian faith. His weekly column in *Dawn*, in which he railed tirelessly against corruption, bigotry and the swelling forces of radicalisation, had become a lodestar for Pakistani progressives. For Cowasjee, it was a way of coming to terms with a country that had betrayed its promises to him.

He pulled a photograph from his pocket. Taken in the 1940s, it showed a fresh-faced young man – Cowasjee – at the wheel of a jalopy with Jinnah in the back seat. A fervent supporter of the *Quaid* in his youth, he now used his weekly column to defend Jinnah's legacy. When I suggested that Jinnah had failed to articulate a clear vision for Pakistan, Cowasjee banged his fork on the table. 'You don't know much, do you?' He summoned a servant to bring a tome of Jinnah's speeches. 'They re-write history to suit themselves, the stupid bastards,' he said of his countrymen, flipping through the pages. 'But you can't blame Jinnah. Someone else fucked it up.'

A police van idled outside his front gate. Cowasjee had enjoyed VIP protection for years, but he viewed cops like Chaudhry Aslam as part of a bigger problem he was determined to solve. For years, Karachi had been devoured by the 'land mafia', a broad class of politicians, army generals, policemen and mafioso business types who enriched themselves through rampant illegal development of public land. Parks, playgrounds, beach promenades, even the mangroves along the Arabian Sea – no corner was safe from their insatiable appetites. To oppose them was a risky business. Campaigners faced threats and beatings; a handful had been murdered. Cowasjee railed against their depredations in his columns and he financed court actions that stalled new construction.

After lunch, we went for a drive, twisting through the chaotic traffic of Shahrah-e-Faisal, a busy highway, before turning into a compact, upscale neighbourhood named Kidney Hill. Cowasjee's four-wheel-drive vehicle halted outside a small park, about fifty acres of wild grass hemmed in on two sides by capacious villas. It was a breezy afternoon, and palm trees rustled gently in the wind, the city stretching out before us – a vast panorama of grey apartment blocks, mobile-phone towers and tangled highways. We took a stroll. Kidney Hill was one of Karachi's last green lungs, but it was being eaten up by illegal development. Political parties nibbled off plots to sell or to build houses for their supporters, he said; one-third of the land had disappeared. The mullahs were also in on the act. Inside the park gates, we passed a clutch of worshippers prostrated in prayer outside a ramshackle, recently constructed mosque. 'It's like children nibbling on a biscuit,' grumbled Cowasjee. 'They won't stop until it's all gone.'

We headed back towards his car, passing a newly constructed extension at the side of a large mansion, which jutted into the park. It belonged to the chairman of the Pakistani Senate, Cowasjee said, without emotion. 'If there was no Central Park, there'd be no New York,' he said. 'But try telling these people.' He shuffled towards his vehicle. 'Philistines.'

✵

The suicide bomb attack that destroyed Chaudhry Aslam's suburban villa in early 2011 was not only a worrisome milestone for a cop who was burning through his proverbial nine lives – it announced that a new gang was vying for control of Karachi.

The Pakistani Taliban had been arriving quietly since about 2008, hiding amid a flood of Pashtun civilians fleeing the military's anti-Taliban operations in Swat, Waziristan, and other corners of the tribal belt. After a spate of bank robberies, police investigators reviewing surveillance footage noticed that the robbers often wore *shalwar* trousers that were hitched above the ankle, and handled their guns with practised ease. Then the militants became more brazen, kidnapping businessmen for ransom, extorting money from Pashtun haulage companies, and – in a sure sign they had arrived – becoming players in the property rackets. In Sohrab Goth, a labyrinthine Pashtun shanty town on the outskirts of Karachi, Taliban clerics established informal *sharia* courts to settle disputes; the Awami National Party, a secular party that had traditionally represented Pashtuns in Karachi, was drummed out of town.

I became aware of how serious the situation had become when I tried, and failed, to visit a famous Sufi shrine at Manghopir, on the northern edge of Karachi. There, a green pool surrounding the tomb of a saint is filled with luxuriating crocodiles who feast on sweets and morsels of meat offered by devotees who believe the leathery reptiles possess sacred powers. The shrine's guardians are the Sheedi, descendants of African slaves who were transported to South Asia by Arabs, Persians and other invaders over many centuries. Every year, the Sheedi hosted a festival at the shrine, where pilgrims danced before the crocodiles, showering them with rose petals, anointing them with saffron and feeding them sacrificial goats.

But when I tried to visit Manghopir months after the attack on Chaudhry Aslam, I was told it was impossible. Fixers, policemen, even the local MQM parliamentarian, advised against it. 'It's too dangerous,' the parliamentarian told me when we met at Nine Zero. The Taliban had seized control of the area, taking up positions on a nearby hilltop. The local police were cowering in their station. The famous shrine had closed, leaving the crocodiles in the care of charity workers who sneaked in to feed them. Even so, some crocodiles died.

When the security forces – army-led paramilitaries from the Sindh Rangers, working with the intelligence agencies – took action they turned to Aslam as their partner. Acting on information provided by the ISI, his team raided dozens of Taliban hideouts, seizing arms caches and making hundreds of arrests. The militants hit back hard. In 2013, 138 policemen were killed in the line of duty in Karachi, the highest toll ever. Taliban commanders regularly phoned Aslam directly with insults and death threats. He repaid them in kind. 'Get lost, sisterfucker,' he told Ehsanullah Ehsan, the main spokesman for the Pakistani Taliban.

After the attack on his home in Defence, Aslam sold the property and moved his family to the Naval Housing Colony, a modest yet better protected military housing development. He started to vary his routes to work, as a security precaution. The authorities lauded Aslam's actions. President Asif Ali Zardari decorated him with the *Tamgha-i-Imtiaz*, one of Pakistan's highest civilian awards, and gave him a bulletproof jeep. But friends worried Aslam had gone too far. 'He was under immense stress,' a senior police officer told me. 'It looked like the situation had gone beyond his control.'

On the night of 8 January, 2014, Aslam led a raid on a Taliban lair in Manghopir, a mile from the crocodile shrine. Three militants died in the operation, he told a press conference early the following morning, supposedly after succumbing to their injuries on the way to hospital. His old deputy, Irfan Bahadur, watching on television, phoned Aslam. 'Aslam *yaar*,' he said, 'this is enough. Please distance yourself from the press. Get yourself posted to another job.'

Later that day, after taking a rest, Aslam left his home in the Naval Housing Colony. His armoured jeep was in the garage, being serviced, so he travelled in an unprotected vehicle. As it turned onto the Lyari Expressway, a major highway that sweeps across Karachi, the driver of a waiting pick-up truck gunned his engine. Two hundred kilos of explosives, packed in blue barrels, were strapped into the vehicle. It hurtled towards Aslam.

The blast tossed Aslam's jeep across the road like a toy, where it burst into flames. When an emergency rescue team reached the scene, they found a pile of charred, twisted metal. Three people had been killed: two police officers and Aslam.

Hours later, the Taliban spokesman, Ehsanullah Ehsan, claimed responsibility for the hit – payback, he said, for the militants who had been tortured and executed in detention under Aslam. 'He was on the top of our list,' said Ehsan.

The godfathers of Karachi – gangster politicians, police chiefs, army generals and former president Asif Ali Zardari – attended Aslam's funeral, standing together to pay their respects to a man who, for his many faults, helped bind their chaotic city together. I followed the news from London, watching on television. As Aslam's shattered body was lifted into an ambulance, I noticed that he was dressed in his usual white tunic, now drenched in blood. It made me think of the remark Aslam made on our first meeting. He had fulfilled his own prophecy – his *shalwar kameez* had become his shroud.

Portrait of Nawab Akbar Khan Bugti

9

War of the Flea

Balochistan's Fifth Rebellion

The Pakistan International Airlines turboprop aeroplane banked hard and nosed down as it crossed the deserts of western Pakistan on a bright winter morning in 2011, the roar of its engine filling the cramped cabin. Quetta came into view, a low concrete sprawl under a line of serrated hills. The plane bumped along the runway and jolted to a halt; emerging from the cabin, I shielded my eyes from the harsh sunlight, the thin air scratching my throat. In the battered airport terminal, plainclothes intelligence men loitered by the luggage carousel, scanning every face. Foreigners got extra scrutiny. I grabbed my bag and made a break for the exit, striding purposefully through the doors. I almost made it. In the car park, a scowling man in an ill-fitting suit marched up to my driver. 'Who is this? What is he doing here? Where is he staying?' he demanded, yanking a thumb at me. I gave the name of a hotel that the spook scribbled into his notebook. We drove off, into central Quetta, where I checked into a different hotel.

Quetta was the hardest place to work in Pakistan, a city of shadows and secrets that yielded easily to nobody. Militants skulked in its streets, plotting their next atrocity. Drug kingpins lorded it up in glitzy mansions while heroin addicts squatted in a storm drain that snaked through the city centre. A heavy military presence overlaid everything. Foreigners were discouraged from visiting Quetta, and those who made it were generally presumed to be spies.

The air of intrigue was a product of Quetta's place as the capital of Balochistan, an elephantine province wedged between Pakistan's long and porous borders with Afghanistan and Iran. Balochistan covers 44 per cent of Pakistan's landmass but accounts for just 6 per cent of its people, and its abundance of wide-open space makes it a magnet for mischief-makers of every stripe. Armed convoys burn through its deserts by night, smuggling Afghan heroin to Iran and then the West. Iranian dissidents shelter inside its western border, plotting against the regime in Tehran. On the coast, skiffs loaded with contraband slip onto remote beaches under moonlight. Inland, scruffy little towns boast incongruously long runways built by sheikhs from Saudi Arabia, Qatar and the United Arab Emirates. The Gulf royals fly in every winter for *shikar*, the winter hunt, on cargo planes loaded with jeeps, luxury tents and hunting falcons. Their prey is the houbara bustard, a ducky little bird that the Arabs believe aids their lovemaking. In 2004 the CIA repurposed one of these airstrips as a secret drone base for its campaign of airstrikes against al Qaeda in Waziristan.

Quetta squats in the north-eastern corner of Balochistan, fifty miles from the border with Afghanistan. In the nineteenth century, the city was at the heart of the Great Game, the imperial contest between the British Raj and Tsarist Russia. A devastating earthquake levelled it in 1935, killing 60,000 people. Today its fault lines are human – ethnic, sectarian, political.

The most overtly ruthless attacks are perpetrated by Lashkar-e-Jhangvi, a Sunni supremacist jihadi outfit dedicated to wiping out minority Shias. Lashkar is particularly strong in Quetta, where the Shias are ethnic Hazaras, easily distinguished by their Central Asian features. In recent decades, sectarian militants have sprayed gunfire on Shia religious processions; flung bombs into crowded markets and snooker halls; and dragged Shia pilgrims off buses headed to holy sites in Iran to be executed on the roadside.

In the West, though, Quetta is better known as the home of the Quetta Shura, the Afghan Taliban ruling council that found sanctuary here, with ISI support, after the American invasion of Afghanistan in 2001. As Western pressure on Pakistan over their presence in Quetta grew, those fighters vanished from the streets. But on my first trip to the city, in 2004, they circulated openly. At the Talib Cassette Centre, a store in the main bazaar that sold audiotapes of anti-Western sermons and posters of Osama bin Laden, I bumped into a pair of cheery young men in black turbans. They were back from a stint fighting American soldiers in Uruzgan, they told me, and had come to Quetta for a little R&R. The Taliban fighters took me for a stroll in a nearby park, where they offered tea and a lecture on the virtues of jihad.

But it was Quetta's third schism that I had come to explore in the winter of 2011. After my frosty welcome at the city airport, I checked into the Gardenia, a modest hotel in the military cantonment, where I got a room overlooking a deserted playground. That night, as the temperature plunged, the heater in my room spluttered and died. A receptionist came to my door with a blanket and an explanation: Separatist rebels, who wanted independence for Balochistan, had blown up the city's gas pipeline.

The Baloch insurgency had been rumbling on for about six years by then, little noticed by the outside world. The fighting was led by a patchwork of small, obscure rebel groups that targeted remote army checkposts, trains and energy infrastructure. Their cause attracted little publicity, or sympathy, in Pakistan's national press. But I had heard that the war was far more serious, and dirtier, than was widely known – which was why I had come.

The following morning, I went to see the provincial home secretary, a polished bureaucrat named Akbar Hussain Durrani. The revolt was under control, he assured me at his office – just a few tribal malcontents with little appetite for a real fight. 'This is just a matter of politics. It won't last long,' he said. But his office was dark, and his computer screen blank, because hours earlier the separatists had also knocked out Quetta's power grid.

Later that day, we crossed the city, my fixer glancing in the mirror to make sure we weren't being followed, and turned down a narrow, high-walled street. A gate swung open and a man ushered us into an empty house where, for the rest of the day, a stream of people came to see me, slipping through the gate in twos and threes to avoid suspicion. They were relatives of the 'disappeared', suspected Baloch separatists who had vanished into military custody. Their stories followed a pattern: young men abducted at army checkpoints or from their workplaces who vanished for months, sometimes years. Then one day a body would turn up, usually dumped on a desolate mountainside, bearing signs of terrible torture. The relatives scrolled through photos on their phones of those bodies: smashed bones, pulped faces and gouged eyes cut by knives or punctured with drills, barely recognisable. Some had been sprinkled with scalding lime, others half-eaten by wild animals.

Lal Bibi, a distraught mother with trembling hands, held aloft a tiny photo of her son, Najibullah. He was just twenty-one when the soldiers dragged him away, she said. His body surfaced three months later, dumped at the playground outside my room at the Gardenia. 'He had just two teeth left,' Lal Bibi said, her head-scarf slipping to reveal tear-glazed cheeks. Her father, a gummy old man in a turban, grimaced silently.

It was Balochistan's fifth uprising since 1947, and everyone agreed it was the worst. Schoolchildren refused to sing Pakistan's national anthem; university students burned their books on Pakistani history; and on 14 August, Independence Day, Baloch nationalists hung black flags outside their doors. Despite its low profile, it seemed a consequential conflict – another quivering strand of Pakistan's DNA that threatened to pull the country apart.

How did it get so bad? One answer was offered by a grandiloquent Baloch chieftain – a tribal aesthete, poetry lover and insufferable snob whom I had met six years earlier, in the course of an unusual English lesson.

❈

An elderly tribesman with kindly eyes and a dagger tucked into his waistband cleared his throat and spoke. 'Hell hath no few-ry like a . . . woman scorned,' he intoned in halting English, stumbling over the words as if they were rocks in the desert. 'Love and . . . Attach-ment. Tides. Of. Life.'

His teacher, a bespectacled man with flowing white hair, harrumphed impatiently.

'Essay titles,' said Akbar Bugti, turning to me. 'I set them an essay every ten days or so, in English or in Urdu. Cash prizes for first, second and third. Just to give them an idea, you know – to agitate their minds.'

It was February 2005. We were sitting, cross-legged, in the courtyard of a bullet-pocked fortress on the eastern edge of Balochistan. Nawab Akbar Shahbaz Khan Bugti was the *sardar*, or chieftain, of the Bugti, who numbered perhaps 150,000 souls.* Gathered around him, in the manner of a classroom, were his *waderas*, or subchiefs. The older ones sat up front, with billowing pantaloons and elaborately brushed beards adorned with twirls and combed lines. The young guns lingered at the

---

* A Baloch tribal leader is formally titled *Tumandar* but commonly referred to as a *sardar*.

rear, weapons at their feet, looking bored. This was the *haal*, the Nawab explained – the tribal telegraph. The chiefs had been arriving since dawn by foot, horse and camel. 'They bring the news – rains, deaths, murders. Anything of consequence since the last time.'

If the assembled *waderas* recalled a scene from another era, the Nawab wouldn't have been out of place at a country club. In his late seventies, he wore large rimmed glasses and a Pringle lambs-wool sweater, with a shawl flung rakishly over his shoulder. He sat upright against a wall, projecting an air of hauteur. The *haal*, he continued, was also an opportunity to give some instruction. The Nawab had taken it upon himself to teach English to the *waderas*. He handed me a copy of one exam: a list of sentences to be translated into Urdu.

1. 'A wing beat – aeons vanish far behind.'
2. 'Is it true that my lips are sweet like the opening bud of the first conscious love?'

And so it went, with quotations from Goethe, Sartre and other classical writers that would have challenged even a gifted trans-lator. The entire class failed. 'It was a difficult standard, I realised later,' the Nawab admitted. 'I gave the test to the vice-chancellor of the University of Balochistan when he came to visit. He failed it, too.'

The call to prayer rang out, causing several waderas to rise and slope off to the mosque. 'The prayerful types,' the Nawab observed with barely concealed disdain. He had little time for religion, he continued. 'God should be a loving God; He must love and respect, not punish. But our mullahs and your priests' – he wagged a reproachful finger in my direction – 'their meal ticket is sin.' His God was literature: the ancient fort behind us, where the Nawab lived with his three wives, was said to contain one of the finest libraries in Pakistan. He read late into the night, devouring the works of English romantics, French philosophers, and Sufi masters. Presently, he informed me, he was rereading Homer's *Iliad*.

I had come to Dera Bugti to discuss more temporal matters. Weeks earlier, this lost corner made national news after a group of tribesmen rained rockets on the gas refinery at Sui, the largest in Pakistan, twenty miles to the south. The Nawab's twenty-two-year-old grandson, Brahumdagh, was said to have led the assault. The army, which guarded the huge plant, was furious, and Musharraf vowed to hit back. Helicopter gunships, tanks and troops had been deployed to the area. Was another clash inevitable?

The Nawab shrugged. '*Que sera, sera,*' he said. 'We have always been in a state of war.'

A voice behind him piped up: 'Doris Day.'

The Nawab's brother, Ahmed, a jowly man in his sixties who had been quietly chain-smoking until then, jerked himself from his stupor. 'Doris Day,' he repeated. '*Que sera, sera*. That was sung by Doris Day.'

The Nawab ignored this non sequitur and pulled a sheet of paper from his pocket. 'A poem,' he announced, about Buddhism. He started to read.

How can it be that Brahm
Would make a world and keep it miserable
Since, if all-powerful, he leaves it so,
He is not good, and if not powerful
He is not God?

God, indeed. In this lost corner of Pakistan, the Nawab was as close to a deity as you could get. He folded the poem and put it back in his pocket. The *waderas* sat as quiet as mice, their hard faces betraying nothing. I was certain they hadn't understood a word.

※

The sardars of Balochistan have always guarded their power jealously. During the British Raj, in the nineteenth century, they banded together in a loose confederacy to strike a bargain: in return for allowing the British to build a railway through Balochistan, carrying troops to Afghanistan, the sardars could run their affairs as they pleased. In recent times, though, they have acquired a notorious reputation as the custodians of a cruel feudal order. Like the Pashtuns, they preside over informal village courts that dispense approximate justice. But while Pashtun society is underpinned by an egalitarian ethos that prizes consensus, the Baloch system is an autocracy that vests immense power in one man. As ever, women suffer most. In 2009, Pakistan's Parliament erupted over reports that three Baloch women had been buried alive, on the orders of a tribal court, for daring to marry the men of their choice.

Nawab Bugti, though, considered himself to be cut from finer cloth.

He came to power in 1939, at the age of twelve, after his father was poisoned to death, probably at the hands of a scheming relative. The young Nawab completed his schooling at Lahore's Aitchison College, where the sons of Indian nobles were taught the King's English, and travelled to London in 1953 for the coronation of Queen Elizabeth II. 'I was struck especially by Queen Salote of Tonga,' he later recalled. 'She was seven feet tall and with her huge bulk, she was an impressive figure indeed.' But later that year, back in Quetta, the Nawab found himself in court facing murder charges. At the trial, which was attended by his wife and his Swedish mistress, he vehemently denied killing his cousin. He would never be so stupid, he argued, to kill a man in the 'settled' areas where regular laws held sway. The judge didn't believe him, and the Nawab spent much of the 1960s in jail, where he developed his appetite for literature.

He produced a tattered volume by Rabindranath Tagore, the esteemed Bengali poet and Nobel Prize laureate, which he handed to me with reverence. 'My constant companion in jail,' he said. 'It sustained me.'

※

I had set off from Quetta before dawn, to avoid being trailed by the intelligence services, in the company of a veteran local journalist. Our jeep bumped across a bone-dry, sometimes alien-looking landscape, with odd-shaped rocks in lurid colours, some-times jolting off the main trail to avoid military posts. In my bag I carried a copy of *The Tigers of Baluchistan*, a jaunty account of life among the Bugti in the 1940s by Sylvia Matheson, an English writer whose engineer husband was helping to build the refinery at Sui. Guided by the splendidly named Mohammed Mondrani of Mut, the Englishwoman spent years documenting the tribe's customs; an introduction to the handsome nineteen-year-old Nawab left her weak at the knees. 'A sight to gladden the eyes of any romantically inclined girl,' she wrote. 'Almost impossibly good looking.' The Nawab, for his part, treated Matheson some-what dismissively and boasted that he had killed his first man at the age of twelve. 'He annoyed me,' he told her. (Years later, he admitted that was a lie – he had been showing off.)

The Nawab's propensity for showmanship and provocation remained undimmed. When we arrived in Dera Bugti after a twelve-hour journey, we were instructed to wait: the Nawab was exercising on his treadmill. He finally emerged hours later, walking through a giant wooden door with his secretary scurrying behind. I introduced myself as a reporter with the *Guardian*.

'Really?' he replied, arching an eyebrow. 'I prefer the *Times* myself.'

That evening, the Nawab held court in a small, pillow-strewn room, where he offered a feast of basted goat meat, oil-soaked vegetables and *kaak*, a delicious crunchy flatbread that is cooked around a roasting stone. As we ate, the Nawab held forth. He was by turn engaging, discussing his love for Shelley and Byron – "To a Skylark" is one of my favourites,' he said – and mildly entertaining. He liked to drop the names of famous Pakistanis he had met, then disparage them with gibes and mocking impressions. Benazir Bhutto was annoyed, he said, when he called her husband, Asif Ali Zardari, 'the son of a camel *wallah*'. But he could also be crude and cruel, and he appeared to take pleasure in the discomfort of others.

Seated beside me was a rotund man named Manzoor Gichki, a minor political leader from the coastal district of Makran, who evidently had angered the Nawab with some perceived show of disloyalty. Throughout the meal, the Nawab periodically mocked and bullied the poor man. In the 1970s, the Nawab declared, the government of Pakistan tried to outlaw the sardars. 'But there was an exception,' he said, lowering his voice to a menacing pitch. 'Those sardars whose services were required. Overnight, hundreds of them spread out their hands to receive the goodies.' He motioned dismissively at Gichki. 'He's one of them. He's not even a real Baloch.'

Gichki shifted uneasily in his seat and tried to shrug off the rebuke with a watery smile. 'Why are you laughing?' the Nawab snapped. The table went quiet. 'Oh, look at him,' he continued in a contemptuous tone. 'You're just a pygmy of a man, aren't you?'

Just as the Nawab had become entirely insufferable, the mask slipped, exposing a man of some sensitivity.

As a child, he recounted, he had been greatly influenced by a German woman named Elsa Kazi. He had lived with Elsa and her husband, the vice chancellor of the University of Sindh, in the 1930s, during his early school years in Karachi. The woman entranced the young chieftain. 'She was a poet, an artist, a painter, a playwright, a philosopher and a storyteller,' he said, his stentorian tone now inflected with a note of tenderness. 'Over dinner she would tell stories like *One Thousand and One Nights*. We were really enthralled. She was head and shoulders over her husband, intellectually. But, being in this society, she had to defer to him.' When Elsa Kazi died, he continued, her heartbroken husband flung himself into the Indus. 'He went to meet her in his suit. People saw his hat floating on the water.' The Nawab's face flashed with sadness.

For all that, he was a firm enforcer of the tribal code. At his nearby private jail, he was holding thirty men from a rebellious subtribe who had defied him. Their beards had been cut and their eyebrows shaved in an act of ritual humiliation. He adjudicated disputes using 'trial by fire', an ancient tradition in which an accused man scuttles barefoot across a bed of burning coals. The innocent cross unscathed, Bugti explained, but the guilty emerge with charred toes. 'Some people can't walk afterward. They have to move on their bottoms,' he said dryly.

He was equally unapologetic about the practice of honour killing, recounting a recent instance. A young couple had attempted to elope, but were caught by their relatives. The man was killed on the spot but the woman was allowed to return to her family. Instead of offering refuge, her mother and sisters took her shawl, fashioned it into a rope, and hanged her from a tree. 'The job was done,' Nawab Bugti said firmly. 'Honour was restored.'

Hardly a just punishment, I countered. The Nawab snorted.

'These laws come from our ancestors. We call it *namus*, which means honour, but it's also more than that. You have to feel it.'

He narrowed his eyes. 'There is no equivalent word in English because you don't possess these qualities, I'm sorry to say.'

A woman's honour was the ostensible trigger for the show-down with Musharraf at the Sui gas plant. A thirty-one-year-old female doctor had accused an army captain of breaking into her quarters and raping her. Instead of investigating the doctor's complaint, the military drugged her and sent her to a psychiatric hospital in Karachi. The Bugtis, led by the Nawab's grandson, Brahumdagh, registered their outrage with a volley of rockets.

Now with an arrest warrant on his head, Brahumdagh sat opposite me at supper, a taciturn, serious-looking young man, with a mop of thick curly hair that poked from a knitted prayer cap. His only contribution to the conversation was to note that the word for 'rape' in the Bugti language was *siachar* – a black deed. 'Our homeland is not a brothel for the Pakistani army,' he said.

The dispute was also driven by less noble considerations. The Sui gas company paid several million dollars in rent to the Nawab every year and provided him with a range of perks, including four-wheel-drive vehicles and a lavish villa in Karachi for one of his four sons. The Nawab could use the company aeroplane, which even was used once to transport a batch of pizzas from Karachi. The trouble started when Musharraf, hoping to expand production at Sui, sent a two-star general to negotiate terms with the Nawab. It didn't go well. The Nawab rejected the general's initial offer – 'Peanuts,' he spat – then subjected him to a stream of inventive, highly personalised insults. Enraged by the Nawab's insolence, Musharraf accused him of orchestrating the rocket attack on Sui as a way of strengthening his hand in those talks. Now, a pair of army field guns had been positioned on a hilltop overlooking Dera Bugti, pointed directly at the fort where we ate supper.

It seemed hopelessly one-sided, I remarked: a few hundred tribesmen against the might of the Pakistani army. 'You're very ignorant, I must say,' the Nawab retorted. He reached for another book: *The War of the Flea*, a study of guerrilla warfare. 'You see, this is the war of the flea,' he continued. 'The flea bites the dog all over, and so he lashes out. But the flea is elsewhere. The dog cannot shake him off.'

It was getting late and the Nawab suddenly looked tired, his voice growing weary. The showdown at Sui was indicative of an older, more fundamental issue, he continued – that Balochistan had never truly been a part of Pakistan. 'If you cut off part of a camel, and attach it to an elephant, how can both be happy? They are alien.' He pulled off his glasses and rubbed his nose, revealing a pair of small, piercing eyes.

'The army may come here and kill a few hundred Bugti,' he continued, 'but the flea is multiplying. It will not go away.'

Much like the Kurds of the Middle East, the Baloch see themselves as a proud people shortchanged by history. By some accounts they originated around the Caspian Sea and migrated in the twelfth century to their current territory at the intersection of Iran, Afghanistan and Pakistan. At the birth of Pakistan in 1947, some Baloch leaders revolted against the new state, and later claimed they had been strong-armed into acceding to it. Scholars say the tale is more complicated, but that didn't matter: a powerful narrative of dispossession was born.

Small-scale uprisings erupted in Balochistan during the 1950s and 1960s, followed by a juddering, province-wide one in 1973. Thousands of tribesmen, led by rebel sardars, rose to protest a stolen election. The Pakistan military, still reeling from the loss of East Pakistan two years earlier, responded with ruthless force. Helicopter gunships on loan from the Shah of Iran (who was also battling Baloch rebels in eastern Iran) strafed the rebels; separatist leaders were flung blindfolded from helicopters; torture was commonplace. By the time the insurgency fizzled out in 1977, about 5,000 Baloch and 3,000 soldiers had been killed. An uneasy peace descended on the province.

In theory, Balochistan should be Pakistan's richest province. Beneath its baked soil lie vast deposits of gold, copper, iron and uranium. Yet little of that wealth has been exploited, and most Baloch live in abject poverty. Half of the population draws its drinking water from a well; education rates are atrocious; and dilapidated hospitals mean that a Baloch woman is twice as likely as another Pakistani woman to die in childbirth. Baloch nationalists blame this woeful state on the army, specifically Punjabi generals they accuse of seeking to steal their mineral wealth, use their land for military bases and treat them with neo-colonial contempt. Famously, gas from Sui was piped to Punjab in the 1950s but only reached Quetta in the 1980s, when the army expanded its cantonment in the city.

The generals, for their part, say the sardars are the problem – petty, money-grubbing autocrats who have purposely sabotaged efforts to develop the province in health, education and commerce to preserve their own godlike privileges. I got a taste of this attitude when I interviewed Musharraf in 2006. A passing mention of Nawab Bugti launched the military ruler into an impassioned, twenty-minute tirade. 'These people are pygmies, and will finish up as such,' he said.

In fact, dozens of Baloch sardars were firmly in Musharraf's camp. But the recalcitrant leaders of three major tribes – the Marris, the Mengals and the Bugti – stubbornly refused his agenda. A few years earlier, Musharraf had announced a slew of ambitious projects for Balochistan: a deep-water port at Gwadar, on the Arabian Sea; a gas pipeline to Iran; and a slew of copper-mining and gas projects including the expansion at

Sui. But these *grands projets* were rejected by the three sardars, who vowed to resist them.

Musharraf snorted. 'The *sardari* system is anti-government, anti-democracy and anti the people,' he declared. 'It must be finished.' He made a chopping gesture with his hands.

※

The morning after my supper with the Nawab, I took a stroll through Dera Bugti, a one-street town with a spaghetti-western air. Tribesmen wrapped in dun-coloured shawls, rifles slung over their shoulders, rolled in off the stony desert. Camels sauntered past. Burlap sacks filled with sugar, salt and spices were stacked outside a line of rudimentary stores. At the top of the street stood a large portrait of the Nawab, resplendent in a Panama hat and dark sunglasses.

I strolled into the town pharmacy – a ramshackle trading post, really, whose walls were filled with images of Lakshmi, Vishnu and other shimmering Hindu deities. The pharmacist, Parsa Ram, was outside the counter with an alarming-looking syringe in one hand, standing over a teenage boy with a painful boil on one eye, who was wincing in anticipation. Parsa looked up, greeted me, and shouted at an underling to bring tea and pistachios. Hindus and Sikhs had been part of life in Dera Bugti for as long as anyone could remember, he said. 'The Nawab holds us close,' he said. 'Nobody dares touch us.' He excused himself, turned back to his patient, and plunged the syringe into the boil.

Dera Bugti's thriving minority was a point of pride for the Nawab. At partition in 1947, when Hindus and Sikhs fled to India in droves, the Nawab insisted that the local community remain behind. 'They have been with us since we were nomads in the desert, part of life and death, gain and loss,' he told me. One local Hindu had been elected to Balochistan's provincial assembly; another served as the Nawab's personal accountant.

They repaid his protection with unswerving loyalty. The pharmacist directed me to a Sikh temple, at the end of an alley, where I found Gobind Singh hunched over a religious text with a gleaming Kalashnikov by his side. The gun was new, Singh said, purchased following the clashes with the army. 'If the time comes,' he declared, 'I will fight alongside the Nawab.'

At the far end of the town I reached the gates of a small Frontier Corps base with a besieged air. At the entrance, soldiers hunched behind a wall of sandbags. Every building in sight was festooned in the colours of the Nawab's Jamhoori Watan political party. A pick-up truck filled with Bugti fighters, rocket launchers poking over the guardrail, cruised past in a slow show of defiance. The base commander, Colonel Furqan, a softly spoken Punjabi, invited me in. The Nawab was making his life miserable, he said, striking up a cigarette, evidently glad of an opportunity to talk with an outsider. Shopkeepers refused to serve his soldiers, locals refused to work on his base, and the army-run school next door – the best for miles around – stood deserted because the Nawab had instructed local children to boycott classes. Even small children ran off screaming when the colonel offered them sweets to celebrate the Eid ul-Fitr holiday. 'They said it was an order from the Nawab,' he said wearily.

It was a matter of irony that the Nawab, derided for decades by his fellow Baloch as an establishment stooge, had emerged as a spearhead of anti-government agitation. He had supported the province's amalgamation with Pakistan in 1947 and served as governor in 1973 during the uprising, at a time when other chieftains were being bombed or were languishing in prison. Even his use of the title *Nawab* – a Raj-era peerage awarded to the leaders of princely states for their services to British India – attracted raised eyebrows among Baloch leaders who went by the title of *Sardar*. Yet his defiance at Sui resonated powerfully across a province that was again stirring against the army. At the construction site of the port in Gwadar, unidentified gunmen ambushed and killed two Chinese engineers helping to build the facility. To the north of Dera Bugti in Kohlu, an oil-rich tribal district, militiamen ambushed army convoys. 'The lava is on the boil,' said Akhtar Mengal, another rebellious sardar, shortly before he was imprisoned.

Before leaving Dera Bugti, I sat with the Nawab's grandson, Brahumdagh. Among the Nawab's forty-odd grandchildren, he was the undisputed favourite. Since the death of Brahumdagh's father when he was seven, the Nawab had managed his schooling and taken him hunting for deer and grouse; now he was grooming him as his successor, to lead the tribe. Brahumdagh, who had just got married, was spending much of his time going from village to village, learning how to preside over disputes. Although quieter and less flamboyant than his grandfather, he shared his antipathy towards the Punjabi-dominated military. The generals had snapped up the best land in Balochistan and coveted its resources, he told me. 'Gas, oil, the coastal areas – this is our natural wealth, and they want it.'

A reasonable army would negotiate, he continued. 'You can come to me, you sit, you ask – and then we will decide whether to give it or not. But if you don't want to talk, and you want to take it by force, well then . . . ' He shrugged and threw his hands in the air, in a gesture of helplessness. 'It's okay.'

Clearly, he did not think it was okay.

***

Two months later, in March 2005, after I had returned to Islamabad, the tensions in Dera Bugti boiled over into open war.

The Nawab's tribesmen pounded the Colonel Furqan and his men with gunfire, who responded with a rain of shellfire on the Nawab's ancient fort. Sixty-seven civilians were killed, including Hindus and Sikhs in the cramped alleyways around the fort walls I had explored, hit by bombs that fell short of their target.

Mediators in Islamabad brokered a hurried truce. But by December the shelling had resumed, and thousands of residents fled. On New Year's Eve, the Nawab joined them, slipping away from his shell-pocked fort at dawn, surrounded by a band of trusted gunmen, and pushed deep into the nearby Zainko Mountains.

At the same time, neighbouring Kohlu district also erupted in revolt. The Marris vehemently rejected the military's plans to drill for oil and build a new military base on their land. When Musharraf visited Kohlu in an effort to persuade them, rockets landed fifty yards from the podium where he was speaking. Days after that, a burst of gunfire cut through a helicopter, wounding the same general who had been insulted by Nawab Bugti. 'It's not the seventies when you can hit and run and hide in the mountains,' Musharraf warned the rebels. 'This time you won't even know what hit you.'

The Nawab and his small entourage roamed across the Zainko mountains, flitting between safe houses and rocky caves. He clambered over rocks with his walking stick and pushed down lonely valleys by moonlight, sitting on a camel, remarkably agile for a man of seventy-nine. Brahumdagh scouted the path ahead, watching for signs of their army pursuers, who were never far away. Pakistani warplanes dropped 1,000lb, American-made bombs in an effort to flush out the group, often coming perilously close. Brahumdagh began to suspect that the military had locked onto the signal from his grandfather's satellite phone, and pleaded with him to flee to Afghanistan, where President Hamid Karzai had offered sanctuary. The Nawab refused. 'I already have one foot in the grave,' he told his grandson. 'I want to die among my people, in my area. Not in my bed.'

In April 2006, four months after the Nawab went on the lam, two journalist friends – Isambard Wilkinson of the *Daily Telegraph* and Carlotta Gall of the *New York Times* – caught up with him. They found him at the mouth of a cave, in a large wooden armchair, wearing a corduroy jacket that gave him the air of a country squire. Beside him sat Balach Marri, the head of the newly formed Balochistan Liberation Army, who had led the attack on Musharraf in Kohlu. The Nawab seemed in high spirits. An old chest served as a desk, stacked with copies of the *Economist* and a stock of chocolate. He recited poetry by John Donne, offered a disquisition on the intricacies of camel copulation, and claimed to relish being on the run. 'What more is there to life than love and warfare?' he said.

As the journalists clambered on to the camels that would take them away, though, the old man appeared wistful, even sad. 'The government says with glee that Bugti is at an end,' he told Isambard. 'Of course, everything comes to an end.'

Four months later, in August, a squadron of Pakistani military helicopters swooped through the arid mountains and landed near a rocky defile. Soldiers converged on a rocky overhang – a sort of half-cave, according to Brahumdagh – where the Nawab, sheltering inside, was finally cornered. A stand-off ensued. For days, soldiers surrounded the cave, urging the Nawab to surrender. On the third day, a military delegation entered the cave, apparently to negotiate. What happened next is disputed. By some accounts, the soldiers fired first; by others, it was the Nawab. Either way, a cacophony of gunfire filled the cavern, and when it was over the Nawab lay dead.

Balochistan convulsed with fury. Across the province, protesters hurled rocks, blocked roads and burned tyres. In deserted Quetta, riot police rumbled through debris-strewn streets in armoured vehicles. Protesters tore down symbols of Pakistan, including a billboard with a photo of Jinnah.

Meanwhile, the Nawab was hastily buried in a secretive ceremony near Dera Bugti. Military officials and pro-government tribal leaders watched as a plain wooden coffin, sealed with cheap Chinese locks, was lowered into a desert grave. Brahumdagh had vanished, and the rest of his family was absent from the funeral. Officials refused permission to view the Nawab's body, prompting speculation that he had survived, so they produced his watch, wallet and glasses as proof of his demise.

Musharraf was jubilant, but it was a hollow victory. The Nawab's failings in the eyes of his fellow Baloch – decades of opportunism, cynicism and arrogance – were washed away in an instant by a tide of public anguish. Instead of smothering the Baloch revolt, Musharraf had breathed new oxygen into it. 'Every sensible person should be filled with deep foreboding,' warned *Dawn*. Unrest spread from the mountains to the sea. Balochistan's fifth uprising was erupting.

❄

In the outside world, few people noticed. Officials in Washington and London, concerned with defeating the Taliban or chasing al Qaeda fugitives, viewed the war in Balochistan as an obscure sideshow in Pakistan's multi-ringed circus of violence. There had been a time, certainly, when the Baloch produced world-class terrorists who seized global attention. In 1993, Mir Aimal Kansi, a Quetta-born migrant to the United States, opened fire outside the CIA headquarters in Langley, Virginia, killing two CIA employees. Al Qaeda's Khalid Sheikh Muhammad, an ethnic Baloch raised in Kuwait, had masterminded the 2001 attacks on America. But the new wave of Baloch nationalists, with their narrow anti-military beef and largely secular politics, didn't fit that mould. Their cause had no ties to global terror, no designs on Pakistan's nukes, and no apocalyptic visions of destroying the West. They were of limited interest.

Yet the revolt that swept Balochistan after Nawab Bugti's death did matter. At first, it echoed earlier risings. From exile in Afghanistan and Europe, the sons of the Marri and Bugti leaders coordinated bands of insurgent tribesmen. The fighters clustered in remote camps, ambushed army checkposts and planted bombs that ripped through trains winding through narrow gorges on the tracks laid by the British a century earlier. But as the conflict wore on, it began to change shape. Fighters from the province's middle classes, abused in previous uprisings, joined the rebellion. Many came through the Baloch Students Organisation. Its most famous graduate was Allah Nazar, a medical student who had been abducted and tortured by the army. On his release, he became the face of resistance for many angry young Baloch. 'What is Pakistan?' Asad Baloch, a wiry twenty-two-year-old medical student, asked during my trip in 2011. 'There are Pashtuns, Baloch, Sindhis, Punjabis, and they cannot live together. Why should the Punjabis steal our land and loot our resources? We want to get them out, and we will fight them out.'

By then, the military had scooped hundreds of young men into its gulag of hidden detention centres, where torture was commonplace. The students I met accepted they could be next. 'I must speak to you now,' one said, 'because in any event, I am dead.'

The army, facing little risk of Western censure, could be surprisingly frank. In Rawalpindi, I went to see General Obaidullah Khan Khattak, commander of the Frontier Corps paramilitaries in Balochistan. Khattak criticised the exiled rebel leaders in London and Geneva – 'They're enjoying the good life in Europe while their people suffer in the mountains,' he said – and brushed off my questions about torture and execution. Such tactics may be illegal, he conceded. 'But you feel less pain in your heart if a murderer is killed.'

Things got nasty on the rebel side, too. Allah Nazar's group denounced ethnic Punjabis who lived in Balochistan as 'settlers' and fifth columnists, even though most had lived in the province for generations. A vicious campaign of intimidation and assassination started up. Militants tossed grenades into the homes of Punjabi teachers and university professors, and shot coal miners in their quarters. Dozens of people were killed.

Matters were further complicated by Indian meddling. New Delhi was quietly stirring the pot in Balochistan, funneling money to the separatists as payback for Pakistan's support to jihadists in Kashmir. In the early days of the fight, a senior Western intelligence official told me, it was an open secret that India's Research and Intelligence Wing was 'handing over bags of dosh' to the Baloch. Later, the Indians sent the money via bank accounts in Dubai. Indian officials barely contained their glee at the trouble the insurgency had caused to their old foes in the Pakistani military. It gave them 'a taste of their own medicine', Vijay Nambiar, a senior Indian security official, told an American diplomat. Infuriated Pakistani generals saw a re-run of 1971, when Indian support to Bengali separatists precipitated the catastrophic secession of East Pakistan. Even so, it was clear that deeply held historical and political grievances, not Indian cash, were driving the fight. Mushahid Hussain, a Musharraf supporter who tried to mediate between Bugti and the army, told me his efforts had ultimately been thwarted by army hardliners. 'There is a mind-set in the Pakistani establishment that is unwilling to concede the legitimate rights of the smaller provinces,' he said.

In 2014, a year after my hasty exit from Pakistan, I met an exiled Baloch activist in London who brought a tantalising piece of information. As we sat in a coffee shop off Oxford Street, he opened Google Maps on his computer and guided me to a strange-looking facility in the remote Kirthar Mountains in the dead centre of Balochistan. The images showed newly cut roads snaking through a rocky mountain range that disappeared into the flanks of a vertiginous slope. There were barriers and checkposts at the tunnel entrances, as well as the outline of a new electricity substation that appeared to power whatever work was going on in the mountain depths. To my untutored eye, the mountain complex resembled the villain's lair in a James Bond film. But nobody had heard of it. The nearest town, Khuzdar, was one of the most dangerous corners of Balochistan, where rebels battled against an army-supported militia. Journalists were regularly caught in the crossfire; Reporters Without Borders listed Khuzdar among the world's ten most dangerous places for reporters. Curious, I forwarded the coordinates of this mysterious complex to experts at the Institute for Science and International Security, a nuclear-security research organisation. A few years later, they released their findings: the complex appeared to be a hardened, secure underground facility that was likely used to store part of Pakistan's nuclear arsenal. Moreover, they noted that it was roughly equidistant from Pakistan's international borders – as far as it was possible to be from India, Iran and Afghanistan – and therefore an ideal location to hide part of Pakistan's counterforce nuclear-strike capability, far from prying eyes, in a place few dared to visit.

The dirty war dragged on. In Quetta, tear-streaked women brandished posters of missing husbands and sons, sometimes flinging stones at passing traffic in frustration, but beyond the province few Pakistanis seemed to care. The war was an unwelcome distraction in a country weary from fighting the Taliban and bickering with the United States. The Pakistani military actively discouraged scrutiny. The human rights activist Asma Jahangir came under fire from the military when she drove into

Balochistan on a fact-finding mission. Most newspapers gave the conflict only cursory coverage.

Well-meaning Pakistanis discussed the situation in Balochistan with mannered sighs and regretful shrugs. The province, as the writer Mohammed Hanif noted, was remote 'not just geographically but in our imagination as well'.

✻

The upstairs lounge of the Grand Hotel Kempinski on Geneva's Quai du Mont-Blanc hummed with understated elegance. Business types huddled on leather sofas, speaking in hushed tones. Waiters circled with trays of drinks. A sweeping panoramic façade overlooked the shimmering splendour of Lake Geneva, with its joggers and bobbing yellow boats and spurting jet fountain. Brahumdagh Bugti sank into his seat.

It was June 2015, a decade since my trip to Dera Bugti. I barely recognised the tribal ingénue with whom I had shared a plate of chicken and *kaak* at his grandfather's mud-walled fort. The intricately brushed beard had been trimmed to a fashionable stubble; a pair of expensive loafers replaced the rubber-soled sandals; we nibbled on club sandwiches. Now thirty-four, Brahumdagh was a father of two young girls, a fitness enthusiast, and – although some disputed his authority – the new Nawab of the Bugti tribe.

'All very nice,' he said, gesturing to the swish hotel lounge, 'but this is a golden cage.'

His had been a peripatetic existence since the death of his grandfather in the wilds of the Zainko Mountains almost a decade earlier. After the army killed the Nawab, Brahumdagh stole across Balochistan, moving at night, until he slipped across the Afghan border near Kandahar. A government military vehicle, sent by President Hamid Karzai, was waiting. His wife, Shomaila, followed weeks later. They moved between safe houses in Kandahar and Kabul, guests of Afghan intelligence, before eventually settling in Wazir Akbar Khan, an upscale Kabul neighbourhood, on a street that housed the British Embassy and the *New York Times* bureau. Brahumdagh shaved his beard, signed up to a gym and hid in open sight. He socialised at bars frequented by Westerners, where he passed himself off as an Indian tourist, and in private with the Afghan intelligence chief, Amrullah Saleh, a trenchant critic of Pakistan. Even so, Kabul was not safe. Musharraf came to learn that Brahumdagh was living there and tried to pressure Karzai to send the young fugitive home. Karzai, happy to pay back the Pakistanis for allowing the Afghan Taliban to take sanctuary in Balochistan's Pashtun belt, feigned innocence. Musharraf's anger swelled. Brahumdagh's status had become a 'neuralgic issue' for the Pakistani leader, one American official noted. When the American conveyed Karzai's assurances of good faith, Musharraf snapped: 'That's bullshit.'

One day, a suicide bomber hit a house on Brahumdagh's street, a few doors down. Saleh, the spy chief, told Brahumdagh that he was the intended target. The bomber had been sent by the Pakistanis, he said, and had failed only because he went to the wrong address.

In 2009, Brahumdagh and his family slipped out of Afghanistan, travelling on an Afghan passport under an assumed name – first to Dubai and then to Switzerland, where I found him. His two girls, born in exile, attended an international school; he treated visitors to meals in some of the city's best restaurants. But if it was a safe and comfortable existence, he found it deeply frustrating. The Pakistanis had blocked his efforts to gain political asylum in different countries – Colombia, France, Ireland – and, because he no longer had a valid passport, he couldn't travel abroad. The Swiss, being the Swiss, did nothing. 'I'm stuck,' he said glumly. He spent his days running the affairs of the tribe, as best he could. The ISI had installed its own sardar in Dera Bugti – a pliant, twenty-something cousin of Brahumdagh – in an effort to bring the tribe to heel. It didn't work: many Bugti rejected the 'official' Nawab, and his supporters were targeted in gun attacks and kidnappings. So Brahumdagh still held sway over much of the tribe, ruling by phone to adjudicate in disputes and occasionally settling them with a prescription of trial by fire. It all seemed ludicrous: a young chieftain, in his loafers and business shirt on the shores of Lake Geneva, ordering tribesmen thousands of miles away to prove their innocence by racing over a bed of glowing coals. Brahumdagh shrugged. 'Personally, I don't agree with it. I've asked our people many times to find another way to discover the truth. But they are stuck with the idea. They say it's our tradition.'

He was coy about Pakistani claims that he was commanding one wing of the Baloch insurgency, although few doubted it was true. 'Sitting here, I can't answer that question,' he said, alluding to his delicate situation with the Swiss authorities. In any event, the insurgency was badly faltering. The rebels had captured little territory and were mostly confined to remote desert camps. His allies, the Marri brothers, were feuding among themselves. And the Pakistani military's counter-insurgency tactics had proven brutally effective: more than a hundred officials from Brahumdagh's small political party had been detained, including its seventy-six-year-old secretary general, Bashir Azeem, who was hung from his ankles and beaten. 'We can torture you or kill you or keep you for years at our will,' his captors told him. 'It is only the Army chief that we obey.'

On my second day in Geneva, Brahumdagh Bugti led a demonstration outside the main United Nations office. It was a motley crowd of a few dozen people, mostly Baloch exiles from across Europe – London cabbies, waiters in Berlin, a couple of stragglers from Norway. An American woman hovered awkwardly on the margins. The wife of a Republican congressman, she had been hired, at considerable expense, to lobby for the Baloch cause in Washington – a Sisyphean task, given the chronic lack of interest. Only the Chinese were interested, for purely commercial reasons. Months earlier, on a visit to Islamabad, President Xi Jinping had announced a $46 billion investment package that included 1,800-mile-long economic corridor – new roads, railway and oil pipelines – spanning Balochistan, linking the port of Gwadar with Xinjiang in western China. The Pakistan army announced a new battalion to protect the corridor.

United Nations officials strolling to lunch in Geneva barely glanced at Brahumdagh or his supporters holding aloft posters of an elderly man who was surely unknown to them: the Nawab, resplendent in a snazzy suede jacket, with a wry smile playing on his snowy whiskers, looking as smug as ever. I wondered what he would have made of the current state of 'The War of the Flea'.

In one sense, he was an anachronism, an exemplar of a fading era. Ardeshir Cowasjee, another crotchety relic of the old Pakistan and an acquaintance of the Nawab, noted that he 'held one sole stern view of life and the world in which he lived, a view that was unshakeable, non-negotiable and non-discussable'. Left alone, that cruel feudal order would surely have collapsed naturally in time, under pressure from the inexorable forces of education, globalisation and urbanisation (even in Balochistan). But the state's brutish efforts pushed many Baloch back into the arms of the sardars and their entitled sons. By some estimates, the insurgency had ebbed to a few hundred hardened fighters. Yet it bubbled along, a revolt fuelled by anger and repression as much as by any unifying idea of what an independent Balochistan might look like.

Not for the first time, the army was trying to hold Pakistan together by force, crushing its critics instead of talking to them. And not for the first time, in squeezing too hard, it seemed to be pulling the country even further apart.

Pakistani army officer, Waziristan

10

Undesirable Activities

A Spy Comes Clean

After my last reporting trip to Balochistan, in 2012, I returned to my house in Islamabad. One of my dogs, Spike, had fallen sick, so I took him to the vet. I caught up on the news from Mazloom, who was in a gloomy mood because his daughter was getting divorced. Then I filed my story about Quetta. Little did I know that I had crossed a red line.

The nature of that line would only be revealed years later, long after my departure from Pakistan, when a mysterious stranger would come forward, out of the blue, offering startling new information about that trip of mine to Quetta, as well as some answers to the question that had haunted me for years – what were the 'undesirable activities' of the letter that the bearded intelligence officer brought to my gate on the eve of the election in 2013, announcing my expulsion? In truth, though, there had been plenty of clues, much earlier, only some of which I understood at the time.

In the months following my abrupt departure from Pakistan, I tried hard to learn what prompted it. Editors at the *New York Times* met with Prime Minister Nawaz Sharif when he visited the United Nations General Assembly in New York. I went to see a senior ISI general at a conference in London. All of them offered emollient handshakes, a sympathetic hearing and promised to look into my case – the classic fob-off. Pakistan's gutter press was a richer source of information. Urdu-language rag sheets – the kind sold at traffic lights for a few rupees, and which took their cues from the intelligence agencies – published lurid accounts of my expulsion. The specifics varied, but their stories had a common theme. FOREIGN JOURNALIST OR SPOOK? read one headline. *Khabrain* revealed that I was a deep-cover CIA agent who had converted to Islam and married a Pakistani woman as a pretext for a years-long clandestine mission to monitor the Taliban. By another account, I had been caught red-handed dropping off a paper bag containing $50,000 at a juice shop in Peshawar, for collection by my jihadi informants. A third story linked me to Raymond Davis, the CIA contractor who had killed two Pakistanis on the street in Lahore in 2011 – even though, at the *Guardian*, I had broken the news that Davis was employed by the CIA, which was unlikely to have made me popular at the agency's Langley headquarters.

Such fairy tales were unsurprising, the quintessential smears of a Pakistani security bureaucracy that routinely blamed 'the foreign hand' for its woes. In the taxonomy of the state, I had moved into the 'anti-Pakistan' column. But it wasn't just the hundred-rupee hacks. Visitors to London brought accounts of dinner-table conversations in Lahore and Islamabad where guests discussed my expulsion with arched eyebrows and knowing glances. No smoke without fire, right? It was disappointing, of course – I counted some of the doubters as friends – but perhaps also the ultimate accolade: after years of tracking Pakistani conspiracy theories, I had become one.

The smear campaign was no accident. It soon became clear that my expulsion was a harbinger of a much wider crackdown targeting the Pakistani news media. Over the preceding years, Pakistan's generals had endured serial humiliations – the Taliban uprising, the fall of Musharraf, the American raid that took out bin Laden under their noses. They urgently needed to re-establish their authority. But how? The traditional solution – a military coup – was no longer so easy, and being in charge would mean direct responsibility for the mess. So they set about quietening their critics. Foreign reporters like me were a minor concern; the priority was to silence Pakistani journalists. One of them was the country's biggest TV star, a man once considered a friend by the military, now its declared enemy.

❧

On a sunny spring afternoon in 2015, Hamid Mir walked into the lobby of the Hilton Hotel on London's Edgware Road. Mir was a celebrity reporter, who had to fend off members of the public seeking selfies. His top-rated show, *Capital Talk*, which aired from a studio overlooking the Parliament building in Islamabad, was essential viewing for aficionados of Pakistan's raucous politics. A garrulous man, with tufts of black hair and playful eyes, Mir ran his studio like a circus ringmaster – one moment goading guests into argument, the next playing the conciliator. He peppered the interviews with juicy nuggets of insider information, gleaned from his deep Rolodex of official sources, that frequently generated controversy. He was ratings gold, and the public's adoration was matched only by the gratitude of his employer, Geo TV, which paid him handsomely.

But the man who crossed the lobby of the Hilton was a very different Mir. He had a grey pallor, walked with a limp, and, after exchanging greetings, dropped heavily into an armchair where he struggled to find a comfortable position – a consequence, Mir said, of the two bullets lodged in his gut.

A year earlier, as Mir was being driven from Karachi Airport, a gunman stepped onto the road. Bullets thudded into the vehicle. Mir dived onto the back seat and yelled at the driver to floor it. As the car zigzagged through the Karachi traffic, Mir speed-dialled his producer. 'They're killing me! They're killing me!' he cried. The car made it to a hospital where Mir was rushed into surgery. He had been shot six times – in the pelvis, bladder, legs, and shoulders.

As doctors operated on Mir, his brother, Amir went on Geo to deliver a sensational *j'accuse*: the ISI was behind the shooting, he declared, singling out the spy agency's director general, General Zaheer ul-Islam, as being personally responsible. Although Amir produced no evidence to support his claim, and General Islam strenuously denied any role, it was an extraordinary moment. ISI chiefs were the sacred cows of the Pakistani media, habitually treated with studied deference; they were never traduced as murderers on live television. In the days that followed, the ISI hit back hard. Geo was forced off the air, while anchors on rival channels launched vicious attacks against Mir that sought to discredit his reporting.

As Mir laid in hospital, he received apologetic texts from other TV presenters he counted as friends. 'They would say, "Sorry, this evening we are going to attack you, otherwise we will lose our jobs",' Mir told me. He had come to Britain for treatment to the extensive nerve damage down his left side. 'Pain has become an integral part of my life,' he said.

There was a time when Mir was the last reporter anyone expected to find in the ISI's crosshairs. In the 1990s, at the start of his career, he was a cheerleader for the military's covert war in Indian-controlled Kashmir. 'To be frank, I am a hardliner,' he told an Indian journalist. In the late 1990s, he travelled to Afghanistan twice to interview the fugitive Osama bin Laden – a feat many Pakistani reporters believed was impossible without a nod from the ISI. I heard a wild story from that time about a jihadi commander from Kashmir who marched into Mir's office in Islamabad, and presented him with the head of an Indian soldier. I presumed it was an apocryphal account but when I mentioned it to Mir he told me it was true. 'He pulled the head from a shopping bag,' he recalled with a puckish smile. 'It was stinking.'

But after Mir moved to television in the 2000s, and his career took off, his relationship with the security establishment began to fray. He helped mobilise public opinion against Pervez Musharraf during the sweeping street protests of 2007, and highlighted the plight of detainees who vanished into ISI custody. When Musharraf forced Geo off the air, Mir hosted *Capital Talk* from a stage on a pavement – a gleeful act of defiance that burnished his reputation as a champion of democracy and the free press.

Critics, though, grumbled that the old Mir hadn't gone far. He was a chameleon, they charged, a reporter who often crossed boundaries of good taste and journalistic ethics, and that it was impossible to know where he stood. 'All his career, he has played both sides against the middle,' one newspaper editor told me. Mir befriended Asma Jahangir, yet lambasted other progressives as 'liberal-fascists', a term borrowed from the American hard right. Even as he defied Musharraf, he adhered to the ISI's agenda on certain national security issues. He could be thin-skinned, as I learned to my cost.

In 2010, soon after Colonel Imam and Khalid Khawaja vanished in Waziristan, a leaked audiotape surfaced of a phone conversation between Mir and the militant commander who was holding the hostages. In the tape, Mir appeared to ingratiate himself with the commander by suggesting that Khawaja had once been on the CIA payroll and was an Ahmadi sympathizer. Weeks later, Khawaja was executed. Mir insisted the tape was a fake but executives at his own channel told me it was real. When I wrote about it for the *Guardian*, Mir flew into a rage, and later sent a message via a mutual friend: we were now foes. A couple of years later, my reporting was the subject of a twenty-minute segment on *Capital Talk* in which retired army generals suggested I took my cues from the United States government. It felt personal.

Even then, Mir was nobody's mouthpiece, and he pressed ahead with gutsy reporting on subjects that other journalists shunned, in particular military-led abuses in Balochistan. Infuriated, the military pressured Geo to rein in its star anchor, who began to receive death threats. It hadn't been long since the unexplained death of the investigative journalist, Saleem Shahzad, who, like Mir, had once been close to the ISI.

In November 2012, Mir returned from his barber's to find a magnetic bomb attached to the underside of his car. Whether the device had failed, or was intended as a message, was unclear.

Then, in January 2014, editors at Geo asked Mir to fly to Karachi for a special edition of *Capital Talk*. As a precaution, he bought an air ticket to Quetta, then at the last minute switched to Karachi. 'I was trying to deceive the enemy,' he explained. But as Mir left Karachi Airport, the gunman was waiting. 'The government has no power in Pakistan these days,' Mir told me in London. 'Everything is being done by the khakis.'

Even as the military was busy trying to tear down the institutions and most recognisable faces of the Pakistani media, it began experimenting with building up its own one. Around the time that Hamid Mir came under fire, a brash new television station announced itself on Pakistan's crowded electronic-media landscape. The station, Bol (Urdu for 'speak'), was fronted by a showy Karachi businessman with military ties named Shoaib Shaikh, who tried to lure the top staff at the main networks, including Hamid Mir, with promises of extravagant salaries, limousines and mansions. Bol presented itself as a patriotic TV network, promising to present a 'positive image' of Pakistan. That, along with its murky finances, led many Pakistani journalists to suspect it was being backed by the army.

From my base in London I started to investigate. The new venture was owned by a thrusting software company called Axact, which operated from an imposing, mirrored-glass office block in an upmarket Karachi suburb. Axact had two thousand employees, billed itself as 'the world's leading IT company,' and listed Microsoft and the Ford Motor Company among the customers. At glitzy presentations, its chief executive, Shaikh, boasted of lavish staff perks including a swimming pool, a movie theatre and a corporate yacht. But in Karachi, Axact was viewed as an enigma. Nobody was sure what kind of software it sold, and journalists who asked hard questions met with aggressive threats of legal action from a company lawyer.

My reporting efforts led me to a former Axact employee named Yasir Jamshaid, who had fled to the United Arab Emirates.

I flew out to meet him. He provided videos and documents from inside the company, and an astonishing account of its operations. Rather than sell software, as Axact claimed, the company was running a vast internet fraud, he said. It had set up hundreds of websites for non-existent American schools and universities that were used to sell fake high school diplomas and college degrees to customers around the world. Sometimes, he added, Axact employees impersonated American diplomats or law enforcement personnel as part of a ruse to extort extra cash from gullible customers.

My story on Axact was published on the front page of the *New York Times* on May 28, 2015, causing a sensation in Pakistan. The following day, police investigators raided three Axact offices where they found stacks of fake degree certificates and records of sales to 215,000 people in 197 countries, one-third in the United States. Shoaib Shaikh and thirteen other executives, including two retired army officers, were arrested and charged with fraud, extortion, and money laundering. Financial records showed that Axact's internet empire was a hugely profitable operation which had raked in $89 million in its last year alone – enough to start a TV station, certainly. A mystery remained: how had it operated openly, evaded prosecution, for so many years?

Shaikh's ties to the Pakistani military may have helped. Journalists told me that senior ISI officials had lobbied them to join Bol. Police investigators uncovered a tangled web of corporate entities – dozens of shell companies and bank accounts, in Caribbean tax havens and other places like Dubai, Cyprus and Singapore – that was used to funnel money back to Pakistan. This vast, money laundering operation could also be useful to a spy service that wanted to shift funds around the world. As they probed the company's accounts, they found that checks signed by Shoaib Shaikh had been used to move money to Waziristan.

Despite the voluminous evidence against Shaikh and his confederates, the case against them trundled torturously through Pakistan's courts. Witnesses recused themselves without explanation. Two judges due to hear the case dropped out. A grenade exploded in the garden of a potential prosecutor, shattering a window and frightening him off. In 2016, an Islamabad trial court judge acquitted Shaikh only to later admit that he had taken a bribe of five million rupees, ($47,000), which invalidated the verdict.

Two years later, after retrial, Shaikh was convicted and sentenced to twenty years imprisonment. But three months later, while his appeal was pending, the Islamabad High Court suspended his sentence. Shaikh walked free.

Ultimately, one Axact executive was held to account – in New York. In August 2017, Umair Hamid, a deputy of Shaikh who helped run the scheme in the United States, was convicted for wire fraud and sentenced to twenty-one months' imprisonment by a court in New York. The FBI estimated the fake degree scheme was worth $140 million.

The prosecution in Pakistan, meanwhile, seemed to be going nowhere. Axact reopened its doors and resumed business.

Incredibly, Hamid Mir was already back at work when I met him in London. Despite our differences, I greatly admired his courage. Colleagues advised him to abandon journalism, and his wife hinted she might leave him if he didn't. Mir insisted he was going nowhere. 'We faced a very difficult period', he chuckled. 'But in the end, I prevailed'.

Like Asma Jahangir, Mir believed that the final straw in his relationship with the Pakistani military was his coverage of Balochistan – a factor that would eventually figure in my story, too.

※

In late 2018, after returning to my base in Cairo from a trip to Yemen, an email arrived out of the blue. 'I'm a former intelligence official and was based in Quetta, Pakistan, when you came there,' it read. 'Your surveillance was our prime objective.' The sender provided a name and some basic details: he was a former ISI agent who had fled to Europe, was seeking asylum and wanted to talk.

I waited a week before responding. Was this a hoax? A trap? Once we started messaging, the contact established his bone fides by providing some startling details from my last trip to Quetta, six years earlier. Did I remember, he asked, a personable police officer named Abdullah who approached me at my hotel? I did. Well, he continued, Abdullah was in fact an ISI officer who had been tasked with surveilling me. He provided the man's real name. Did I remember when 'Abdullah' invited me for coffee at a café near the hotel with his young son? That was when the ISI searched my bags and bugged my hotel room. And when 'Abdullah' took me to interview the Quetta police chief, and I left my laptop in the car? A technician working for the agency seized that opportunity to try to hack into my laptop's hard drive.

'I know many things about you,' he said.

It was a surreal moment – the spy who shadowed me, stepping from behind a curtain like the fictional Stasi officer in *The Lives of Others*, a film about surveillance in communist-era East Berlin. It begged more questions. Why now? What did he want? The ex-spy insisted his motives were pure. 'Maybe you can expose the reality of Pakistan to the world,' he said. That was intriguing enough, but there was another potential upside: perhaps this person could tell me something about the line I had crossed, and why I had been kicked out. At the end of the winter, I flew to meet him.

A freezing wind gusted through the city, where commuters pedalled under battleship-grey skies, their collars upturned. I checked into a small hotel and then headed out to find the contact. After some confused texting, we bumped into each other on a side street, and exchanged awkward greetings. He was younger and less fusty than I expected – in his thirties, clean-shaven, in jeans and a hoodie, with a shock of dark hair and bright, searching eyes. He had just knocked off from his job as a courier, pedalling across the city making deliveries. We wandered through a shopping area, looking for a place to sit. Along the way, he pointed to a place where an Islamist terror attack had occurred years earlier. A clutch of police officers lingered at the spot, burly bearded men and a woman with bright lipstick. The ex-spy shrugged, and kept walking. We settled on a Pizza Hut.

He wanted to be known as Ashraf. His family were small-town Pashtuns, farmers and traders, and he had fallen into a career in intelligence almost by accident. Soon after his graduation from university, Ashraf came across a newspaper advertisement for positions at Pakistan's Defence Ministry. He applied. A year later a reply arrived from a post-office box in Islamabad, inviting him to an interview. At first, he figured it might be a job in the secretive nuclear programme, and it was only after several interviews that he realised it was the ISI. He embraced it as an opportunity: government jobs are the holy grail for many young Pakistanis – a pensionable position for life, job security, often with the potential to make a little cash on the side. The security sector is considered particularly lucrative. Two years later, after a battery of background checks and psychological tests, he was sent to spy school.

The Defence Services Intelligence Academy was Pakistan's version of The Farm, the CIA's covert training facility on a 9,000-acre compound in rural Virginia. It was located on the edge of Rawalpindi, where the city bleeds into the suburbs of Islamabad, at a discreet compound where recruits had to surrender their mobile phones and computers. Next door was an ISI storage depot known as Ojhri Camp, which briefly hit the news in 1988 when a huge stockpile of rockets and other munitions, destined for the mujahideen in Afghanistan, exploded. A hail of flaming munitions fell across a wide area, killing dozens of civilians; despite a wealth of conspiracy theories about sabotage and infiltration, the cause of the disaster was never fully explained.

Ashraf's class was filled with small-town boys like him, from across Pakistan. Over six months, they learned rudimentary tradecraft – lock-picking, phone-tapping and surveillance; interrogation and infiltration; surreptitious entry, clandestine photography. How to divert the attention of an adversary if caught in the act. 'If you caught me covering a target in here,' Ashraf said, gesturing around the Pizza Hut, 'I might pretend that I was stealing a pizza, to divert you from my true purpose.' The trainee spies practised their skills on the streets of Islamabad and Rawalpindi. Deploying in small groups to shopping malls and university campuses, often in disguise, they surveilled unsuspecting citizens and practised 'dead drops' – an espionage technique for secretly passing on messages in public. Other times, the instructors drove the students to towns miles away, dumped them on the roadside without money or papers, and ordered them to make their way back to the Academy using their wits. Sometimes, real life intruded. Once Ashraf and his classmates, in the guise of street vendors, were arrested by police officers who hauled them off to jail for refusing to pay a bribe. The police slapped and threatened the students, who were under strict orders not to break cover. Eventually, a weary ISI instructor turned up to bail them out.

After his graduation, Ashraf was posted to Quetta. He was initially assigned menial duties – running bureaucratic errands for bosses, or depositing payment for sources at the bank – but that afforded a view of the ISI's extensive operations in Quetta. Offices dotted around the city were known by their code names: Section 944 for Operations; Section 9341 for Counter-Intelligence; and, most sensitive of all, Section 21 for the 'Afghan Cell', which liaised with the Afghan Taliban. Like any intelligence organisation, the ISI was supposed to be strictly compartmentalised. But Quetta's compact size, and the loose discipline of its officers, allowed Ashraf to grasp the agency's activities beyond his office. In Meezan Chowk, a bustling downtown intersection, he spotted an ISI officer he knew in beggar's clothes, apparently surveilling a target. On a visit to the ISI headquarters in the city, Section 51, he spotted militants from outlawed sectarian and extremist groups who had apparently popped in for meetings. During tea breaks, fellow officers spoke indiscreetly about their work – swapping notes about their findings, showing off personal photos taken from phones or email accounts and chortling about anything strange or compromising.

The Counter-Intelligence detachment, Section 9341, was charged with surveilling foreigners. Quetta was a city of secrets, and their job was to ensure that snooping visitors didn't expose them. At the Serena, Ashraf explained, ISI officers posed as waiters, hovering near tables in the lobby, or listened through the walls of adjoining bedrooms at night. United Nations officials, Western diplomats, aid workers and foreign correspondents were the typical targets; hotel management, with little choice but to cooperate, pleaded with the spies for discretion. In 2006 those pleas were ignored, when the journalist Carlotta Gall was assaulted in her room at the Serena by presumed ISI goons. But during the visit that Ashraf described in 2012, their methods were more subtle and invasive than I had imagined.

At least four people tailed me. At night, an office in Islamabad sent them a copy of my email correspondence. I felt foolish for not spotting so-called Abdullah, the fake police inspector, who had sidled up to me in the lobby of the Serena, all warm smiles and firm handshakes. He gained my confidence by bad-mouthing the ISI, calling the agency a nuisance to honest-to-God policemen like himself. Still, Ashraf noted, Abdullah's team had struggled to break into my Apple laptop, which was rare in Quetta, so he hired a computer science lecturer from a private college to help with the job. As I had been interviewing Quetta's police chief, Ashraf explained, this man was in the back seat of my car, trying to break my encryption. He didn't know if the man succeeded.

The ISI also tailed its nominal allies. The CIA funded much of the ISI's fancy counterterrorism wing, known as Directorate C, and the two agencies collaborated closely on the hunt for members of al Qaeda. But out in the field, a chasm of mistrust lay between the two agencies, and the gloves came off. A CIA officer who went by the name George, and who came to Quetta to cooperate on counterterrorism, was the subject of an intensive surveillance operation, Ashraf told me. The American's phone was tapped, his car was tailed and his meetings were monitored at the ISI safe house where he was staying. (CIA officials in Pakistan, for their part, had begun to apply 'Moscow Rules', a highly defensive form of spycraft in a hostile country.)

Of likely greatest interest to the Americans was Section 21. Also known as the Afghan cell, Section 21 was part of what American intelligence called Directorate S – the most sensitive, action-oriented branch of the ISI, roughly akin to the CIA's paramilitary Special Activities Division, which had been at the heart of the agency's blackest operations for decades. Colonel Imam had been deputy chief of Section 21 for a period during the 1980s, directing guerilla strikes against the Red Army inside Afghanistan. A sister unit, known as the Kashmir Cell, ran jihadi operations in Indian-occupied Kashmir. In recent decades, officers at Section 21 liaised with the Quetta Shura, the Taliban's exiled leadership council. Even inside the ISI, its work was considered secretive. Most of its officers in Quetta were army officers, Ashraf said, and they tended to work through "cutouts" – paid tribal strongmen who lived in the ethnic Pashtun villages around Quetta, where Taliban fighters sheltered. Ashraf reeled off a list of these cut-outs. One name rang a bell.

In 2006, I had travelled to a village called Bagarzai, north of Quetta, to attend the funeral of a Taliban fighter who had been killed in battle with NATO troops in Kandahar, in southern Afghanistan. As a mullah – who also happened to be Balochistan's minister for health – read the eulogy over a mosque loudspeaker, I sat with the dead man's brother, Naseebullah Agha, one of the Taliban organisers now listed by Ashraf. Now Naseebullah, too, was dead. On his mobile phone, Ashraf called up a newspaper clip from a few years earlier that noted Naseebullah's death in a vehicle accident. Ashraf shrugged. ISI assets often perished under murky circumstances, he said. Some had gone too far with their criminal sidelines, such as kidnapping foreigners. Others knew too much. 'Once that person becomes a problem, the ISI takes care of them,' he said. 'They throw them away like a tissue.'

Darkness was falling over the European city. We left the Pizza Hut and headed out in search of a drink. When Ashraf worked at the ISI, his friends and family were envious of his position. 'They were like "Wow, it's a great job,"' he recalled. 'In our society, people believe that we have the world's number one intelligence agency.' But the junior spy no longer shared their admiration.

Ashraf never gave a single reason for his quitting the ISI, a decision that would eventually send him into exile. Over several conversations, he described his growing disenchantment with a spy agency seen by many Pakistanis as omnipotent and highly competent, but which he came to view, at ground level, as crude, incompetent and corrupt.

His duties included overseeing a small ISI jail, in the basement of an office building, where detainees were held – mostly Baloch separatists, but also people who had just fallen under suspicion. Their mistreatment bothered Ashraf. Detainees were held blindfolded for months on end, tortured by nothing as much as the constant darkness, slowly shrivelling before his eyes. He recalled an Afghan refugee, a man in his thirties, who had travelled for treatment for throat cancer, which caused the ISI to pick him up on suspicion of spying for India. The man was held for months on end, barely able to speak due to a pipe in his throat, and he begged Ashraf to be set free. He knew of at least one detainee who died for want of medical treatment, he said, and he heard from colleagues that others had been driven to remote mountainsides and executed.

Accountable to almost nobody, ISI officers were involved in a wide variety of money-making schemes, he said. They extorted money from the families of detainees and squeezed payments from businessmen with secrets to hide. Their ISI service card was a ticket to pass unhindered through virtually any police checkpoint in the country. At the crossing with Afghanistan, at Chaman, he said, Frontier Corps paramilitaries charged $500 for a car to cross unhindered. ISI officers were also on the take. Nobody seemed to care much what was smuggled, as long as they lined their pockets. 'A lot of it was clothes and car parts,' he said, 'but it could have been drugs, guns, anything.'

Much of Ashraf's disillusionment, though, seemed to be a matter of old-fashioned office politics, with an ethnic twist. He resented the domination of ethnic Punjabi military officers, who only allowed natives of Balochistan to hold menial positions in the ISI. His relationship with his boss, an army colonel, was difficult and they frequently clashed. And as a Pashtun, Ashraf detested the games that the ISI was playing inside that community, tolerating or strengthening the Afghan Taliban. He also worried for his safety. As Quetta grew more volatile, ISI colleagues were killed in the violence. One friend died in a suicide attack near the University of Balochistan; a second was shot dead as he sat in his car at a traffic light.

Ashraf quit. His first years outside the ISI were uneventful, working in an office job. Then he made a mistake. He applied for a job with foreigners, drawing the attention of the ISI. A friend called from inside the agency: they were monitoring him. Ashraf changed his mobile phone, moved in with a relative and got off Facebook. But one day, as he drove away from his parents' house, bullets smacked into his vehicle, leaving him unhurt but shaken. He didn't know who fired those shots. But he grew fearful that the ISI might treat him like a problematic asset.

He slipped out of Pakistan to Europe, studied for a year, and filed for asylum. Then he contacted me.

Ashraf produced letters, certificates and other documents to prove his record with the ISI; ascertaining his motives was harder. Was he shading the truth? Did he abandon the ISI for his stated reasons? Was he just another shape-shifting opportunist in the violent stew of Quetta? It was impossible to know for sure, but he insisted that his goal was merely to shine a light on the reality of Quetta. The Pakistani news media were so cowed, so understandably afraid, he said, that they could never do it.

He spoked excitedly about one such hidden story. A new civil rights movement was rising in the tribal belt called the Pashtun Protection Movement, known as PTM after its initials in Urdu. Led by a charismatic twenty-four-year-old named Manzoor Pashteen, the PTM offered Pashtuns a bracing sense of purpose. After years of being caricatured by outsiders as terrorists or warlike savages, Pashtuns were reclaiming their identity as a dignified people who rejected terrorist violence, and they flocked to rallies where Pashteen, who came from Waziristan, stirred their passions with eloquent oratory.

The PTM thrilled Ashraf, and as we drank beer he spoke of his delight that Pashtuns were finally speaking up. But he lamented that his old employer was trying hard to silence them. The Pakistani military, which viewed any Pashtun political movement as a threat to national security, had tasked the ISI with shutting down the PTM. Large public demonstrations in the northwest received little or no coverage in the Pakistani newspapers. Even when PTM organizers were assaulted or imprisoned, it was barely mentioned. The military's increasingly aggressive press division, Inter-Services Public Relations, had barred Pashteen from appearing on national TV stations, and devoted great efforts to discrediting him, trying to portray him as an agent for India or Afghanistan.

'Army is power over there,' Ashraf said, of Pakistan. 'People are afraid of it. This represents a chance to break it.' He paused to polish off the remainder of his beer. 'Maybe.'

We picked up our jackets and headed into the night.

❈

I stayed in touch with Ashraf for months after our meeting. Sometimes he would call from work, waxing at length about his spy days as he travelled across the European city making deliveries, interrupted by the opening doors of customers and their yapping dogs. Eventually, the conversation turned to the question of my expulsion from Pakistan. What were the 'undesirable activities' that got me kicked out?

For one thing, he said, it wasn't just the rag newspapers that believed I worked for the CIA, he ventured – the ISI did too. When I protested such a preposterous idea, given my profile as a reporter for a major newspaper, he chided me for my naïveté. 'A spy can be under any cover,' he said. Years earlier, he continued, the ISI had found evidence that a French aid worker visiting Quetta was in fact moonlighting for his own government. The man was expelled. My trips to Quetta, he continued, had brought me into focus inside the agency – or, at the least, suggested an irredeemable interest in the parts of Pakistan the ISI wanted to hide. That was especially true in Balochistan. 'Their eyes were on every move you made,' he told me. 'Wherever you went, whatever you did.'

I thought back to the odd question that the Information Minister put to me after I received the 'undesirable activities' letter: 'Have you been to Quetta recently?' Now it made sense, as did a strange warning I received months earlier. An official at the United States embassy had invited me for coffee and to deliver a warning: the United States had intercepted a phone conversation between two men in Quetta, the official said, who talked about killing me and a British journalist with the *Financial Times*. The Americans believed these men were with a jihadi organization, the diplomat said. The warning was concerning, but I set it aside as I did not intend to return to Quetta soon. But on that day following the expulsion letter, when I met the embassy press officer in the garden of the Serena Hotel, she changed their explanation: now she said that one of the men on the intercepted call was with the ISI.

Social media offered more hints that Balochistan was central to the ISI's decision to expel me. After I left Pakistan, progovernment Twitter accounts endlessly focused on my reporting on the province, in attacks that were frequently accompanied by a photo taken during my trip to Dera Bugti, in 2005. In the photo, I posed with a group of whiskery Baloch tribesmen who were guarding Nawab Bugti – proof, in the eyes of these trolls, that I was part of a nefarious 'anti-Pakistan' plot.

As the months wore on, Ashraf grew nervous about his safety. When called home, to chat with friends, he always said he was in a different European city, hoping to push the ISI off the trail if its agents were listening to the call. His family warned him to be careful. 'They're looking for you', a brother said. 'Don't come back.'

I pressed him. Was it definitely Balochistan that got me kicked out? He was not privy to the agency's file on me, he said. 'But it seems logical'. I realized I might never know the whole story – this was the best answer I could get. But it also presented a new riddle.

During my nine years in Pakistan, I'd written about countless sensitive issues – American drones strikes, Pakistan's nuclear weapons program, the SEAL raid that killed bin Laden, the internal workings of the ISI. So why was 'the war of the flea' – a scrappy insurgency in a remote province that barely concerned the outside world – the story that so angered the ISI that it was worth pushing me out?

It made little sense. The Baloch insurgency posed a puny military threat to Pakistan's military, the world's sixth-largest, with 800,000 men under arms. Western apathy toward the plight of the Baloch left Pakistan's generals free to fight the rebels as they pleased. And yet, Balochistan had become the biggest chip on their shoulders.

Why? Certainly, the province had strategic value – vast mineral resources and remote locations suitable for hiding nuclear weapons – and was the focus of a multi-billion-dollar economic corridor funded by China. On top of that, the army had a reflexive contempt for tribesmen it viewed as impudent upstarts. But perhaps, also, it came down to less tangible factors buried deep in the Pakistani psyche. The secession of East Pakistan in 1971, when a bungled counter-insurgency campaign cost Pakistan half of its territory, shattered the military's self-image as the guardian of the nation, and furrowed deep scars in its thinking. Subsequent attempts by other ethnic groups to claim greater independence – Baloch, Pashtuns and Sindhis, among others – met with a neuralgic response. Balochistan was the most glaring example of this weakness – a huge chunk of the country's land mass that, seven decades after independence, was under tenuous central control. And that, in turn, bespoke the psychosis of instability that had plagued Pakistan from the beginning. In a land of broken maps, Balochistan had the most fissiparous borders.

Military graduation ceremony, Abbottabad

11

A House on a Hill

Two Nations

In the winter of 2013, six months after my expulsion from Pakistan, I paid a visit to the Indian megalopolis of Mumbai. The city felt instantly familiar. A salt breeze whipped in off the Arabian Sea; street carts offered tangy snacks outside mould-stained buildings; the papers carried reports of gangster wars – unmistakable notes of Karachi, 500 miles up the coast. I had come to speak at a literary festival that took place on the stages of an old movie studio, famous in the 1950s when Indians and Pakistanis flocked to the same films. Afterwards, eager Indian schoolchildren peppered me with questions about their estranged cousins from that exotic, volatile land across India's northern border.

There had been a time when Pakistanis could afford to sneer at India, with its heavily centralised economy and suffocating bureaucracy, a land of cheap polyester *kurtas* and wheezing old rattletraps. Pakistan had smoother roads, smarter airlines and flashier hotels. 'The only part of an Indian car that doesn't make a noise is the horn,' went one Pakistani joke in the 1990s. But their fortunes starkly diverged after 2001, when Pakistan plunged into conflict and India's economy soared. Now, Indians were sending satellites into space and snapping up British luxury carmakers, and it was the Pakistanis who looked sclerotic. One night I was invited to a party at a chic residence on Marine Drive.

An antique lift transported guests up to a lavishly appointed salon where Mumbai's great and glamorous, dressed to the nines, sipped gin on a balcony overlooking the inky blackness of the Arabian Sea. As I left, I passed the city's most famous residence: a gleaming mansion that reached twenty-seven storeys into the sky, with helicopter pads and hundreds of staff, built by India's richest family on the site of a former orphanage at a cost of one billion dollars. This real-estate monstrosity had become a perverse source of pride to Mumbaikars (as Mumbai's residents are known), a neck-straining folly to be admired and mocked. Further along, outside a Rolls-Royce showroom, silvery light fell gently on beggars curled up on the pavement.

The following day I took a taxi to Malabar Hill, a well-heeled neighbourhood of old money and steep slopes on the south side of the city. At the wheel was a taciturn, half-shaved man named Maqbool, one of India's 180 million Muslims – nearly as many as in Pakistan. Maqbool's old car chugged to the top of a hill, passing high walls draped with blazing flowers, and halted outside a pair of slumping gates. NO PARKING, read a sloppy sign. I peered through the rusting bars, drawing the attention of a dishevelled guard. No, I could not take a look, he said curtly, muttering something about official permission before turning on his heel. As he vanished into the gloaming, I could make out the lines of a crumbling mansion hidden behind a cluster of unkempt trees. Its grand windows were smeared with dirt. Its balustrades sagged. And there was no evident trace of the man who had built it eighty years earlier: Muhammad Ali Jinnah.

This was South Court, Jinnah's principal residence in the decades leading to partition in 1947. Key events of those hectic years unfolded inside these walls – the huddled parleys that forged the destiny of a subcontinent and its 400 million people, a population now surpassing 1.7 billion. The dining room was the stage for stormy confrontations between Jinnah and his nemesis, Jawaharlal Nehru of the Congress Party. Lord Mountbatten, the pomp-loving viceroy, took brooding walks in South Court's European-style garden, with its sweeping sea views. In the autumn of 1944, Jinnah held crucial talks here with Mahatma Gandhi, the spiritual guide of Indian independence and his fellow Gujarati, once Jinnah's steadfast ally and now his implacable foe.

Jinnah bought the property from a departing Scottish colonial officer in 1912, when Mumbai was known as Bombay. At the time, a modest bungalow, built in the Goan style, stood in the grounds. Six years later, after their hurried wedding, Jinnah's new wife, eighteen-year-old Ruttie Dinshaw, was distinctly unimpressed with this dingy bachelor pad. 'A fun-forsaken house,' she declared, before setting about transforming it into one of Bombay's most fashionable homes, with Chinese vases, Persian rugs and bronze casts of ancient animals. The silver-haired Muslim barrister and his vivacious wife quickly became fixtures of Bombay's high society. Jinnah held court in the library while Ruttie entertained guests on the veranda, drinking sherbet as they overlooked the sea. They loved each other. Jinnah indulged Ruttie's whims, and she doted on him as 'J'. A daughter, Dina, was born. But style and elegance failed to bridge the deep gulf of temperament between them, and in 1928, after years of blazing rows, they separated. Ruttie plunged into depression and, a year later, was found dead after swallowing a fistful of sleeping pills. Jinnah, grief-stricken, was devastated. For months, his servants noted, he would sit with her belongings in his upstairs bedroom, trapped in sorrow. In 1931, he shut up South Court and moved to London.

On his return to India, four years later, Jinnah razed the tired old bungalow and built a spectacular mansion in its place. He spared little expense. Italian workmen installed the marble façades, the walnut panelling was pure British, and a majestic peepal tree filled the driveway. 'Oh, it is a dream!' marvelled one awestruck visitor. But South Court was also a loud political statement. During his long exile in London, word reached Jinnah that Gandhi had written him off as 'a spent force'. Now he was back, catapulted to the pinnacle of politics as the uncontested leader of India's 100 million Muslims. There was talk of a new country named Pakistan.

Through the early 1940s, as World War II raged, Jinnah, Gandhi and Nehru would mug for the cameras on the steps of South Court before retreating inside to do battle over the future of the subcontinent. Jinnah was embroiled in arguments with his family, too. A rift erupted with his daughter, Dina, over her plans to marry a Parsi industrialist named Neville Wadia – a union that Jinnah feared would bruise his popularity with Muslim voters. 'There are millions of Muslim boys in India, and she could have anyone she chose,' he raged. Dina called out his hypocrisy. 'Father, there were millions of Muslim girls in India,' she shot back. 'Why did you not marry one of them?' For a time, Jinnah referred to his daughter frostily as 'Mrs Wadia', but within himself he was anguished. 'For two weeks he would not receive visitors,' his driver told the celebrated writer Saadat Hasan Manto. 'He would just keep smoking his cigars and pacing up and down in his room. He must have walked hundreds of miles in those two weeks.'

Even in the feverish summer of 1947, amid the torn maps and blood-soaked rampages of the burning British empire, Jinnah believed he might keep his magnificent residence. Once Pakistan had been created, he intended to return to South Court at weekends, and perhaps even retire there once things settled down. That quixotic hope was a reflection of Jinnah's broader expectation that Pakistan and India would be friendly neighbours, like the United States and Canada, with open borders and free trade, and perhaps even mutual defence arrangements. When it became clear, so horribly quickly, that they would be more like feuding cousins, Jinnah held on to South Court thanks to a magnanimous gesture from his old nemesis. Ignoring protests from hardliners in his cabinet, Nehru ensured that South Court was not designated as 'evacuee property', which would have caused it to be occupied by Hindus or Sikhs who had fled Pakistan. The house would remain in Jinnah's name but be rented to British diplomats.

By the time I reached South Court in 2013, it was in a state of near-collapse. Newspapers reported that bats fluttered through its empty corridors, snakes slithered in the weed-infested gardens and the proud walnut panelling had crumbled to mulch. The property had been vacant for three decades, locked in a three-way legal battle. Dina, now in her nineties and resident in New York, was suing for possession, hoping to spend her final years in the house where she had grown up. The Pakistani state argued that it was the rightful owner, and said it would use the house to house a future Mumbai consulate — whenever that might be possible, given the dire relations between the two countries. India's government, unsure which way to turn, left the dispute to the courts — which was to say that it might drag on for years, or decades.

In Mumbai's overheated real-estate market, the land alone was worth $400 million. But South Court was stuck, trapped in a bitter and intractable dispute, the haunted house of partition. And like so much of the state of rancour between Pakistan and India, nobody seemed to have the imagination, much less the will, to find a way out of the mess.

❧

The two countries come face to face, every day, for an exquisitely choreographed martial ballet. At about four in the afternoon, on a narrow patch of no-man's-land at the Wagah border crossing, ten miles from Lahore, Pakistani and Indian troops come together to perform the Beating Retreat, a seventeenth-century military drill they inherited from the British. The tallest soldiers from both countries, wearing the most elaborate fantail turbans, march back, forth and around each other, shouting and stamping, preening and pouting. Apparently selected for their ability to comically eyeball one another, they brandish fists and perform preposterously high kicks to loud roars from spectators gathered in giant bleachers on either side of the border. The spectacle is camp, glorious and depressing: decades of history reduced to a *desi* (South Asian) version of TV wrestling, the difference being that these combatants might one day start fighting each other for real. When the show is over, the gate slams shut, the crowds melt away and soldiers on both sides beat a retreat to a cup of tea.

It's hard to imagine now, but relations between India and Pakistan were once civil, even warm. In the early years after partition, citizens of both countries enjoyed visa-free travel and their leaders were on chummy terms. In 1959, Pakistan's military ruler, Field Marshal Ayub Khan, stopped off at New Delhi Airport to negotiate a water treaty with Jawaharlal Nehru, the leader of independent India. A year later, Nehru received a hero's welcome in Karachi, where 100,000 Pakistanis lined the route crying, '*Nehru Zindabad!*' ('Long Live Nehru!') But then came the 1965 war over Kashmir, when Pakistani tanks rolled through the sugarcane fields of Punjab and Indian jets bombed the Lahore suburbs. The long spiral into conflict had begun. Today, Wagah is the only border crossing between Pakistan and India, a narrow aperture that permits a dribble of trucks to cross every day, leaving untapped the two countries' vast potential for trade.

It's a shame, if only because Pakistanis and Indians hold so much in common: Bollywood movies, fast-bowl cricket, a scattering of languages, even playful arguments over who produces the juicier mango. They share a word, *desi*, that signifies a person or cultural concept from the subcontinent; when they meet in Western cities or on African peacekeeping missions, Pakistanis and Indians automatically gravitate towards one another. But the wounds of history cut deep, and their security establishments are trapped in a loop of grievance, recrimination and chest-beating. Nothing is resolved. Indians portray Jinnah as a vampiric figure, driven by a cold ego to dismember the subcontinent. Pakistanis wallow in slights and resentment – did Edwina Mountbatten sleep with Nehru? India caused the humiliation of East Pakistan! – and seethe at Western allies who refuse to take their side, especially the Americans. Both countries have enough nuclear firepower to blow their respective capitals to smithereens.

'It all comes back to India,' as the American ambassador to Pakistan, Anne Patterson, told me before she left. We were in her office, mulling over why Pakistan's military continued to play with fire by supporting 'good' jihadis. The perceived threat from India lay at the heart of this confounding strategy, she concluded. 'I don't think it's justified, but they do. And the longer you are here, the more you are convinced that's the key to the whole problem.'

It was certainly true that the trauma of partition, and the confusions of faith and identity it created, lurked behind the most enduring pathologies I encountered in the land of broken maps. Although Pakistan was built on faith, Islam offered an incomplete identity. Negation of India filled the void. Viewed through this lens, so much of what Pakistan did – the coddling of jihadis, the scheming in Afghanistan – seemed to stem from a gnawing insecurity. Pakistan had to be everything India was, and was not.

As we chugged through rush-hour traffic, Maqbool the taxi driver pointed out a quiet stretch of shoreline that recalled a sinister moment. On a calm evening in November 2008, a small boat carrying ten heavily armed Pakistanis landed here. After splitting into pairs, the Pakistanis headed for central Mumbai, where they set about killing as many Indians, Jews and Western tourists as possible. 'Brothers, make it burn,' their handler instructed.

The gunmen belonged to Lashkar-e-Taiba, or 'The Army of the Pure', the most lethal of several militant groups established by the ISI in the 1980s to carry out attacks in Indian-held Kashmir. After 9/11, Lashkar fighters turned their guns against American troops in Afghanistan. But the *jihad* against India remained their priority. By the end of the assault on Mumbai, sixty hours later, 166 people lay dead and hundreds were injured. It was a staggering global terrorist spectacle, arguably the most audacious since 2001, and it unfolded live on television, leaving indelible images of a blazing five-star Taj Mahal Palace hotel and bloodied bodies strewn around the Leopold Café, which was popular with foreign tourists. And all of it had been remotely directed from a house in the Karachi suburbs.

A single attacker survived. Ajmal Kasab was a high-school dropout from a Punjabi backwater who had joined Lashkar a year earlier, seeking fame and adventure. In the iconic image of the massacre, Kasab strides through the packed Chhatrapati Shivaji railway station, an assault rifle under his arm, spraying gunfire at helpless commuters. The Indian police captured him two hours later as he drove in a stolen car towards Malabar Hill. The semi-literate militant was unlikely to have grasped the historical irony of his mission: to carry out a massacre of rich

Indians in the name of Pakistani nationalism, in the shadow of Muhammad Ali Jinnah's abandoned mansion.

At the magnificent Taj Mahal Palace hotel, where Lashkar gunmen had corralled guests into the ballroom to be slaughtered, a magazine publisher named Ashok Advani showed me around. A Hindu in his seventies, Advani was born in Pakistan before his family moved to India in 1947. We climbed the sweeping staircase, all traces of blood washed clean, then took tea in the lush gardens, at tables where tourists had once cowered in terror. The air was heavy with delicate fragrances. 'One day,' Ashok said, 'our countries will need to find a way out of this. So much hate. So much utterly pointless hate.'

I had met the face of that hate. Earlier that year, in January 2013, I interviewed the effective leader of Lashkar-e-Taiba, Hafiz Saeed, at his spacious Lahore residence. Uniformed police officers stood guard outside. The United States had announced a $10 million bounty for Saeed's arrest, adding to earlier United Nations sanctions. Saeed, who formerly ran a large health and education charity, affected an air of indifference. 'I move about like an ordinary person,' he said, reclining on a bolster as he picked from a heaped plate of *biryani*. 'My fate is in the hands of God, not America.'

As the police guard indicated, Pakistan's military continued to coddle Lashkar-e-Taiba, whose portly leader was their most prominent asset. The army chief, General Kayani, swore he had no role in the Mumbai attack. But his proxy's fingerprints were all over the gun. Before he was executed, Ajmal Kasab told Indian investigators of a rousing speech delivered by Saeed at a training camp in the Pakistani-controlled part of Kashmir. 'If you die waging jihad, your faces will glow like the moon,' Saeed told the Mumbai attackers, his hands resting across his chest as if in prayer. 'Your bodies will emanate scent. And you will go to paradise.' When I repeated that account to Saeed, he dismissed it with deadpan mockery. 'Who knows why Kasab was in Bombay?' he mused, referring to Mumbai by its old name. 'Maybe he went to see a movie?'

I knew countless Pakistanis who yearned for peace with India, a country they secretly loved. But their voices were drowned out by the gunmen and their military backers. I showed Saeed the photo of Kasab striding through the crowded railway station, gun in hand. He shrugged. 'These days, you can create anything you want on a computer,' he said, and turned back to his supper.

❧

Just as Pakistan's pretensions of economic superiority were being shattered, so were India's notions of itself as a bastion of secular tolerance. The election of Narendra Modi, a populist Hindu nationalist, as prime minister of India in 2014 signalled more than a rightward lurch – it shook India's ideological foundations to their core. Until then, Indian politicians had prided themselves on being the heirs to Nehru's vision of India as a country of rich pluralism, where Hindus, Muslims and Sikhs co-existed peacefully and shared political power (even if reality often fell short of that goal). The rise of Modi's Bharatiya Janata Party (BJP), which surfed to power on a wave of pent-up Hindu resentment, changed all of that. Modi had entered politics through the RSS, the Hindu supremacist group whose member, Nathuram Vinayak Godse, had assassinated Gandhi in 1948. Within a few years of Modi becoming prime minister, the civil and political rights of India's Muslim minority came under sustained assault.

It started with a symbolic issue. Cows had always been a marker of cultural and religious difference in India: Hindus worshipped bovines; Muslims ate them. 'The cows I want to eat, the Hindu stops me from killing,' Muhammad Ali Jinnah remarked. After Modi came to power, that distinction became a pretext for communal violence. Hindu mobs lynched Muslims who worked with cows under the noses of indifferent police officers. The Hindu supremacists turned to other issues. Muslim romantics were accused of waging 'love jihad' against Hindu women. State governments curbed their civil liberties. In December 2019, Modi passed a law that blatantly restricted Muslim citizenship. Two months later, Hindu mobs set upon Muslims in New Delhi, in a wave of destruction and arson that left fifty people dead, and had chilling echoes of partition. Such flagrant discrimination was strikingly similar to the intolerance of Pakistan's Islamists. Modi himself was riding a larger wave, as the South Asian flag-bearer for the wave of right-wing populism washing across the globe. 'This is extraordinary. This is unprecedented,' Modi told diaspora supporters in the United States in September 2019, before grasping the hand of President Donald Trump.

India's lurch into belligerent Hindu nationalism suggested an uncomfortable historical vindication. For decades, Pakistani progressives had revered Jinnah but scoffed at his two-nation theory – the idea, used by Muslim leaders to justify the creation of Pakistan, that Muslims and Hindus could never peacefully coexist. Now those assumptions were being re-examined. In 2019, Muslims were literally written out of Indian history, when Modi officials drafted new school textbooks with a 'Hindu First' focus that stressed the country's Hindu heritage, and played down the older multicultural narrative. In Muslim-majority Kashmir, Modi revoked the region's special constitutional position, arrested its political leaders and cut off the internet. To Pakistani eyes, this revived the old fears of Hindu majoritarianism, or 'Hindu Raj', touted by Jinnah and his supporters seventy years earlier. Maybe, some ventured, the old man had been right all along. #ThankYouJinnah read a popular hashtag on Pakistani Twitter.

Amid those changes, Jinnah's tumbledown Mumbai mansion lurched back into the headlines. A powerful politician named

Mangal Prabhat Lodha launched a crusade to break the deadlock over South Court. He was a politician for the times, a brash billionaire and real-estate mogul whose projects had included Mumbai's Trump Tower, a seventy-five-story behemoth of shimmering gold. He had survived investigations for tax evasion and corruption. MAKE MUMBAI GREAT AGAIN, declared his website. Lodha was the Mumbai head of the Baharatiya Janata Party, a position he attained by stoking crude anti-Muslim sentiment. He specialised in outlandish ideas like his campaign to bar Muslim men from marrying Hindu women. Now he turned on South Court.

As 'the place from which the conspiracy of partition was hatched', Lodha told the Maharashtra legislative assembly, the house should be seized by the Indian state and razed to the ground. To sweep aside the tangle of legal claims, Lodha hoped to exploit recent changes to the Enemy Property Act, which governed property abandoned during partition. The changes appeared to invalidate the longstanding claim by Jinnah's daughter, Dina. In place of Jinnah's hated house, Lodha proclaimed, the government should erect a cultural centre to celebrate the glories of India's Hindu heritage.

But the Hindu supremacist faced a second obstacle: the special order about South Court that prime minister Nehru had enacted seven decades earlier, as a favour to his old foe Jinnah, insulated the house from any changes in the law. At the legislative assembly, Lodha demanded that the government abolish those protections so that Jinnah's crumbling mansion could be formally, and finally, declared 'enemy property'.

❋

My own house in Islamabad was also in limbo, a symbol of my desired return. I held onto it for two years after my expulsion, hoping to find a way back. Mazloom fed the dogs and dusted my room; my housemate, a journalist for the Guardian, continued to host dinner parties. In London, I met with Pakistani diplomats and ISI officials, to petition for a new visa. If nothing else, I wanted closure, an opportunity to say farewell to the country that filled my life for a decade. No such luck. A Pakistani newspaper reported that I had been placed in 'Category One' of an official blacklist of people barred from entering the country. Later, my photo was posted on the immigration counters at Karachi Airport, alongside images of various 'miscreants', presumably to stop me from trying to slip back in. I got the hint.

The *New York Times* posted me to Cairo and I arranged a sale of my belongings in Islamabad. (My 1968 Volkswagen Beetle went back to its original owners, who promised to let me drive it if I ever returned.) I found a new home for two of my dogs, Luna and Pookie, at a farmhouse outside Islamabad. Spike was already dead, following a bone disease. I bade an emotional farewell to Mazloom over the phone. 'Sir, we miss you here,' he said.

My expulsion did, however, have one happy outcome. My girlfriend had been visiting when the Pakistanis kicked me out. Days later, she welcomed me into her flat in London and, two years after that, we were married in a grand celebration in a field under a mountain in the west of Ireland. One-third of the guests were Pakistani, and they danced in a tent through the night until the neighbours, despite their high tolerance for drunken carousing, complained about the noise. You could say we owed the ISI that much. I offered the generals a silent toast.

✳

There have been so many hollow predictions of Pakistan's demise – Tariq Ali's fine book from 1983, for example, was titled *Can Pakistan Survive?* – that the most pertinent question might be not whether Pakistan will fail, but how it has survived this long. The doom-tinged forecasts of my early years in Pakistan did not come to pass. Militants did not seize power or snatch a nuclear warhead. War with India was averted. Pakistan's relationship with the United States stumbled on. The state did not collapse and, best of all, the Taliban were pushed into retreat.

A high-school massacre proved a turning point. In December 2014, six militants rampaged through the Army Public School in Peshawar, flinging grenades and spraying gunfire that killed 149 people, mostly children. Under intense public pressure, the military jolted into a higher gear. A wave of unremitting anti-Taliban operations cleared the militants from their strongholds in the tribal belt and Karachi. The rate of violence plunged. In 2013, Pakistan had forty-six suicide attacks and 2,400 deaths from militant attacks; in 2019, there were four suicide attacks and 350 deaths. In Karachi, pilgrims flocked to the reopened Manghopir shrine, where the sacred crocodiles once again luxuriated in its murky green waters, feasting on small bags of meat. 'Peshawar opened the world's eyes,' said a policeman posted outside the shrine.

And yet.

The decade of mayhem that followed the Red Mosque siege in 2007 had exacted a fearsome toll. Some 63,000 Pakistanis had been killed and 66,000 injured in violence of various kinds – Taliban bombings, American drone strikes, sectarian bombings, the war in Balochistan and fighting on the border with India, among other causes. Over a thousand schools had been destroyed, and the land's ancient lattice of religious diversity had been ripped to shreds. Even the glowing, 800-year-old Sufi shrine at Sehwan Sharif did not escape: in 2017, a blast ripped through a crowd of pilgrims gathered before its golden gates, slaughtering ninety people. Although the Taliban were on the run, many other jihadi outfits roamed freely. The ISI's double games continued.

The United States also bore a measure of responsibility for Pakistan's chaos. The CIA drone campaign in the tribal belt wiped out the top tier of al Qaeda militants, but it also killed hundreds of civilians. The lengthy, inconclusive American intervention in Afghanistan had badly destabilised Pakistan by creating fertile ground for its jihadi groups. No firm evidence was produced, in Washington or elsewhere, to prove accusations that the Pakistanis had been sheltering Osama bin Laden in Abbottabad. But a poisonous distrust endured, demonstrating more than ever that Washington and Islamabad were joined by their hard interests rather than any shared values.

Bigger questions loomed. With more than 200 million inhabitants, one-third under the age of fourteen, Pakistan had become the world's fifth most populous country. The figure was projected to double by 2050. One day, experts joked, Pakistan would be a standing-room-only kind of country. Environmental damage and climate change added to the strain. In the winter, a poisonous smog blanketed Lahore, injuring children and forcing schools to close; in the summer, Karachi laboured under hellish, increasingly frequent heat waves that, in 2015, killed 400 people in a matter of days. Melting ice caps in the Himalayas threatened food production. The economy stumbled on, lagging ever further behind India. It all raised anxious questions. What would those legions of jobless young Pakistanis do in the future, as they chafed at the frustrations of their poverty-stricken lives? Who would they blame it on? And what ideas would guide them?

Pakistan's identity crisis is not unique. In his 1995 book *Inventing Ireland*, the historian Declan Kiberd traced how the poet W. B. Yeats and other intellectuals purposefully forged an Irish identity in the early twentieth century, before independence from Britain. Was it Jinnah's fault, as Salman Rushdie has charged, that he insufficiently imagined his creation? Perhaps. But blame – or adulation – of Jinnah is no longer of much use to those Pakistanis seeking to imagine a better future. Husain

Haqqani, a former diplomat, has suggested that its leaders should jettison the ideology of jihad, abandon the pointless pursuit of parity with India, and see Pakistan as a trading nation rather than a warrior one. Already, Pakistanis possess many advantages and strengths: a huge number of educated, ambitious and resourceful young people; an extended family system that provides a social safety net; surprising pockets of tolerance, even in the most conservative quarters; and deep stores of resilience. Above all, Pakistanis are survivors.

Yet a country, like a person, may only have nine lives. Rather than wait for fate to overtake them, some of the people I met in the Insha'Allah Nation took matters into their own hands.

Shakir Husain, the software entrepreneur from Karachi, moved his family to San Francisco. His wife could no longer stand Pakistan's volatility. His firm has thrived.

Karachi's political don, Altaf Hussain, fared less well. A concerted army operation shattered his hold on Karachi, fracturing his MQM party and disbanding his gangs of armed street enforcers. Still stranded in exile, Hussain's speeches became increasingly erratic, and one day his posters vanished from the Karachi monument with the inscription 'Distance Does Not Matter'. The monument was renamed.

On the frontier, Anwar Kamal's brother, Akhtar, assumed the leadership of the Marwat tribe. With the Pakistani Taliban on the run, Akhtar told me, the Marwat *lashkar*, or private army, was less busy. The villagers of Shah Hassan Khel began to play volleyball again.

After five years of brutal captivity, Salmaan Taseer's kidnapped son, Shahbaz, made a dramatic escape in 2016. On his return to the family home in Lahore, he cited his father's words: 'I am not made of wood that burns easily.' But he came back to a family split in two. A bitter inheritance dispute had erupted between the children of Taseer's two wives, who traded accusations of forged wills and other underhand tactics. 'It's gloves off – the whole shit,' one of Taseer's sons told me, in terms that were reminiscent of his father.

The Christian blasphemy convict, Asia Bibi, was finally released in 2018, after nine years in prison. She eventually fled to Canada, where she was granted political asylum. 'They said change your faith, and you'll be freed,' she told one interviewer, of her time in prison. 'But I said no. I will live my sentence. With my faith.' In Islamabad, devotees still flocked to the glittering tomb where Taseer's assassin lay buried. A donation box by the door solicited funds for a new *madrassa*, where, presumably, future Malik Mumtaz Qadris could be educated.

In Karachi, the police tracked down the Taliban military commander thought to have masterminded the hit on Chaudhry Aslam. Perhaps predictably, he did not make it to court, having been shot dead by the police in yet another 'encounter'. The government gave $460,000 in compensation to Aslam's widow and offered his oldest son a job with the Karachi police. The son declined.

At the Red Mosque in Islamabad, the bullet holes were filled and plastered over, and its iconic dome was repainted in a bright shade of scarlet. The mosque's sour-faced chief cleric, Maulana Abdul Aziz, resumed his duties. More than thirty criminal charges, including murder and kidnapping, had been dropped – lack of evidence, the authorities claimed – and a new batch of poverty-stricken teenagers enrolled at Abdul Aziz's new *madrassa* in central Islamabad. The seminary library was named after Osama bin Laden.

Things ended less well for Maulana Sami ul Haq, the cleric known variously as the 'Father of the Taliban' and 'Sami the Sandwich'. In late 2018, an unidentified assailant broke into the cleric's Rawalpindi home and stabbed him to death. The motive for the crime was unclear, and it seemed destined to join

Pakistan's lengthening list of unsolved murders, the most prominent of which was still that of Benazir Bhutto.

Her son, Bilawal, took control of the Pakistan Peoples Party; her husband, Asif Ali Zardari, faced fresh corruption charges after stepping down as president. Zulfikar Ali Bhutto Junior – Benazir's nephew, who was named for her famous father – announced himself as a queer performance artist. He appeared on stage in San Francisco wearing a shimmering dress and dancing to a beloved Pakistani pop song.

The portly militant leader of Lashkar-e-Taiba, Hafiz Saeed, was finally arrested in July 2019 on charges of financing terror. Few expected he would be kept in prison for long.

Imran Khan was elected prime minister in 2018 but struggled to deliver on his heady promises. Instead of ending corruption and dynastic politics, the former sports star ruled with an authoritarian touch, and, as feared by his critics, abdicated control of key areas – national security, Afghanistan and India – to the military. A second marriage, in 2014, to a British-Pakistani television presenter, soon ended in divorce. His ex-wife wrote an explosive tell-all memoir that was filled with salacious details about Khan's sex life and his allegedly voracious appetite for intoxicants. (Khan dismissed the accusations and called the marriage the biggest mistake of his life.) Three years later he remarried again, this time to a Sufi faith healer who appeared in public in an all-covering white burka. Unable to see their first lady's face, some Pakistanis nicknamed her 'the ghost'.

Nawaz Sharif's third term as prime minister was marred by tensions with the military, and he was jailed on corruption charges in 2018. A year later, he was allowed to fly to London for medical treatment. He did not return.

After the criminal case against Axact fell apart, Bol TV went on air, offering its viewers a diet of reliably pro-military programming. Among its stars was the retired dictator Pervez Musharraf, who hosted a show called *First and Foremost, Pakistan*. In 2018, Axact sued the *New York Times* in Pakistan's courts for defamation; two years later, the case was still pending.

Ardeshir Cowasjee, the charming curmudgeon of Karachi, penned his last article for *Dawn* in December 2011, at the age of eighty-five. 'Tired and disillusioned with a country that just cannot pull itself together in any way,' he wrote, 'I have decided to call it a day.' Eleven months later, Cowasjee died. Mourners of all faiths streamed into his Bath Island residence, where one woman wore a burka and another clutched a set of rosary beads. His remains were transferred to the Tower of Silence – a raised structure where, as the Parsi faith dictates, the bodies of the dead are left to be eaten by birds of prey.

The insurgency in Balochistan limped on. With little coverage for their cause in the Pakistani media, separatists posted gory photographs to social media websites that showed the mutilated remains of men they claimed had died in custody. In the desert outside Nawab Bugti's destroyed fort in Dera Bugti, the watchtower still stands above the Nawab's grave, manned by soldiers charged with ensuring that nobody would dare to visit it.

In November 2017, Jinnah's daughter, Dina, died in New York at the age of ninety-eight. The fate of her father's Malabar Hill mansion remained unresolved. The news made me think back to another of Jinnah's houses, his summer residence in the juniper-covered hills over Quetta, where he spent his agonising final months in 1948. For decades, the two-storey wooden house was a museum where schoolchildren came to learn about their country's enigmatic prodigal father. Then one night in 2013, as Pakistan shuddered under the force of its own contradictions, it became another symbol to be torn down.

A group of masked Baloch separatists on motorbikes, armed with assault rifles and grenades, pulled up by the front door of the deserted old house. Guided by torchlight, they stormed inside.

A video filmed by a militant cameraman captures the final moments of the assault. The militants gather the paintings into a bonfire, douse it with petrol and set it alight. Moving outside, they tear down a Pakistani flag and run a rebel standard up the flagpole. Behind them, the wooden structure crackles as flames lick its walls. A window shatters. Dogs bark. The masked men vanish into the night as the house of Jinnah burns silently.

Waziristan as seen from a Pakistan army helicopter

ACKNOWLEDGEMENTS

This book took a long time to write and taxed the patience of family, friends and editors. Its working title was *Insha'Allah Nation*, which I loved yet came to rue. "Insha'Allah book," they would tease. But those people, and many others, helped in so many ways to get it over the line.

Peter Bergen planted the seed for a book over a drink in my garden in 2008; John Freeman at *Granta* published my first longform stories on Pakistan, which were skilfully edited by Ellah Allfrey; Rukhsana Siddiqui, a friend and professor at Quaid-i-Azam university, brainstormed the original title. James Astill, my predecessor as *Guardian* correspondent, pointed me toward Pakistan in 2004, and Kate Jones, a brilliant agent and a wonderful person, was the first person to believe in the project. She died soon after, tragically young.

Friends offered beds, desks, dinners: Romaine Lancaster in London, Jason Burke in Paris, David Leigh in Scotland, Ghaith Abdul-Ahad in Istanbul, and Rick Snelsire in Milan. I had the good fortune to get a place on two fabulous writer's residency programs. Thanks to Pilar Palacia and the staff at the Rockefeller Foundation's Bellagio Center, on Lake Como, where I spent an idyllic three weeks; and thanks to D.W. Gibson for a last-minute place at the Art Omi residency at Ledig House in Hudson, New York. Additionally, I spent a few winter weeks at the cosy Tyrone Guthrie Centre in Annaghmakerrig, Ireland. My thanks also to the smart, inspiring writers I met on those stays, as well as to the staff at the British Library, where I did the final stretch of writing.

Growing up as a teenager in Ballina, in the west of Ireland, lapping up every newspaper I could lay my hands on, I never imagined that I would one day be lucky enough to work for the best of them. At the *Guardian*, Harriet Sherwood hired me as Pakistan/Afghanistan correspondent, Ian Katz brought me to London to cover the WikiLeaks cables, and Alan Rusbridger offered support when things got tricky. Thanks especially to Jamie Wilson, David Munk, Paul Hamilos and Julian Borger, as well as to Charlie English, Ewan MacAskill, Peter Beaumont, Simon Tisdall, Richard Norton-Taylor, Roger Tooth, Heather Mercer, Karen Plews, Max Benato, Martin Hodgson, Mark Rice-Oxley, Sean Smith, Rory McCarthy, Malik Meer and Chris Elliot.

At the *New York Times*, Jane Perlez made the introductions, Susan Chira invited me to New York, and Joe Kahn hired me. Jill Abramson was a fierce advocate with the Pakistanis after I was expelled, as was Dean Baquet who allowed me to continue covering Pakistan from London, where John F. Burns and Steven Erlanger were welcoming hosts. Tyler Hicks brought cakes to my hotel room when I was detained in Lahore; Jim Yardley offered a bed in New Delhi; David Furst always ensured the strongest images. Bill Keller kindly invited me for an eventful weekend with his family in the Hamptons. Michael Slackman guided me to Egypt and provided new opportunities. Special thanks to all the editors who guided Pakistan coverage, but especially Doug Schorzman, whose fine judgements and unwavering support steered the trickiest stories onto the page — a true reporter's editor.

Thanks to my editors: Tom Mayer at W. W. Norton, who plunged into the material, offered incisive feedback, and was a ready source of elegant solutions to knotty narrative problems; Michael Fishwick at Bloomsbury who brought his tremendous enthusiasm and experience to the project, as well as Lauren Whybrow who was patient with a flurry of last-minute changes. And the agents: Patrick Walsh at Conville & Walsh (now PEW Literary), Sloan Harris at ICM in New York, and especially the formidable Karolina Sutton at Curtis Brown, my mainstay throughout.

Most of my 'nine lives' died tragically early, so I am indebted to their family members who helped flesh out biographical details: Munizae and Sulema Jahangir, Shaan and Shehrbano Taseer, Akhtar Munir Khan. For Chaudhry Aslam Khan, Omar Shahid Hamid was an invaluable resource and Saba Imtiaz interviewed one of his colleagues for me. Thanks to Allen Ezell, Zahid Jamil and Javed Hassan for helping with the Axact story. Charles Berman, a former British soldier, shared his memories of Waziristan in the 1940s with assistance from his daughter, Sandy. Former CIA officers Art Keller, Bob Grenier, Milt Bearden offered their insights on the ISI. Ameena Saiyid at the Oxford University Press in Karachi provided a copy of an elusive book. In Mumbai, Ashok Advani and Gayatri Rangachari Shah offered hospitality and advice. Henrik Moltke helped with research. Others who helped with research cannot be identified, but I am no less in their debt.

I drew shamelessly on the expertise of others to read chapters: Abubakar Siddique, Michael Semple, Shehryar Fazli, Hassan Zaidi, Sabrina Tavernise, Zaffar Abbas, Griff Witte, Alex von Tunzelmann, Doug Schorzman, David Kirkpatrick, Aarish Khan, Zia ur Rehman, Fahad Desmukh, Taha Siddiqui, Shah Meer Baloch, and Salman Siddiqui. Sanam Maher helped weed the clichés from the manuscript. I owe a special debt to my friend Sarah Lyall, who edited chapters and offered encouragement when mine flagged; to Omar Waraich, who was generous with his encyclopaedic knowledge of Pakistan; and especially to Madiha Sattar, who carved out entire weekends to read and edit chapters. Her incisive, careful feedback improved the text greatly and I remain in her debt. Needless to say, any errors that remain are entirely my own.

A decade is a long time to cover a country, and whatever I know stems partly from endless conversations with Pakistan's many analysts, writers and academics: in Lahore, I.A. Rehman, Raza Ahmed, Ahmed Rashid, Najam Sethi, Jugnu Mohsin, Hasan Askari Rizvi, Rashid Rahman and Salman Rashid; in Islamabad, Pervez Hoodbhoy, Muhammad Amir Rana, Imtiaz Gul, Zahid Hussain, Tanvir Ahmed Khan and Samina Ahmed; in Peshawar, Rahimullah Yusufzai and Idris Khattak; in Karachi, Haris Gazdar, Asad Sayeed, Nadeem Farooq Paracha; in Boston, Adil Najam and Beena Sarwar; in Washington, Shamila N. Chaudhary, Vali Nasr, Stephen P Cohen and Jeff Hayes; and in London, Dr. Farzana Shaikh, Victoria Schofield, Umber Khairi, Huma Yusuf and Mustafa Qadri. Ayesha Siddiqa offered analysis on jihadis and a crate of juicy mangoes from her farm in Bahawalpur every summer; Ayaz Amir provided succinct quotes and rollicking company; Hameed Haroon introduced me to the richness of the country's art; Shuja Nawaz helped to decipher the inner workings of the military.

Thanks to able and brave colleagues at the *New York Times* in Pakistan: Salman Masood, Ismail Khan, Zia ur Rehman, Ihsanullah Tipu Mehsud and Waqar Gilani. Sana ul Haq, a stringer in Swat, sent a photo of his prize-winning snowwoman based on Queen Elizabeth II that I still cherish. I wouldn't have gotten far in Quetta without the unflappable Shahzada Zulfiqar. The photographer Andrea Bruce took a dingy train ride across Pakistan with me, and Diego Ibarra Sanchez illustrated other stories. During my 18 months covering Pakistan from London, Saba Imtiaz and Taha Siddiqui helped with reporting. For guidance and friendship, thanks to Abbas Nasir, Pir Zubair Shah, Murtaza Ali Shah and Shoaib Hasan, and especially to Zaffar Abbas and Cyril Almeida.

Thanks to officials at the Pakistan government's External Publicity Wing especially the gracious Nighat Shah; thanks to ambassadors Wajid Shams ul Hassan in London and Maleeha Lodhi in New York; and to diplomats Imran Gardezi, Syeda Sultana Rizvi and Colonel Zulfiqar Ali Bhatty. Among the politicians and officials who helped were: Sherry Rehman, Afrasiab Khattak, Tariq Aziz, Farahnaz Ispahani, Mushahid Hussain, Shoaib Suddle, Farooq Sattar, Nafisa Shah, Sanaullah Baloch, and Husain Haqqani. Thanks especially to Rehman Malik for renewing my visa in 2013 when others tried to cancel it.

If this book is in places critical of Pakistan's military and intelligence services, that is no reflection on the military officials, serving and retired, who generously offered their time, explained their perspective, and whose patriotism I never doubted. Retired general Talat Masood was a master of the pithy quote; General Tariq Hyatt Khan was always thoughtful and considerate; Athar Abbas was a gentlemanly army spokesperson; former ISI chiefs Javed Ashraf Qazi, Hamid Gul and Asad Durrani patiently answered my questions, as did the former chief of army staff, Jehangir Karamat. Thanks also to Shaukat Qadir at the National Defence University, the late Brigadier Niaz Ahmed and to Asad Munir, a retired ISI officer and proud Pashtun who tragically took his life in 2019.

Among the many foreign diplomats who worked on Pakistan, thanks to Adam Thomson, Mark Lyall Grant, Liz Colton, Barry Shapiro, Jonathan Pratt, Richard Hoagland, Anne Patterson, Alexander Evans, Rebekah Grindlay and Michael Koch.

For company, camaraderie and laughs, thanks to Owen Bennett-Jones, Omar Waraich, Griff Witte, Sabrina Tavernise, Sebastian Abbott, Rob Crilly, Shakir Husain and his father,

Irfan, Adnan Malik, Anam Mansuri, Saima Mohsin, Ali and Asma Saigol, Mosharraf Zaidi, Nadia Naviwala, Saeed Shah, Huma Imtiaz, Orla Guerin, Carlotta Gall, Kate Brooks, Nicholas Schmidle, Danny Kemp, Emmanuel Giroud, Jane Perlez, Matthew Green, Michael Georgie, Jennie Matthews, Zahir Riaz, Mehreen Zahra-Malik, Baker Atyani, Ali Faisal Zaidi, Imran Khan, Kim Barker, Nick Schifrin, Francoise Chipaux, Tim McGirk, Kathy Gannon, Carol Grisanti and Nadia Blétry. My house-mate Eric de Lavarene was a wonderful source of terrible jokes. Alice Albinia turned up one day, on her way to Waziristan, and became a dear friend. A press conference hosted by Angelina Jolie led to Shehryar Mufti, his brother Shahan, and their band, Bumbu Sauce. Jon Boone kindly packed my belongings after I was expelled. Isambard Wilkinson was, at all times, the best of company.

I owe special thanks to my friend and editor extraordinaire Faiza Sultan Khan, who nurtured the idea of a book, read drafts and spurred the project over the finish line. Writers who offered invaluable advice and encouragement included Mohammed Hanif, Kamila Shamsie, Pankaj Mishra, Alex von Tunzelmann, Basharat Peer and Nadeem Aslam. Thanks also to Jalal Salahuddin, Lyse Doucet, Mishal Husain, Victoria Schofield, Moni Mohsin, Farzhana Naek, Michael and Rachel Dwyer, Siraj ul Mulk, Roshaan Khattak, Kashif and Sujatha Zafar, Imran Aslam, Talat Aslam, Mir Ibrahim Rahman, Riffat Hussain, Surti Singh, Moeed Peerzada and Tammy Haq. Andrew Testa took the jacket photo.

For the nine years I was in Pakistan, Ismail Jan steered me across the country in his Toyota Corolla. Ismail was unflappable, incredibly hard-working and seized with a sense of mission that went far beyond the call of duty. During the military campaign in Swat in 2009, when the roads were blocked, he walked through a deserted valley with me for days, carrying his

ACKNOWLEDGEMENTS

belongings in a suitcase. Some stories would never have been done without him. I also owe a great debt to Mazloom Raja, a gentle soul who managed the house and welcomed my friends, no matter how many or how late. We lived a lot together, in both good and hard times, and I miss him.

More than anybody else, Ali Dayan Hasan and Sahr Atta Ullah helped make sense of Pakistan, and brought me into their wider family: Samar, Najji, Shahid, Bunta, Mariam, Nash and Cheanie, not to forget the lovely Zainab and Zahra. They carried me through joy and sorrow, helped to untangle the gnarled threads of their country, and left me with a sense of being rooted in it — a great and special privilege.

I owe a special debt to my parents, Paddy and Mary Walsh, who as children brought us on sweaty holidays to France that whetted my appetite for travel. They taught me the value of open-hearted curiosity, and any success I have is shared with them. During my last year I met my future wife, Nisreen Malik, who pushed me to keep reporting even after I got the expulsion notice, and then provided a new home in London. Nisreen read chapters, endured stolen weekends without complaint and, as the manuscript was being finished, gave birth to two boys, Eamonn and Samuel. They brought hope and joy and smashed the curse of "Insha'Allah book".

NOTES AND SOURCES

Prologue

Pakistan has a rich political lexicon. Other than the euphemism 'angels', ISI officers are also commonly referred to as 'aliens' and 'the boys', while the mysterious machinations of the powerful are attributed to 'sensitive institutions' or 'invisible hands'. The expulsion letter that was hand-delivered to my house was written on Ministry of Interior letterhead. The fate of Nawaz Sharif's unfortunate tiger, Sandra, was a matter of heated dispute in the closing days of the 2013 election campaign. Although animal rights activists said the tiger had died, Sharif's family insisted it was alive and well. Party officials brought reporters to a farm where, according to Yaroslav Trofimov of the *Wall Street Journal*, they were led into an air-conditioned shed and shown a snoozing tiger said to be Sandra. The dispute was never resolved.

The $5-million demand refers to a legal notice I received in May 2011 from lawyers representing former president Pervez Musharraf over an article in the *Guardian* that detailed a secret agreement, struck a decade earlier, between Musharraf and President George W. Bush that permitted an American raid to capture Osama bin Laden. The suit never made it to court.

Several books and articles have reported the *Dawn* headline of December 17, 1971, marking the fall of Dhaka, as VICTORY ON ALL FRONTS. The edition in the *Dawn* archives in Karachi, though, records it as WAR TILL VICTORY.

1. *Insha'Allah* Nation

For more on the abuses by Pakistani troops and their allies during the secession of East Pakistan in 1971, see Gary J. Bass's book *The Blood Telegram*. I obtained details of Jackie Kennedy's trip to Pakistan in 1963 from an article by Tariro Mzazewa in the *New York Times* on 10 October 2019. The BBC World Service 2013 Country Ratings Poll, a survey of about 26,000 people around the world, rated Pakistan as the second most unpopular nation after Iran. Thomas Friedman expressed his discomfort about 'cold stares and steely eyes' in an article for the *New York Times* in November 2001. To understand why the reference to depictions of rabid-looking protesters is literal, see the 31 October 2017 cover of *Newsweek* magazine, showing smoke and snarling faces. The account of Maulana Sami 'The Sandwich' ul Haq and his sexual adventures was provided by a Pakistani source with close ties to the country's intelligence chiefs (some were his poker partners). Details of the corruption accusations against Benazir Bhutto are from an article by John F. Burns in the *New York Times* on 9 January 1998. Fatima Bhutto described her aunt as 'a nasty piece of work' during an interview in Karachi in October 2007, and she accused Benazir and Zardari of having a hand in her father's death in her book *Songs of Blood and Sword*. *Sifarish* was an indispensable part of my life in Pakistan, but I first read about it in my dog-eared copy of Emma Duncan's perspicacious book *Breaking the Curfew*, which prompted me to consider writing my own account. Alas, it's now out of print.

2. Red Zone

I visited the Red Mosque numerous times during the tumultuous spring and summer of 2007 – I still have my copy of *Best of Baghdad* – and I drew on the work of reporters including Zahid Hussain, Saeed Shah, Griff Witte and Nicholas Schmidle to describe those events. The reference to 'chicks with sticks' is from an article by Somini Sengupta in the *New York Times* of 24 July 2007. The account of Sayyid Ahmad and the battle of Balakot is taken from *Partisans of Allah* by the historian Ayesha Jalal. The reference to Mullah Powindah as a 'pestilential priest' is from the book *Resistance and Control in Pakistan* by Akbar S. Ahmed, another eminent scholar on Pakistan. General Zia's quote about his fondness for prayer is from Hussain Haqqani's book *Between Military and Mosque*. Steve Coll's *Ghost Wars* was the starting point for my research on Pakistan's role in the anti-Soviet jihad of the 1980s and its support to the Taliban in the 1990s. I supplemented it with interviews with key figures from that era, including retired generals Hamid Gul, Asad Durrani and Javed Ashraf Qazi, as well as Colonel Imam, Khalid Khawaja and others.

History lecturer Naeem Qureshi called Abdul Rashid Ghazi a 'well-adjusted young man' in an Associated Press profile by Matthew Pennington published on 10 July 2007; he provided me with other details in a later interview. Ghazi recounted his trip to meet Osama bin Laden in Kandahar to numerous journalists, including me, but the story about drinking from bin Laden's glass came from Zahid Hussain. Background on Farid Esack, the South African scholar who knew Ghazi in his final months, is from a profile published in *Focus*, a journal of The Helen Suzman Foundation. Ghazi's role as an HIV campaigner is mentioned in a November 2004 document published by UNICEF and the Pakistani Ministry of Health titled 'The Role of Religious Leaders in the Prevention of HIV/AIDS'.

I travelled to Sehwan Sharif with my friend Isambard Wilkinson of the *Daily Telegraph*, who wrote an account of the same trip in his book, *Travels in a Dervish Cloak*. (It records my unpoetic reaction to the magic of the festival: 'It's a fucking rave!') The translation of Sheikh Zauq's poem about the mullah who 'loves to screw' is from the anthology *Celebrating the Best of Urdu Poetry* by Khushwant Singh. Details on the diversity of Sufi thought are from an *Economist* article in December 2008.

The International Crisis Group has produced numerous detailed – and alas often ignored – reports about Pakistan's *madrassas* and the need for reform. Abdul Aziz's comment that 'someone's got to fill' the governance vacuum in Pakistan is from the documentary *Insha'Allah Democracy*, directed by Mohammed Naqvi. For more on the underreported subject of clerical sexual abuse of children in religious seminaries, Kathy Gannon of the Associated Press wrote an important story that was published on 21 November 2017.

President Hu Jintao received constant briefings during the massage-parlour drama, according to Andrew Small in his book *The China–Pakistan Axis*. Musharraf's quote about being ashamed before his Chinese hosts is from a speech he gave in November 2007. The Ghazi Force militant group that sprang up to avenge the Red Mosque siege was described by Syed Manzar Abbas Zaidi in the journal *CTC Sentinel* in July 2010. The description of Abdul Rashid Ghazi's funeral is from a Reuters report by Asim Tanvir on 11 July 2007, and from video footage posted to the internet.

3. The Prodigal Father

Numerous texts about Jinnah and partition informed this chapter, among them Nisid Hajari's *Midnight's Furies*, Alex von Tunzelmann's *Indian Summer* and Dilip Hiro's *The Longest*

August. Other invaluable works included Ayesha Jalal's *The Sole Spokesman* and *The Pity of Partition*; Akbar S. Ahmed's *Jinnah: Pakistan and Islamic Identity*; and Yasmin Khan's *The Great Partition*. I spotted the technically blasphemous image of the Prophet Muhammad in the halls of Lincoln's Inn during a dinner hosted by the Pakistan Society in 2013. Everyone was too polite to mention it, which seemed apt. Jinnah's predilection for ham sandwiches is a staple of every profile, although it should be noted that it is disputed by some historians.

I attended the polo festival at Shandur with the inimitable Siraj ul Mulk, of the royal family of Chitral, who also provided a history of the tournament. Mountbatten's admission about his own conceit is from an obituary by Albin Krebs in the *New York Times* on 28 August 1979; his view of himself as the 'most powerful man on earth' is from an article by Alex von Tunzelmann in the *New York Times* on 2 September, 2007. General Joseph Stilwell's impatience with the 'endless walla-walla' surrounding Mountbatten is from an article by Pankaj Mishra in the *New Yorker* on 6 August 2007. Cyril Radcliffe's fear of eighty million Indians tracking him down is from Lucy Chester's *Borders and Conflict in South Asia*. The Mountbattens decided to watch *My Favorite Brunette* according to Hajari's book. Jinnah's comment, 'My dear boys, don't be in a hurry,' is from Hiro, *The Longest August*.

Background on Saadat Manto came from Ayesha Jalal's *The Pity of Partition*; an article by Tariq Ali in the *London Review of Books* on 13 January 2012; and interviews given by Manto's family for a radio documentary, 'Manto: Uncovering Pakistan', which first aired on the BBC World Service on 16 June, 2016. In that documentary, one of his daughters recounted how a veiled threat from a Hindu prompted Manto's flight to Pakistan, but the actor Shyam's comment that 'I could have killed you' are from Jalal's account. Shyam, whose real name was Sunder Shyam

Chadha, himself married a Muslim, but died in 1951 after falling off a horse during a film shoot.

Although Jinnah was born a Shia, there is strong evidence that he had become a Sunni Muslim by the end of his life, according to Akbar S. Ahmed. Sheela Reddy's book *Mr and Mrs Jinnah* was the main source for Jinnah's relationship with Ruttie, including Ruttie's letter begging Jinnah to 'remember me beloved as the flower you plucked.' I also spoke with the author in 2019 for supplemental detail and context. Phillips Talbot's observation about Muslims being 'a little frightened and belligerent' in the run-up to partition is from his book *An American Witness to India's Partition.* The British diplomat who described Pakistan's political parties as 'a collection of gangs' is mentioned in Ayesha Jalal's *The State of Martial Rule.* Pervez Musharraf's memories of partition are from his memoir, *In the Line of Fire*, and from my interview with him at his apartment in London in 2009. An iconic Henri Cartier-Bresson photograph of Nehru, Mountbatten and Edwina, taken on the steps of a Lutyens building in New Delhi, offers a wonderfully suggestive glimpse into their complicated relationship. Mountbatten and Edwina's open marriage came under fresh scrutiny in August 2019 when the historian Andrew Lownie described previously unseen FBI files for his book *The Mountbattens.*

4. Arithmetic on the Frontier

I interviewed Anwar Kamal in Peshawar, Lakki Marwat and Islamabad between 2007 and 2012, when he died. I confess that the comparison with George MacDonald Fraser's peacocky anti-hero, Harry Flashman, offers an imperfect parallel – Kamal could be just as entertaining and roguish as Flashman, yet with none of the loutish behaviour or, as far as I knew, serial womanising. His brother, Akhtar Munir Khan, and his son,

Nasir, were also helpful. Salim Saifullah, the business tycoon in Lakki Marwat, graciously hosted me in Islamabad despite his mild annoyance that I wrote about his Prada loafers.

I took the figure for violent deaths in northwestern Pakistan in 2009 from the annual report of the Pak Institute for Peace Studies. Fearing retribution from the Pakistani authorities, Kamal initially denied to local journalists his encounter with the group's leader, Baitullah Mehsud. Kamal later gave me a full account of the meeting.

The account of British wars on the frontier came from several books, including Jules Stewart's *The Savage Border* and Charles Allen's *Soldier Sahibs*, and a paper by Paul Titus in *Modern Asian Studies* in 1998. The journalist Abubakar Siddique, who is from North Waziristan, and his book *The Pashtun Question*, provided excellent background about Pashtun history and culture, and a necessary antidote to certain stereotypes. Olaf Caroe's book *The Pathans*, although dated, was a useful reference, and an article by James Astill on *Pashtunwali* in the *Economist* in December 2006 was stimulating. An Israeli study on the Pashtuns as 'lost Jews' was the subject of numerous newspaper reports in early 2010 but never completed, according to an article in the science magazine *GeneWatch* published in February of that year. The UNICEF-funded study revealing shocking levels of child sexual abuse in northwestern Pakistan was conducted by the NGOs Coalition on Child Rights in 1999. Joshua T. White's paper, 'Pakistan's Islamist Frontier', which was published in 2008 by the Institute for Global Engagement, provided a useful overview of Islamist politics at that time. Amnesty International wrote several reports on human rights abuses in Pakistan's northwest. State Department cables published by WikiLeaks provided information about American efforts to find Osama bin Laden at that time.

My knowledge of the Faqir of Ipi comes principally from Alan Warren's 2000 book, *Waziristan, the Faqir of Ipi, and the Indian*

Army; a *New Yorker* profile of the Faqir by Christopher Rand on 19 February 1955; a fascinating account of his near-dalliance with the Nazis by Milan Hauner in the *Journal of Contemporary History* of January 1981; and an interview with Charles Burman, a retired British soldier who had been posted to Waziristan in the 1940s as a radio operator. Burman sent me a letter after reading one of my reports from Waziristan; in shaky handwriting, he described the terror of British road convoys that ran the gauntlet of Pashtun guerrillas. 'When you went out on the road, you never knew what would happen,' he wrote.

5. The Fabulous Senorita

Asma Jahangir gave several frank and revealing interviews in the later years of her life that, along with my interviews, informed much of this profile. She spoke in detail about her relationship with Benazir Bhutto in a talk in Lady Margaret Hall at Oxford in February 2018, six days before her death. Her daughters, Munizae and Sulema, provided information about their wider family. Jahangir described the tensions in her marriage and the desire of her in-laws for 'an ideal wife' in a frank interview with the BBC World Service's Outlook programme in 2010. Jahangir's childhood memories are from a profile by William Dalrymple published in the *New Yorker* in July 2007. Her description of the law court as 'a place where you dressed up' is from a September 2016 profile by Saroop Ijaz in the *Herald* magazine, which ceased publication in July 2019. Her observation that she had 'less to lose' than ordinary Pakistanis was made in an interview with the BBC's Newshour programme in 2013.

Condoleezza Rice's fear that Musharraf would 'do something stupid' in 2007 is from her memoir, *No Higher Honor*. The United States ambassador, Anne Patterson, reported on

Musharraf's rambling address to Western diplomats and his comment that Jahangir was 'mentally unbalanced' in a State Department cable sent on 5 November 2007, and later released by WikiLeaks. 'Teach the bitch a lesson' is from an article by Ali Dayan Hasan in the *New York Times* on 15 June 2005. The claim by the Maula Jatt producer, Sarwar Bhatti, that his character represented the 'true culture of Pakistan', is from an interview with the *Express Tribune* on 28 February 2013. Fouad Ajami's observation about the American predilection for charming dictators is from his review of Musharraf's memoir, *In the Line of Fire*, in the *New York Times* on 7 January 2007. The 'shining swords' boast of newspaper proprietor Majid Nizami is from an article in *Nawa-i-Waqt*, a newspaper he owned, on 19 October 2009.

Samia Sarwar's father was quoted about his notions of honour in an article by Suzanne Goldenberg in the *Guardian* on 26 May 1999. Asma Jahangir said that 'many of these things are crimes' in an interview with me. The drunken New Year's Eve Ball in Lahore took place in December 2008. I attended the opening of the city's Porsche dealership at the Royal Palm Golf and Country Club in April 2006. 'Our folklore is about passionate love . . .' is from a talk Jahangir gave at the University of Pennsylvania in May 2015. The Pakistan Centre for Philanthropy estimated in 2018 that Pakistanis give $2 billion to charity every year. The clothes designer who fired her tailors, Ayesha Hashwani, was quoted in *Sunday* magazine, which was published with the *Daily Times*, in November 2010. Moni Mohsin's book, *The Diary of a Social Butterfly*, offers sharp satire on upper-class Lahore.

General's Zia's boast, 'The bastard's dead!' is from Mary Anne Weaver's profile of Benazir Bhutto in the *New Yorker* on 4 October 1993. My account of the negotiations leading to Benazir Bhutto's 2007 return to Pakistan comes from interviews with British and American diplomats. The doctored photos of Benazir in the 1988 election were mentioned by Mohammed Hanif in the *New York Times* on 30 December 2007. Benazir told the American lobbyist Mark Siegel of Musharraf's warning that 'your security is a function of your relationship with me', which Musharraf later angrily denied saying. Jahangir mentioned the 'Don't come back' text message in her 2018 Oxford speech. Details of Bhutto's last hours and death are from the final report of a United Nations Commission of Inquiry that was published on April 15, 2010. The historian Ayesha Jalal, a close friend of Jahangir, provided an account of how they both learned of Benazir's death on the set of a television show. Jahangir's assertion that 'everyone is saying the army killed Benazir' is from her interview with an Indian news outlet. The Taliban leader Baitullah Mehsud's comment that it was 'really brave boys who killed her' is from a transcript of a phone call released by the Pakistani government on 28 December 2007.

Jahangir's comment that 'we all live dangerous lives' is from an interview with NPR on 31 May 2011. Details about Saleem Shahzad's career are from a profile by Dexter Filkins in the *New Yorker* published on 12 September, 2011. In July 2011, Admiral Mike Mullen, the top officer in the United States military, publicly accused Pakistan of sanctioning Shahzad's death. A source with access to United States government documents leaked by Edward Snowden provided a copy of the intelligence report about the ISI plot to assassinate Asma Jahangir. The idea that the plot to kill Benazir stemmed from anger among senior military officers about her comments on the nuclear programme came from Owen Bennett Jones's BBC radio series *The Assassination*, which aired between December 2017 and February 2018. Najam Sethi, a veteran journalist and old friend of Jahangir, told me that Asma bought a bulletproof four-wheel-drive vehicle after learning of the ISI plot to kill her.

6. The Good Muslim

Salmaan Taseer's children have written extensively about the circumstances around his death. I drew on interviews with his son, Shaan and his daughter, Shehrbano, as well as on the High Court judgment at the end of Mumtaz Qadri's murder trial, which was issued on 9 March 2015, and on the Supreme Court ruling of 7 October 2015. I interviewed Taseer in Lahore with Omar Waraich of *Time* magazine, who knew him well, and I culled details about both Taseer and Qadri from Waraich's writings. Taseer outlined his views on extremism in an interview with Shehrbano in *Newsweek Pakistan* on 15 November 2010.

The media blog *Cafe Pyala* wondered whether the Taseer family was living in 'la la land' in a post published on November 13, 2010. Aatish Taseer's account of his stay at his father's home in Lahore comes from his book *Stranger to History*. A subsequent novel by Aatish, *Noon*, features events that are loosely based on the Taseer family. Taseer's remark about 'spineless bloody judges' and the details of how he became involved with Asia Bibi are taken from 'Blasphemy and the Governor of Punjab', a BBC drama-documentary by Owen Bennett-Jones that aired in 2012. In the same programme, Tariq Ali recounted Taseer's justification for taking high office: 'At least I wouldn't have to bribe myself.' Ali wrote about his childhood friendship with Taseer, including their protest outside the American Consulate, in the *London Review of Books* on 20 January 2011. In an interview in December 2019, Ali explained how he learned that Taseer betrayed him to the police when they were teenagers. Imran Khan's comment that Taseer lacked a 'moral anchor' is from a profile of Khan by Aatish Taseer published in *Vanity Fair* on 12 September, 2019.

A senior Pakistani official told me that Malik Riaz, a real estate tycoon with close ties to the ISI, made the $2 million payment to secure the release of the imprisoned CIA contractor Raymond Davis. The understanding was that Riaz would later be reimbursed by the United States. But relations continued to decline between the CIA and the ISI chief, Shuja Pasha, and it was unclear if the money was ever repaid. Details of the confrontation between Asia Bibi and the women in the field, and of her conditions in prison, are taken from the books *Blasphemy, A Memoir,* and *Free at Last,* both written by Asia Bibi with the French journalist Anne-Isabelle Tollet. Jon Boone of the *Guardian* reported on the Islamabad mosque that doubled its congregation by taking Qadri's name in 2014. The speech by the cleric Hanif Qureshi that is alleged to have incited the death of Taseer was available online for a time; the Middle East Media Research Institute published an edited transcript of his remarks on 19 October 2011. Shehryar Taseer said Qadri was 'just the bullet' in an interview with Aleem Maqbool of the BBC on 10 January 2011. I drew on Pakistani news articles for details of Qadri's trial and execution. Asia Bibi told a Christian organisation, Life for All, that she had to cook her own meals to avoid being poisoned.

7. Lost in Waziristan

For the history of the ISI, see Owen L. Sirr's *Pakistan's Inter-Services Intelligence Directorate: Covert Actions and Internal Operations,* and Hein Kiessling's *Faith, Unity, Discipline.* Details about Walter Cawthorn are from an entry in the *Australian Dictionary of Biography,* volume 13, published in 1993. Steve Coll's books *Ghost Wars* and *Directorate S* are the indispensable references to Pakistan's role in Afghanistan since the early 1980s. C. Christine Fair's book *Fighting to the End* and Shuja Nawaz's book *Crossed Swords* are excellent resources on the Pakistani military. Ayub Khan's grumbling about the failure of the ISI to anticipate an assassin is taken from *Diaries of Field Marshal Mohammad Ayub Khan, 1966–1972*, edited by Craig Baxter. The Mikhail Evstafiev quote is from his novel *Two Steps from Heaven*, about the trials of an elite Soviet officer named Oleg Sharagin during the Afghan war.

I learned that the ISI was monitoring my communications from Western officials in Islamabad, and, later, from an ISI officer involved in my surveillance. Imam told me he got the Berlin Wall memento from 'the Americans' but Milt Bearden, the CIA station chief in Islamabad in the late 1980s, told me it had been presented by an American intelligence officer who went by the alias 'Jud Falcon'. (Incidentally, Imam's old ISI boss, Hamid Gul, had a similar Berlin Wall memento that he received from Germany's BND foreign intelligence service.) The Afghan diplomat's outburst against Imam is taken from the record of the United Nations on 5 October 1995. Imam's statement that 'My boys and I are riding into Mazar-i-Sharif' is from an article by Douglas Frantz in the *New York Times* on 8 December 2001. The reference to Imam in Uruzgan is from a *Time* magazine article by Rory Callinan on 24 January, 2008. Afrasiab Khattak, a veteran Pashtun human rights activist and politician, told me that Imam's Pashto was poor.

The detail about Ayman al-Zawahiri crossing the Pakistan–Afghanistan border on horseback comes from a *New Yorker* article by Lawrence Wright published on 16 September 2002. David Headley's observations about foreign jihadis in Waziristan is culled from prosecution documents filed in the Northern District of Illinois, Eastern Division, on 11 October 2009. I learned that the CIA had a small base in Wana from Art Keller, a former CIA officer posted to Waziristan in 2006. Robert Grenier, the former CIA station chief in Islamabad, wrote about his encounter with Colonel Imam in October 2001 in his book, *88 Days to Kandahar*, and later described it to me in an interview.

The remark that American 'shackles were unleashed' after the suicide attack on a CIA camp in 2009 is from Joby Warrick's book *The Triple Agent*.

I relied on my interview with Asad Qureshi and on his book, *165 Days*, for many of the details about his captivity in Waziristan. The video of Hakimullah's speech and Colonel Imam's execution was available online for several years. Michael Semple helped me understand the symbolic importance of the speech.

8. Minimum City

In a city of such tangled politics, and torn between such a wide array of ethnic, criminal and political gangs, fiction provides a useful entry point. I benefited much from *The Prisoner*, a novel by Omar Shahid Hamid, who drew on his experiences as a senior officer in the Karachi police to paint a gritty, insightful picture of the force and the city's seedy underbelly. Hamid worked with Chaudhry Aslam and provided key details about Aslam's career, his thinking and his morality code. The title of the chapter derives from *Maximum City*, Suketu Mehta's brilliant non-fiction book on Mumbai, which also features a police anti-hero.

Hussain Haroon, the politician who got Aslam into the police force (and later became Pakistan's ambassador to the United Nations) provided details of his early life. Saba Imtiaz interviewed Aslam's friend and colleague, Irfan Bahadur, on my behalf in March 2016 at Karachi police headquarters. (Saba's first novel, *Karachi, You're Killing Me*, published in 2014, offers a racy, humorous portrait of the city.) Police 'encounters', as extrajudicial executions are known in Pakistan and India, are openly discussed in the news media. The number of Karachi cops on VIP duty is from an editorial in

Dawn on 3 August 2012. An International Crisis Group report in January 2013 entitled 'Policing Urban Violence in Pakistan' provided wider context about the force. The Anti-Extremism Cell headed by Aslam was re-named the Counter-Terrorism Department in 2015.

Details of Karachi's history, including its Jewish councillor Abraham Reuben, are from the book *Kurrachee: Past, Present, and Future*, published by the *Dawn* media group. The cited population figure is from the 2017 census. Bernard-Henri Lévy's description of Karachi as a 'black hole' is from his book *Who Killed Daniel Pearl?* The defiant 'our city takes no shit' comment is from a Karachi resident on Twitter. Zaffar Abbas, the editor of *Dawn*, and Irfan Husain, a *Dawn* columnist, gave a detailed picture of Karachi under the MQM in the 1990s. (Zaffar was beaten up by MQM thugs over his reporting; both journalists are themselves *mohajirs*.)

The American estimate of 10,000 MQM supporters under arms appeared in a State Department cable of 22 April 2009 titled 'The Gangs of Karachi', later published by WikiLeaks. The Human Rights Commission of Pakistan described the MQM as a 'frightening military organisation' in its 2007 report, *Carnage in Karachi*. The reference to Altaf Hussain's golden sword and his supporters' pledge of allegiance are from Oskar Verkaaik's book *Migrants and Militants*. The Karachi monument with the inscription 'Distance Does Not Matter', an enduring symbol of Altaf Hussain's grip on the city, was actually dedicated to Pakistan's first prime minister, Liaquat Ali Khan, a mohajir, when Hussain inaugurated it by video link from London in August 2009.

After Taliban leader Mullah Omar's death was confirmed in 2015, Afghan intelligence joined a long list of sources who claimed, without much proof, that he had been living in Karachi. In 2019, a report by the Dutch reporter Bette Dam, citing sources that included Mullah Omar's bodyguard, concluded he had in fact been in seclusion in southern Afghanistan.

The disturbing account of Arshad the assassin comes from a paper by Nichola Khan in the journal *Economic and Political Weekly* on 23 June 2007. I interviewed Shoaib Suddle in Islamabad and drew other details about the police and army operations against the MQM during the 1990s from news reports of that time. Details of Karachi's criminal underworld are from an article by Ghulam Hasnain in *Newsline* magazine on 10 September 2001. Omar Shahid Hamid provided me with a spreadsheet listing 273 Karachi police officers killed supposedly by the MQM between 2000 and 2011. Several police officers and crime reporters in Karachi, who cannot be named, provided details of how bribery and other corruption work inside the force. Sebastian Abbot and Adil Jawad's excellent profile of the police officer Waseem 'Beater' for the Associated Press in March 2013 fleshed out those details. Aslam's 'Who are we?' quote is from the reporter Shoaib Hassan.

For an account of Karachi's free-wheeling past in the 1970s, see Shehryar Fazli's book, *Invitation*, and numerous articles in *Dawn* by Nadeem F. Paracha, the foremost chronicler of that period. In 1985, Hanif Kureishi wrote a finely observed article for *Granta* magazine, 'Erotic Politicians and Mullahs', that remains a relevant commentary on Karachi society and social mores. Princess Abida Sultaan's book, *Memoirs of a Rebel Princess*, provided biographical detail that I supplemented with interviews with family members. Successful entrants in the short-story competition run by Faiza were published in the *Life's Too Short* literary review.

Ardeshir Cowasjee gave many interviews, often hilariously curt or plain rude, but most of the quotes are from my meetings with him. His comment about Karachi as a 'tinderbox' comes from a column he wrote in *Dawn* in November 2009, following the killing of land campaigner Nisar Baloch. Much to my chagrin, I never actually made it to the crocodile shrine at Manghopir. Chaudhry Aslam's colleagues provided details about his anti-Taliban operations in the run-up to his death.

9. War of the Flea

There is a lamentable dearth of good general texts on Balochistan – a reflection, perhaps, of the province's marginalisation in the story of Pakistan. But the province has provided ample material for human rights researchers, journalists and specialist writers on the Pakistani military's complex entanglements with jihadist militancy.

For Nawab Bugti's early life, I relied on an old copy of *The Tigers of Baluchistan* by Sylvia A. Matheson. I took details of the early trouble at Sui from an article in *Newsline* magazine by Massoud Ansari in September 2006. The poem about Brahm quoted by the Nawab is from *The Light of Asia* by the British poet and journalist Edwin Arnold. I developed the idea of Quetta's multiple identities from a paper by Haris Gazdar, Sobia Ahmad Kaker and Irfan Khan of the Collective for Social Science Research, published in February 2010. The city (known as 'Q') provides the surreal setting for the opening part of Salman Rushdie's 1983 novel *Shame*, in my opinion his finest work.

The Pakistani news magazines *Herald* and *Newsline* consistently provided some of the best reporting from Balochistan during the death of Nawab Bugti and in the following years. Willem Marx's book, *Balochistan: At a Crossroads*, provides a unique glimpse into the insurgency. Amnesty International's 2008 report, 'Denying the Undeniable', and Human Rights Watch's 2011 report, 'We Can Torture, Kill, or Keep You for Years', were key resources on enforced disappearances, including Bashir Azeem's account of being tortured by Pakistani security officials. Human Rights Watch documented violence by Baloch separatists against Punjab settlers in its report 'Their Future Is at Stake' in December 2010. A briefing paper on Balochistan by the International Crisis Group (Asia briefing number 69), published on 27 October 2007, provided political context. Matthew Green investigated the province's drug trade in a study for Reuters published on 5 September 2012. President Pervez Musharraf launched into a tirade against the sardars, calling them 'pygmies', when I interviewed him at Army House in Rawalpindi in May 2006. The death toll from the army attack on Bugti's fort on 17 March 2005, and the attack on civilians by a helicopter gunship on 31 December of that year, is from a report by the State Department's Bureau of Democracy, Human Rights, and Labor, published on 8 March 2006.

Mohammed Hanif's short book on human rights violations, *The Baloch Who Is Not Missing & Others Who Are* was also useful, as was testimony provided by Ali Dayan Hasan of Human Rights Watch to a hearing of the United States House Committee on Foreign Affairs on 8 February 2012. Carlotta Gall wrote about her adventurous reporting trip to interview the fugitive Nawab Bugti at his cave in the *New York Times* on 2 April 2006, as did Isambard Wilkinson in an article for the *Daily Telegraph* of 21 March 2006, and subsequently in his book *Travels in a Dervish Cloak*.

President George W. Bush's observation that Karzai and Musharraf nearly came to blows over supper at the White House in 2006 was recorded in Condoleezza Rice's memoir, *No Higher Honor*. Musharraf's rejection of Karzai's assurances as 'bullshit' was recorded in a State Department account of a meeting with Richard A. Boucher on 12 January 2007 that was later published by WikiLeaks. The comment by Vijay Nambiar, then India's deputy National Security Adviser, that Balochistan was 'a taste of their own medicine', is from an American diplomatic cable dated 9 January 2006 that was published by WikiLeaks.

David Albright of the Institute for Science and International Security helped me make sense of the mysterious satellite images of apparent tunnels in the Kirthar Mountains in central Balochistan. In August 2017, Albright authored a report with Sarah Burkhard, Allison Lach and Frank Pabian that identified the underground complex as a likely ballistic-missile and nuclear-warhead storage site. The report is available on the institute's website.

In an interview with Murtaza Ali Shah for the *News*, published on 24 April 2015, Brahumdagh Bugti claimed to have inherited $100 million from his grandfather. Brahumdagh's tortured party secretary, in an interview with Human Rights Watch, said the military threatened to imprison him for years. Andrew Small's book, *The China–Pakistan Axis*, outlines China's ambition to exploit Balochistan's natural resources and warm-water ports in conjunction with the Pakistani military.

10. Undesirable Activities

Hamid Mir wrote about the suffering of his Kashmiri family during partition, and how that influenced his political views, in an article published in the *Daily Star* of Lebanon on 26 March 2010. He described himself as a 'hardliner' in an interview with Rediff. com on 13 July 2001. His claim to have interviewed Osama bin Laden in Afghanistan in late 2001 met with scepticism from some American journalists, whose doubts were summarised by Timothy Noah in *Slate* on 13 November 2001. Mir is adamant the meeting took place. Mir described the perils of journalism in Pakistan in an article for *Pique*, a now-defunct monthly Pakistani magazine, on 14 April 2014. I interviewed Mir several times in Pakistan and in London, where he told me about his tense interview with a stressed-out President Asif Ali Zardari in his bedroom, and about a confrontation with ISI Director General Ahmed Shuja Pasha following the Mumbai attacks in 2008. Khaled Ahmed noted Mir's use of the phrase 'liberal-fascist' in an article published in the *Express Tribune* on 5 February 2011.

The account of the attack on Mir is from an interview with him and eyewitness testimony, including his driver and his security guard, to the judicial commission that was set up to investigate the attack. Saroop Ijaz described the battle between the ISI and Geo TV following the attack in an article for the *Express Tribune* newspaper on 3 May 2014. A profile of Mir in the *Washington Post* on 26 July 2015 provided background details. So did a paper by Razeshta Sethna on the perils of journalism in Pakistan for the Reuters Institute for the Study of Journalism that was published online in 2015. The Indian press named the soldier whose head was presented to Mir as Bhausaheb Maruti Talekar of the 17 Maratha Light Infantry. He was killed on 27 February, 2000, at the age of twenty-four. The advocacy group Media Matters for Democracy wrote about the final report of the Hamid Mir Judicial Commission in April 2016.

My initial investigation of Axact was based partly on an account and documents provided by Yasir Jamshaid, an ex-employee cited in my first *New York Times* story on the subject in May 2015. Details from the police raid – the stacks of fake degrees, the customer database, and the company's income during its previous year of operations – are from police records filed in court against Axact, as well as from a database of the company's customers that I obtained from a legal source. The police records listed Axact-controlled shell companies and bank accounts in at least 19 countries, including the British Virgin Islands and the other countries cited in the text. Details of Shaikh's acquittal, retrial and subsequent conviction are from Pakistani press reports.

The reference to CIA officers employing 'Moscow Rules' in Pakistan is from Mark Mazzetti's book, *The Way of the Knife*.

Details of the military's accusations against Manzoor Pashteen of the Pashtun Protection Movement (formally known as the Pashtun Tahafuz Movement) are from an article by Hasib Danish Alikozai published on the Voice of America website on 6 May 2019.

Apart from his name, I have not altered any facts about the former ISI agent Ashraf, but I did omit certain details to safeguard his security in exile. He provided me with documentation that confirmed his employment with the ISI, and I was able to corroborate other details independently through my own reporting. The account he provided of my surveillance dovetailed with my own memory of that time, and his description of the Taliban commander I had coincidentally met at a funeral in 2006 was a perfect match with my story notes. But some assertions, including accusations against his former ISI co-workers at the Quetta office, were essentially unverifiable.

11. A House on a Hill

Sheela Reddy's book *Mr and Mrs Jinnah* was invaluable on the history of South Court; an article she wrote for livemint.com in August 2017 brought the story up to date. Jinnah's wish to retire at South Court was recorded in the memoirs of Sri Prikasa, India's first High Commissioner to Pakistan. *India Today* estimated South Court's value at $400 million in April 2017. Jinnah's remark about Hindus and cows is taken from Larry Collins and Dominique Lapierre's book, *Freedom at Midnight*.

Stephen Tankel's book, *Storming the World Stage*, is a strong guide to Lashkar-e-Taiba and its relationship with the ISI. Hafiz Saeed's quote about militant faces that 'glow like the moon' is from Cathy Scott-Clark and Adrian Levy's book, *The Siege*, which also provided details of the bloodshed inside the Taj Hotel.

Imran's Khan's second wife Reham Khan detailed his alleged drug abuse in her memoir, *Reham Khan*; Aatish Taseer made similar accusations in a profile of Khan published in *Vanity Fair* in September 2019. I also drew on profiles of Khan by Pankaj Mishra in the *New York Times Magazine* on August 16, 2012 and by Max Rodenbeck in the *New York Review of Books* on November 22, 2018.

The rise to power of Narendra Modi in 2014 has prompted some fierce, brilliant writing about India's rightward lurch and the state of its relations with Pakistan. Articles that influenced me included a reflection on partition by William Dalrymple in the *New Yorker* on 29 June 2015, and an article on India's seventieth anniversary by Pankaj Mishra in the *New York Times* on 11 August 2017. The sketch of the Trumpian property developer Mangal Prabhat Lodha, including his use of the slogan MAKE MUMBAI GREAT AGAIN, is drawn from a profile by Vidhi Doshi for the *Guardian* on 5 April 2017.

Estimates of the number of Pakistanis killed and injured in violence since 2007 are from the annual reports of the Pak Institute for Peace Studies, which draws on newspaper articles, official publications and field sources. The United Nations predicted that Pakistan will have 408 million people by 2050 in its World Population Prospects 2019 report.

Asia Bibi's quote about keeping her faith is from an interview with Mishal Husain broadcast on the BBC in February 2020. Husain Haqqani sketched his ideas for Pakistan's future in his book *Magnificent Delusions*.

Details of the attack on Jinnah's residence in Ziarat, Balochistan, on 15 June 2013, are from Pakistani press reports and a video posted online by the Balochistan Liberation Army, which claimed the assault. The government renovated the house and reopened it a year later on 14 August, Pakistan's Independence Day.

PHOTO CREDITS

Page ii.   Mourners walk away from the Bhutto family mausoleum following the funeral of Benazir Bhutto in Garhi Khuda Baksh, December 2007. PHOTO BY DECLAN WALSH.

Page xxii.   Pilgrims wash themselves in the Indus during the annual religious festival at Sehwan Sharif in Sindh Province, September 2007. PHOTO BY DECLAN WALSH.

Page 22.   Abdul Rashid Ghazi holding a press conference at the Red Mosque to call for the imposition of Islamic rule in Pakistan, February 2007. PHOTO BY DECLAN WALSH.

Page 48.   An iron portrait of Pakistan's founder, Muhammad Ali Jinnah, stands over the highway between Islamabad and Rawalpindi. "Unity, Faith, Discipline" is the national motto of Pakistan. PHOTO BY DECLAN WALSH.

Page 74.   Anwar Kamal Khan addresses the Marwat *lashkar*, or militia, to rally his constituents against Pakistani Taliban fighters spilling out of the nearby tribal belt, June 2007. PHOTO BY DECLAN WALSH.

Page 104.   Asma Jahangir addressing a press conference in the garden of her Lahore villa, advocating for the right of women to participate alongside men in road races, May 2005. PHOTO BY DECLAN WALSH.

Page 136.   The governor of Punjab, Salmaan Taseer, at Governor's House in Lahore, May 2009. PHOTO BY NIKLAS HALLE'N.

PHOTO CREDITS

Page 162. Retired Brigadier Sultan Amir Tarar, widely known as Colonel Imam, at his home in Rawalpindi, January 2010. PHOTO BY DECLAN WALSH.

Page 190. Chaudhry Aslam Khan at the Karachi police headquarters, November 2011. PHOTO BY DECLAN WALSH.

Page 218. Nawab Akbar Khan Bugti standing in front of his fort in Dera Bugti, Balochistan Province, February 2005. PHOTO BY DECLAN WALSH.

Page 248. A Pakistani military officer in Spinkai Raghzai, South Waziristan, during a media briefing about anti-Taliban operations in the area, May 2008. PHOTO BY DECLAN WALSH.

Page 270. A Pakistani military officer at the passing out parade of the 116th long course at the Pakistani Military Academy in Kakul, Abbottabad, October 2007. PHOTO BY DECLAN WALSH.

Page 291. Waziristan as seen from a Pakistan army helicopter. PHOTO BY DECLAN WALSH.

INDEX

325

A NOTE ON THE AUTHOR

Declan Walsh covered Pakistan for over a decade for the *Guardian* and the *New York Times*. The Pakistani authorities expelled him in 2013, citing unspecified 'undesirable activities'. Walsh has reported from sub-Saharan Africa, Afghanistan, the United States and across the Middle East. He lives in Nairobi.

A NOTE ON THE TYPE

The text of this book is set in Fournier. Fournier is derived from the romain du roi, which was created towards the end of the seventeenth century from designs made by a committee of the Académie of Sciences for the exclusive use of the Imprimerie Royale. The original Fournier types were cut by the famous Paris founder Pierre Simon Fournier in about 1742. These types were some of the most influential designs of the eight and are counted among the earliest examples of the 'transitional' style of typeface. This Monotype version dates from 1924. Fournier is a light, clear face whose distinctive features are capital letters that are quite tall and bold in relation to the lower-case letters, and *decorative italics, which show the influence of the calligraphy of Fournier's time.*